I0885425

Metaverse Applications for New Business Models and Disruptive Innovation

Muhammad Anshari
Universiti Brunei Darussalam, Brunei

Muhammad Syafrudin
Sejong University, South Korea

Ganjar Alfian
Universitas Gadjah Mada, Indonesia

A volume in the Advances in E-Business Research (AEBR) Book Series

IGI Global
PUBLISHER of TIMELY KNOWLEDGE

Published in the United States of America by
IGI Global
Business Science Reference (an imprint of IGI Global)
701 E. Chocolate Avenue
Hershey PA, USA 17033
Tel: 717-533-8845
Fax: 717-533-8661
E-mail: cust@igi-global.com
Web site: http://www.igi-global.com

Copyright © 2023 by IGI Global. All rights reserved. No part of this publication may be reproduced, stored or distributed in any form or by any means, electronic or mechanical, including photocopying, without written permission from the publisher.
Product or company names used in this set are for identification purposes only. Inclusion of the names of the products or companies does not indicate a claim of ownership by IGI Global of the trademark or registered trademark.

Library of Congress Cataloging-in-Publication Data

Names: Anshari, Muhammad, 1977- editor. | Syafrudin, Muhammad, 1990- editor. | Alfian, Ganjar, 1987- editor.
Title: Metaverse applications for new business models and disruptive innovation / Muhammad Anshari, Muhammad Syafrudin, and Ganjar Alfian, editors.
Description: Hershey, PA : Business Science Reference, [2023] | Includes bibliographical references and index. | Summary: "With metaverse expected to be the next generation of the Internet and its online activities., this book explores its fundamental study and application from the business information systems perspectives"-- Provided by publisher.
Identifiers: LCCN 2022034111 (print) | LCCN 2022034112 (ebook) | ISBN 9781668460979 (hardcover) | ISBN 9781668460986 (library binding) | ISBN 9781668460993 (ebook)
Subjects: LCSH: Business information services. | Disruptive technologies.
Classification: LCC HF54.5 .M48 2023 (print) | LCC HF54.5 (ebook) | DDC 658.4/038--dc23/eng/20220729
LC record available at https://lccn.loc.gov/2022034111
LC ebook record available at https://lccn.loc.gov/2022034112

This book is published in the IGI Global book series Advances in E-Business Research (AEBR) (ISSN: 1935-2700; eISSN: 1935-2719)

British Cataloguing in Publication Data
A Cataloguing in Publication record for this book is available from the British Library.

All work contributed to this book is new, previously-unpublished material.
The views expressed in this book are those of the authors, but not necessarily of the publisher.

For electronic access to this publication, please contact: eresources@igi-global.com.

Advances in E-Business Research (AEBR) Book Series

In Lee
Western Illinois University, USA

ISSN:1935-2700
EISSN:1935-2719

MISSION

Technology has played a vital role in the emergence of e-business and its applications incorporate strategies. These processes have aided in the use of electronic transactions via telecommunications networks for collaborating with business partners, buying and selling of goods and services, and customer service. Research in this field continues to develop into a wide range of topics, including marketing, psychology, information systems, accounting, economics, and computer science.

The **Advances in E-Business Research (AEBR) Book Series** provides multidisciplinary references for researchers and practitioners in this area. Instructors, researchers, and professionals interested in the most up-to-date research on the concepts, issues, applications, and trends in the e-business field will find this collection, or individual books, extremely useful. This collection contains the highest quality academic books that advance understanding of e-business and addresses the challenges faced by researchers and practitioners.

COVERAGE

- E-CRM
- E-procurement methods
- Evaluation methodologies for e-business systems
- Virtual Collaboration
- Telework and Telecommuting
- Social Network
- E-business standardizations
- Collaborative commerce
- Trust, Security, and Privacy
- Mobile Business Models

IGI Global is currently accepting manuscripts for publication within this series. To submit a proposal for a volume in this series, please contact our Acquisition Editors at Acquisitions@igi-global.com or visit: http://www.igi-global.com/publish/.

The Advances in E-Business Research (AEBR) Book Series (ISSN 1935-2700) is published by IGI Global, 701 E. Chocolate Avenue, Hershey, PA 17033-1240, USA, www.igi-global.com. This series is composed of titles available for purchase individually; each title is edited to be contextually exclusive from any other title within the series. For pricing and ordering information please visit http://www.igi-global.com/book-series/advances-business-research/37144. Postmaster: Send all address changes to above address. Copyright © 2023 IGI Global. All rights, including translation in other languages reserved by the publisher. No part of this series may be reproduced or used in any form or by any means – graphics, electronic, or mechanical, including photocopying, recording, taping, or information and retrieval systems – without written permission from the publisher, except for non commercial, educational use, including classroom teaching purposes. The views expressed in this series are those of the authors, but not necessarily of IGI Global.

Titles in this Series

For a list of additional titles in this series, please visit: http://www.igi-global.com/book-series/

Digital Technologies for Entrepreneurship in Industry 4.0
Elena G. Popkova (MGIMO University, Russia)
Business Science Reference • © 2022 • 270pp • H/C (ISBN: 9781668442654) • US $250.00

Driving Transformative Change in E-Business Through Applied Intelligence and Emerging Technologies
Hamed Taherdoost (University Canada West, Canada)
Business Science Reference • © 2022 • 307pp • H/C (ISBN: 9781668452356) • US $250.00

Virtual Technologies and E-Collaboration for the Future of Global Business
Jingyuan Zhao (University of Toronto, Canada) and Joseph Richards (California State University, Sacramento, USA)
Business Science Reference • © 2022 • 273pp • H/C (ISBN: 9781668450277) • US $250.00

Navigating Digital Communication and Challenges for Organizations
José Gabriel Andrade (University of Minho, Portugal) and Teresa Ruão (University of Minho, Portugal)
Business Science Reference • © 2022 • 325pp • H/C (ISBN: 9781799897903) • US $230.00

Handbook of Research on Smart Management for Digital Transformation
Belem Barbosa (University of Porto, Portugal) Sandra Filipe (University of Aveiro, Portugal) and Claudia Amaral Santos (University of Aveiro, Portugal)
Business Science Reference • © 2022 • 614pp • H/C (ISBN: 9781799890089) • US $325.00

Handbook of Research on Digital Transformation, Industry Use Cases, and the Impact of Disruptive Technologies
Martin George Wynn (University of Gloucestershire, UK)
Business Science Reference • © 2022 • 487pp • H/C (ISBN: 9781799877127) • US $360.00

IGI Global
PUBLISHER of TIMELY KNOWLEDGE

701 East Chocolate Avenue, Hershey, PA 17033, USA
Tel: 717-533-8845 x100 • Fax: 717-533-8661
E-Mail: cust@igi-global.com • www.igi-global.com

Editorial Advisory Board

Abdullah Al-Mudimigh, *Dar Al Uloom University, Saudi Arabia*
Yunifa Miftachul Arif, *Universitas Islam Negeri Maulana Malik Ibrahim Malang, Indonesia*
Imam Fahrurrozi, *Gadjah Mada University, Indonesia*
Egi Firmansyah, *Padjadjaran University, Indonesia*
Mia Fithriyah, *Indonesia Open University, Indonesia*
Norma Latif Fitriyani, *Sejong University, South Korea*
Ahmad Fathan Hidayatullah, *Universitas Islam Indonesia, Indonesia*
Muhammad Rifqi Maarif, *Tidar University, Indonesia*
Muhammad Sait, *Universiti Brunei Darussalam, Brunei*
Triyo Supriyatno, *Universitas Islam Negari Maulana Malik Ibrahim Malang, Indonesia*
Maria Ulfah, *Universitas Islam Negeri Sunan Kalijaga Yogyakarta, Indonesia*
Condro Wibawa, *Gunadarma University, Indonesia*
Abubakar Yakasai, *Universiti Brunei Darussalam, Brunei*

Table of Contents

Detailed Table of Contents

The metaverse can be described as the largescale societal shift from flat media viewed in the third person to immersive media experienced in the first person. While there is nothing inherently dangerous about immersive media technologies such as virtual and augmented reality, many policymakers have raised concerns about the extreme surveillance capabilities that powerful metaverse platforms could wield over users. What is often overlooked, however, is how surveillance-related risks become amplified when platforms are allowed to simultaneously target users with promotionally altered experiences. When considered in the context of control theory, the pairing of real-time surveillance and real-time influence raises new concerns, as large metaverse platforms could become extremely efficient tools for deception, manipulation, and persuasion. For these reasons, regulation should be considered that limit the ability of metaverse platforms to impart real-time influence on users based on real-time surveillance.

The purpose of this chapter is to make assessments of the metaverse's utility in urban policies. Within the scope of the study, the role of the metaverse in increasing people's quality of life, increasing efficiency in business processes, and creating policies that will meet expectations by changing the understanding of service delivery in public administration will be discussed. A literature review was conducted in this context in order to develop a theoretical framework for the concept of the metaverse. In the literature review, articles, book chapters, proceedings papers, websites, and reports were used. In the application part, the projects carried out by the municipalities on the metaverse were examined in detail within the scope of city management.

Companies are beginning to utilize the metaverse to broaden their service network and create new co-creation value for their clients. To better understand how the metaverse phenomena could impact corporate sustainability, investigative research should be conducted. In this chapter, the authors looked at the moral issues raised by businesses using metaverse to gain a competitive advantage. An exploratory evaluation of business ethics and a metaverse business model were used. Users, the general public, and consumers have a right to be fully informed of and understand that their data cannot be used by a third party for any reason in accordance with the consequentialist utilitarian principle and the notion of moral unity. Finally, those working in the disciplines of technology and public policy, including academics, entrepreneurs, and legislators, are expected to use the study.

The metaverse has become of paramount importance within the last several years, being a virtual universe where individuals and companies can interact. While the metaverses are still in their nascent stage, there has been increasing interest and capital inflow into these universes. For Shariah-compliant focused financial investors and participants, this represents a considerable challenge given the existing lack of Islamic financing frameworks for the metaverses. This chapter outlines options for providing Shariah-compliant financing in the metaverse, outlining the challenges and aspects that have to be taken into account for creating Shariah-compliant financing

The term metaverse refers to a virtual environment that exists beyond the physical world we live in but, at the same time, is similar to the real world. This chapter intends to investigate the impact of the metaverse for future business scenarios and whether there are other uses for the metaverse besides for business and entertainment purposes. The research for this chapter explains the potential and challenges of the metaverse, ways to create and maintain a strategic information systems, and the role of big data analytics in Industry 4.0. The significant findings indicate that the metaverse creates business opportunities for both consumers and sellers due to the growth of digital commerce since shopping can become more immersive with the option to buy physical or digital goods. However, digital footprints may be tracked from the metaverse to disclose the real-world identity of the user and other private information, which can be an invasion of privacy.

By offering both technical and nontechnical courses, educational systems have tried to prepare students. However, with video games, there is the opportunity to create specific metaverses that can assist in educating soft skills, including during informal pleasures. The research will provide a set of design approaches for metaverse and video games in order to foster soft skills. Although there are several soft talents that one may learn, this chapter will concentrate on a few, based on certain games and research. Some data will be gathered from the data to back up the model and justifications. The chapter will help game designers create inventive games, and users will learn soft skills that will help them in both their professional and social lives.

Every year, the metaverse grows to make the world more efficient and easy to use for all societies and industries. When connecting the virtual world to the real world and digital information, privacy and security are two of the most talked-about topics. This is because the metaverse has a lot of sensitive information. This chapter talks about some privacy and security problems in the metaverse and how they will affect the future. At the same time, even though the metaverse has become more advanced, its complexity produces a new situation where it raises the issues of privacy and security again. This chapter also explores and suggests countermeasures to combat privacy and security issues.

The goal of this chapter is to present information on sports technology, specifically how the metaverse will affect the sports world and how well sports will adapt to life in the metaverse. The findings of the study conducted for the literature review have been described in the chapter, and the chapter has also investigated all the possible target outcomes. It has been proven that the sports industry is ready to enter the metaverse and has already taken action to do so as it guides the sporting world into the future.

The virtual world was made possible by big changes in computer hardware, graphics software, and computer software. Considering the function of a metaverse, which is a 3D virtual world with computing infrastructure that is available to everyone. By making products and services that are much better, more affordable, and easier to use, disruptive technologies can grow the industries they are already in or start whole new ones. Disruptive technology offers a big change in how things are done or processes are run. The metaverse uses a number of useful technologies to give users 3D experiences that are both immersive and unique. Marketing, education, travel, and healthcare are among the industries that the metaverse might have an impact on. This chapter discusses how these technologies could be used in digital medicine and the future of the medical metaverse. The authors also talk about the research that is being done to speed up the metaverse's adoption in global education and make it a better place to learn and teach.

This research is about the metaverse as the next evolutionary step in doing business. In addition, the purpose of this research is to get to know more about the metaverse, ranging from positive and negative impacts to business opportunities and business strategies in the metaverse. This metaverse is a proof of the technological development that occurs and does not only refer to one type of technology. However, it leads to ways to utilise the technology. The metaverse is important because it has stylistic ideas that might help us organise society to be more productive, shared standards, and protocols that bring different virtual worlds (the metaverse) and augmented reality into one open metaverse that can help people work together. The study revealed that the metaverse is very important to expand business reachability so that users can explore this virtual world in real life. The metaverse will be co-created and responsibly built so that any type of business can be realised in the future.

Preface

Metaverse is expected to be the next generation of Internet applications, transitioning from 2D online activities to 3D virtual worlds that will serve as the foundation for a massive online business platform, promising more engaging user experiences. Therefore, it might alter people's behavior, which will have an impact on businesses' decisions to choose the metaverse as their primary business platform. The edited book "Metaverse Applications for New Business Models and Disruptive Innovation" examines the recent developments in the metaverse and their implications for business, as well as the challenges and best practises for adopting this technology in the business sector. This reference work is essential for business administrators, managers, data scientists, researchers, academia, practitioners, educators, and students, as it includes themes such as virtual reality, business ethics, security, and business models. Let's present a summary of the collection of twelve chapters of this book.

Chapter 1, titled "The Metaverse: The Ultimate Tool of Persuasion" (by Louis Rosenberg), states that the metaverse is the shift from flat, third-person media to immersive, first-person media. Immersive media technologies like virtual and augmented reality are not inherently hazardous, but many politicians are concerned about the extraordinary surveillance possibilities of strong metaverse platforms. Surveillance-related dangers are heightened when platforms target users with promotionally changed experiences. Real-time monitoring and influence present new challenges in control theory, since enormous metaverse platforms might be used for deception, manipulation, and persuasion. For these reasons, rules should limit metaverse platforms' power to influence users based on real-time observation.

Chapter 2, titled "Metaverse Applications as a Tool in Urban Policy Design" (by Abidin Kemeç), discusses Metaverse's role in urban policy. The research will explore the role of Metaverse in improving people's quality of life, enhancing business process efficiency, and formulating policies that satisfy expectations by transforming public administration service delivery. A literature review was done to develop a theoretical basis for metaverse. Articles, book chapters, conference papers, websites, and reports were utilised. In the application portion, municipal metaverse projects were investigated for city management.

Chapter 3, titled "Ethical Concerns in the Metaverse Business" (by Muhammad Anshari, Muhammad Syafrudin, Norma Latif Fitriyani, and Abdullah Al-Mudimigh), discusses that businesses should evaluate the ethics of their data collection and use strategies. Business ethics analysis cannot be ignored since it influences how sustainable metaverse-using businesses evolve. An investigative study is needed to determine how the metaverse affects business sustainability. This chapter examines the moral difficulties created by firms exploiting the metaverse to achieve a competitive edge. exploratory business ethics evaluation and a metaverse business model are employed. The research also looks at how corporations use the metaverse to make decisions. Any organisation must have a clear Metaverse policy to support ethics. Users, the public, and customers have a right to know that a third party cannot exploit their data for any reason, according to consequentialist utilitarianism and moral unity. This study will inspire a constructive discourse on the ethical problem posed when a firm exploits consumer data. Academics, entrepreneurs, and lawmakers working in technology and public policy should use the study.

Chapter 4, titled "Islamic Compliant Frameworks for the Metaverse: An Opportunity for More Equitable Finance in the Metaverse" (by Klemens Katterbauer, Hassan Syed, Laurent Cleenewerck de Kiev, and Sema Yilmaz Genc), states that Metaverse is a virtual universe where people and organisations may interact. Metaverses are relatively young, but interest and investment are growing. Shariah-compliant investors and players have a hurdle given the lack of Islamic finance mechanisms for metaverses. This chapter describes Shariah-compliant funding possibilities in the metaverse, including obstacles and considerations. The system adapts Murabaha and Sukuk to the metaverse, enabling Shariah-compliant contracts and crypto-payments. The framework helps generate Shariah-compliant metaverse funding.

Chapter 5, titled "The Acceptance of the Metaverse as a Platform for Knowledge Creation and Sharing in the Workplace" (by Abdul Hafiiz Idris), discusses how innovation has always driven societal transformation and workplace efficiency. Today, integrating the internet into a company's activities is important. This research examines the adoption of Metaverse now and makes forecasts for the future, where its integration has been the next big thing since the internet's inception. The technology acceptance model predicts whether people will accept or reject a new technology. The Metaverse is a hardware-created parallel universe with enhanced immersion. It is a virtual reality simulation. Such technology has appeared in modern culture. The technology is still young and needs refining before it can become a societal standard or a business tool. This would allow us to study the technology's acceptability using the TAM. SECI will assist comprehend Metaverse as a platform for knowledge production through its adoption and the CATWOE overview.

Chapter 6, titled "The Development of a Metaverse App for a Blended Learning in Higher Education Institutions" (by Nabillah Masnadi), states that COVID-19 has led to blended learning and global innovation. Innovations include Metaverse in schooling. The article introduces a metaverse app to Brunei Darussalam students, instructors, and visitors. The programme aims to alleviate online learning challenges and allow safer physical learning. The article employs the CATWOE framework to show how education reforms effect student learning. This article includes a road plan for using knowledge management to construct the metaverse app. This paper will also explore metaverse app problems and limits.

Chapter 7, titled "Potentials and Challenges of Metaverse" (by Dk Farhanah Japar and Muhammad Anshari), states that the word "metaverse" refers to a virtual world that exists outside of the real world we live in, but is still similar to it. This chapter will look into how the metaverse will affect business in the future and whether or not it can be used for things other than business and entertainment. The research for this chapter explains the potential and problems of the metaverse, how to make and maintain strategic information systems, and the role of big data analytics in Industry 4.0. The important findings show that the metaverse creates business opportunities for both buyers and sellers because digital commerce is growing and shopping can become more immersive when you can buy both physical and digital goods. But digital footprints can be followed from the metaverse to find out who the user is in the real world and other private information. This can be an invasion of privacy.

Chapter 8, titled "Metaverse and Soft Skills Development Through Video Games" (by Mohd Abi Syarillizam Sabtu), states that educational systems have made an effort to prepare pupils by providing both technical and nontechnical courses. Video games, however, provide the chance to develop specialised metaverses that can help with soft skill training, especially during informal pleasures. In order to promote soft skills, the project will offer a collection of design strategies for video games and the metaverse. Although there are many soft skills that may be developed, this chapter will focus on a handful, using some games and research. From the data, certain information will be acquired to support the model and reasoning. Users will gain soft skills that will aid them in both their professional and social lives from this chapter, which will also assist game creators in creating imaginative games.

Chapter 9, titled "Privacy and Security Concerns in the Metaverse" (by Muhd Hakeem Pg Haji Muhd Japar, Muhammad Anshari, and Wardah Azimah Sumardi), states that Metaverse grows to make the world more efficient and easier to use for all societies and industries. When connecting the virtual world to the real world and digital information, privacy and security are two of the most talked-about topics. This is because the metaverse has a lot of sensitive information. This article talks about some privacy and security problems in the metaverse and how they will affect the future. At the same time, even though the metaverse has become more advance, its complexity produces a new situation where it raises the issues of privacy and security again. This chapter also explores and suggests countermeasures to combat privacy and security issues.

Chapter 10, titled "Sports in Metaverse" (by Muhamad Danial Asyraf Mohamad), discusses about sports technology, especially how the Metaverse will impact the sports world and how successfully sports will adapt to life in the metaverse. In addition to describing the findings of the study done for the literature review, the article investigates all potential goal outcomes. As it steers the sporting world into the future, it has been demonstrated that the sports sector is prepared to enter the metaverse and has already taken action in that direction.

Chapter 11, titled "Applications of the Metaverse as Disruptive Innovation," by Nur Nazihah Assyakirah Haji Isa, affirms that significant advancements in computer technology, graphics software, and computer software made the virtual world conceivable. Considering the purpose of a metaverse, which is a 3D virtual environment with accessible computational infrastructure by creating far superior, more affordable, and simpler-to-use goods and services, disruptive technologies can expand the sectors they are presently in or create entirely new ones. Disruptive technology significantly alters how things are performed or processes are managed. The metaverse employs a variety of beneficial technologies to provide consumers with immersive and distinctive 3D experiences. The metaverse may have an influence on the marketing, education, tourism, and healthcare industries, among others. This chapter examines the potential applications of these technologies in digital medicine and the future of the medical metaverse. The chapter discusses the adoption of the metaverse in global education and how to improve it as a place to study and teach.

The last chapter of the book, titled "Business Future With Metaverse" (by Tazkia Tahira and Fien Zulfikarijah), informs about the Metaverse as the next evolutionary step in the future of business. In addition, this study is to learn more about the metaverse, including its positive and negative effects, business opportunities, and business strategies. Metaverse is evidence of technical advancement and does not refer to a single sort of technology. Nonetheless, it leads to methods of utilising the technology. The Metaverse is significant because it contains stylistic ideas that may help us organise society to be more productive, as well as shared standards and protocols that unite different virtual worlds and augmented reality into a single, open Metaverse that facilitates collaboration between individuals. The research found that the Metaverse is crucial for expanding company accessibility so that users can explore this virtual environment in the real world. The Metaverse will be co-created and constructed ethically so that any future business model can be realised.

Muhammad Anshari
Universiti Brunei Darussalam, Brunei

Muhammad Syafrudin
Sejong University, South Korea

Ganjar Alfian
Universitas Gadjah Mada, Indonesia

Acknowledgment

Alhamdulillah, all praise be to Allah (SWT) for giving us the strength to complete this book in the midst of the COVID-19 pandemic. We are grateful to all the contributors to this book for their valuable contributions. We would like to thank the reviewers for taking the necessary time and effort to review the manuscript. We sincerely appreciate all your valuable comments and constructive feedback, which helped improve the quality of the chapters. Last but not least, the editors also acknowledge the guidance and assistance provided by IGI Global.

Chapter 1
The Metaverse:
The Ultimate Tool of Persuasion

Louis B. Rosenberg
Unanimous AI, USA

ABSTRACT

The metaverse can be described as the largescale societal shift from flat media viewed in the third person to immersive media experienced in the first person. While there is nothing inherently dangerous about immersive media technologies such as virtual and augmented reality, many policymakers have raised concerns about the extreme surveillance capabilities that powerful metaverse platforms could wield over users. What is often overlooked, however, is how surveillance-related risks become amplified when platforms are allowed to simultaneously target users with promotionally altered experiences. When considered in the context of control theory, the pairing of real-time surveillance and real-time influence raises new concerns, as large metaverse platforms could become extremely efficient tools for deception, manipulation, and persuasion. For these reasons, regulation should be considered that limit the ability of metaverse platforms to impart real-time influence on users based on real-time surveillance.

DOI: 10.4018/978-1-6684-6097-9.ch001

Copyright © 2023, IGI Global. Copying or distributing in print or electronic forms without written permission of IGI Global is prohibited.

INTRODUCTION

The United Nations Human Rights Council recently adopted a draft resolution entitled Neurotechnology and Human Rights (UN, n.d.). It's aimed at protecting humanity from devices that can "record, interfere, or modify brain activity." To describe the risks, the resolution uses euphemistic phrases like *cognitive engineering*, *mental privacy* and *cognitive liberty*, but what we're really talking about is mind control.

I applaud the U.N. for taking up the issue of mind control, but neurotechnology is not our greatest threat on this front. That's because it involves sophisticated hardware ranging from "brain implants" to wearable devices that can detect and transmit signals through the skull. Yes, these technologies could be very dangerous, but they're unlikely to be deployed at scale anytime soon. In addition, individuals who submit themselves to implants or brain stimulation, will likely do so with informed consent.

On the other hand, there is an emerging category of products and technologies that could threaten our *cognitive liberties* across large populations, requiring nothing more than consumer-grade hardware and software from trusted corporations. These seemingly innocent systems, which will be marketed for a wide range of positive applications from entertainment to education, targeting both kids and adults, could be dangerously misused and abused without our knowledge or consent.

Unless regulated, the metaverse could become the most dangerous tool of persuasion ever created. To raise awareness about the issues, I've written many articles about the hidden dangers and the pressing need to protect human rights (Rosenberg, 2022), but I have not explained from a technical perspective, why immersive technologies could be as dangerous to our cognitive liberties as brain implants. To do so, I'd like to introduce a basic engineering concept called *Feedback Control.*

It comes from a technical discipline called Control Theory, which is the method used by engineers to control the behaviors of a system. Think of the thermostat in your house. You set a temperature goal and if your house falls below that goal, the heat turns on. If your house gets too hot, it turns off. When working properly, it keeps your house close to the goal you set. That's feedback control.

Of course, engineers like to make things more complex than they need to, so the simple concept above is generally represented in a standard format called a *Control System Diagram* as follows (Wikimedia Foundation, 2022).

Figure 1. Generic "Control System" Diagram – (credit) Wikipedia

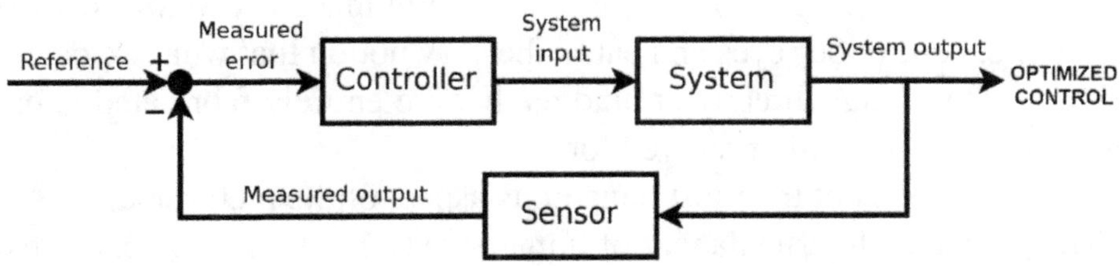

In the heating example, your house would be the SYSTEM, a thermometer would be the SENSOR, and the thermostat would be the CONTROLLER. An input signal called the *Reference* is the temperature you set as the goal. The goal is compared to the actual temperature in your house (i.e., *Measured Output*). The difference between the goal and measured temperature is fed into the thermostat which determines what the heater should do. If the house is too cold, its heater turns on. If it's too hot its heater turns off. That's a classic control system.

Of course, control systems can get very sophisticated, enabling airplanes to fly on autopilot and cars to drive themselves, even allowing robotic rovers to land on mars. These systems need sophisticated sensors to detect driving conditions or flying conditions or whatever else is appropriate for the task. These systems also need powerful controllers to process the sensor data and influence system behaviors in subtle ways. These days, the controllers increasingly use AI algorithms at their core.

If we strip away the hype, the metaverse is about transforming how we humans interact with the digital world. Today we mostly consume *flat media* viewed in the third person. In the metaverse, digital content will become immersive experiences that are spatially presented all around us. This shift to *first-person interactions* will deeply alter our relationship with digital information, changing us from outsiders peering in to participants engaging content presented naturally in our surroundings. Thirty years ago I described the potential like this (Rosenberg, 1994) – *"Given the ability to draw upon our highly evolved human facilities, users of virtual environment systems can obtain an intimate level of insight and understanding."*

I still believe those words, but the power of immersive media can work in both directions. Used in positive ways, it can unlock insight and understanding. Used in negative ways, it could unleash the most powerful tool of persuasion and manipulation we've ever created (Robertson, 2022). That's because immersive media can be far more impactful than traditional media, targeting our perceptual channels in the most personal and visceral form possible – as experiences (Breves, 2021). And because we humans evolved to trust our senses (i.e. believe our eyes and ears), the very notion that what we can see, hear, and feel things directly around us that are entirely fabricated is not a situation we're mentally prepared for.

And yet, that's not the most dangerous aspect of the metaverse.

To appreciate the true danger of immersive technologies, we can use the basics of Control Theory. Referring back to the standard diagram above, we see that only a few elements are needed to effectively control a system, whether it's a simple nightlight or a sophisticated robot. The two most important elements are a SENSOR to detect the system's real-time behaviors, and a CONTROLLER that can influence those behaviors. The only other elements needed are the *feedback loops* that continually detect behaviors and impart influences, guiding the system towards desired goals.

Referring back to the standard diagram above, we see that only a few elements are needed to effectively control a system, whether it's a simple thermostat or a sophisticated robot. The two most important elements are a SENSOR to detect the system's real-time behaviors, and a CONTROLLER that can influence those behaviors. The only other elements needed are the *feedback loops* that continually detect behaviors and impart influences, guiding the system towards desired goals.

As you may have guessed, when considering the danger of the metaverse, *the system* being controlled is you – the human in the loop. After all, when you put on a headset and sink into the metaverse, you're immersing yourself in an environment that has the potential to *act upon you* more than you *act upon it*. Said another way, you become an inhabitant of an artificial world run by a third party that can monitor and influence your behaviors in real time. That's a very dangerous situation.

In the figure above, *System Input* to the human user are the immersive sights, sounds, and touch sensations that are fed into your eyes, ears, hands, and body. This is overwhelming input – possibly the most extensive and intimate input we could imagine other than using surgical brain implants. This means the ability to influence the system (i.e. you) is equally extensive and intimate. On the other side of the user in the diagram above is the *System Output* – that's your actions and reactions.

This brings us to the SENSOR box in the diagram above. In the metaverse, sensors will track everything you do in real-time – the physical motions of your head, hands, and body. That includes the direction you're looking, how long your gaze lingers, the faint motion of your eyes, the dilation of your pupils, the changes in your posture and gait – even your vital signs are likely to be tracked in the metaverse including your heartrate, respiration rate and blood pressure.

For example, a recent headset deployed by META can accurately track your facial expressions and eye motions (Johnson, 2022). The potential goes beyond merely sensing the expressions that other people notice, but also includes subconscious expressions that are too fast or subtle for human observers to recognize. Known as "micro-expressions" these events can convey emotions that users had not intended to express and are unaware of revealing (Li et al., 2017). Users may not even be aware of feeling the emotions, leading to situations where the system literally knows the user better than he or she knows himself.

In addition, AI technology can be used to infer deeply personal information that is not directly detected by sensors. Researchers at META showed that when processing "sparse data" from just a few sensors on your head and hands, AI technology could accurately predict the position, posture, and motion of the rest of your body (Winkler, 2022). Other researchers have shown that body motions such as gait can be used to infer a range of medical conditions from depression to dementia (Wang et al., 2021; Jacobs, 2022).

In addition to tracking basic physical information, metaverse technology already exists to infer your emotions in real-time from your facial expressions, vocal inflections, gestures and body posture. Other technologies exist to detect emotions from the blood-flow patterns on your face and the vital signs detected from sensors in your earbuds (Benitez-Quiroz et al., 2018). This means when you immerse yourself into the metaverse, the sensor in the system diagram above will be able to track almost everything you do and say in that world and accurately predict how you feel during each action, reaction, and interaction.

Figure 2. Control System Diagram for Metaverse Environments

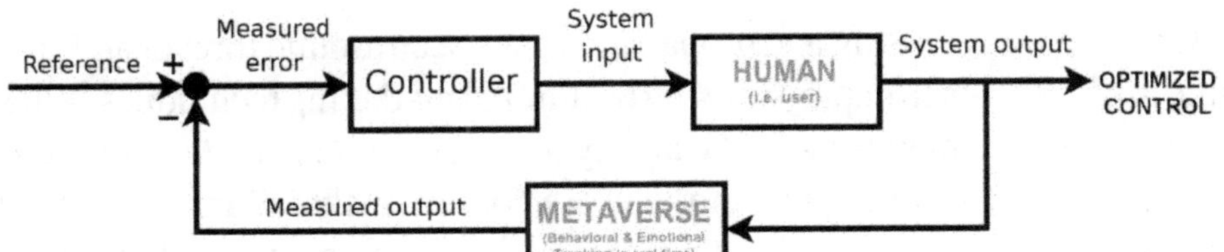

In addition, the behavioral and emotional data described above could be stored by metaverse platforms over time. When processed by AI algorithms, this data could be turned into behavioral and emotional models that enable platforms to accurately predict how users will react when presented with target stimuli (i.e. System Input) from a controller. And because the metaverse is not just virtual reality but also augmented reality, the tracking, storing, and profiling of users will occur not just in fully simulated worlds but within the real-world embellished with virtual content. In other words, metaverse platforms will be able to track and profile behaviors and emotions throughout our daily life (Rosenberg, 2022).

Of course, the danger is not simply that platforms can track and profile the behaviors and emotions of users, it's what they can do with that data. This brings us to the CONTROLLER box in the diagram above. The controller receives a Measured Error, which is the difference between a Reference Goal (a desired behavior) and the Measured Output (a sensed behavior). If metaverse platforms are allowed to adopt and deploy similar business models as those used by social media, the Reference Goal could easily be the AGENDA of third parties that aim to impart influence over users (see diagram below). The third party could be a paying sponsor (or state actor) that desires to persuade a user to buy a product or service, or to believe a piece of propaganda, ideology, or misinformation.

Figure 3. Control System Diagram with Third Party Agenda

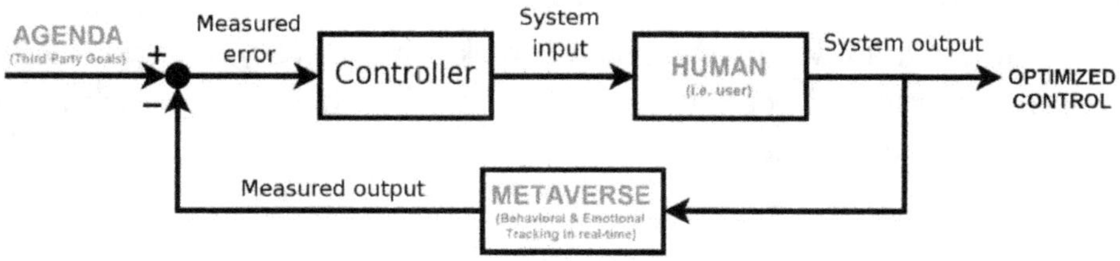

Of course, advertising and propaganda have been around forever and can be quite impactful when deployed using traditional marketing techniques. What's unique about the metaverse is the ability to create high-speed *feedback loops* in which user behaviors and emotions are continuously fed into a controller that can adapt its influence in real-time to optimize persuasion. This process can easily cross the line from marketing to manipulation. To appreciate the risks, let's dig into the controller.

At its core, the CONTROLLER aims to "reduce the error" between the desired behavior of a system and the measured behavior of the system. It does this by imparting System Input as shown on the diagram above as an innocent looking arrow. In the metaverse, this innocent arrow represents the ability of platforms to modify the virtual or augmented environment the user is immersed within.

In other words, in an unregulated metaverse, the controller can alter the world around the user, modifying what they see and hear and feel in order to drive that user towards the desired goal. And because the controller can monitor the user in real-time, it will be able to continually adjust its tactics, optimizing the persuasive impact, moment by moment, just like a thermostat optimizes the temperature of a house.

To make this clear, let's give some examples:

Imagine a user sitting in a coffee house in the metaverse (virtual or augmented). A third party sponsor wants to inspire that user to buy a particular product or service, or believe a piece of messaging, propaganda, or misinformation. In the metaverse, advertising will not be the pop-up ads and videos that we're familiar with today but will be immersive experiences that are seamlessly integrated into our surroundings (Rosenberg, 2022). In this particular example, the controller creates a virtual couple sitting at the next table. That virtual couple will be the System Input that is used to influence the user.

First, the controller will design the virtual couple for maximum impact. This means the age, gender, ethnicity, clothing styles, speaking styles, mannerisms, and other qualities of the couple will be selected by AI algorithms to be optimally persuasive upon the target user based on that user's historical profile. Next, the couple will engage in an AI-controlled conversation amongst themselves that is within earshot of the target user. That conversation could be about a car that the target user is considering purchasing, possibly framed as the virtual couple discussing how happy they are with their own recent purchase.

As the conversation begins, the controller monitors the user in real-time, assessing micro-expressions, body language, eye motions, pupil dilation, and blood pressure to detect when the user begins paying attention. This could be as simple as detecting a subtle physiological change in the user correlated with comments made by the virtual couple. Once engaged, the controller will modify the conversational elements to increase engagement. For example, if the user's attention increases as the couple talks about the car's horsepower, the conversation will adapt in real-time to focus on performance.

As the overheard conversation continues, the user may be unaware that he or she has become a silent participant, responding through subconscious micro-expressions, body posture, and changes in vital signs. The AI controller will highlight elements of the product that the target user responds most positively to and will provide conversational counterarguments when the user's reactions are negative. And because the user does not overtly express objections, the counterarguments could be profoundly influential. After all, the virtual couple could verbally address emerging concerns before those concerns have fully surfaced in the mind of the target user. This is not marketing, it's manipulation.

And in an unregulated metaverse, the target user may believe the virtual couple are avatars controlled by other patrons. In other words, the target user could easily believe they are overhearing an authentic conversation among users and not realize it's a promotionally altered experience that was targeted specifically at them, injected into their surroundings to achieve a particular agenda (Rosenberg, 2022).

And that's a relatively benign example. Instead of pushing the features of a new car or toy, the third-party agenda could be to influence the target user about a political ideology, extremist propaganda, or outright misinformation or disinformation. In addition, the example above targets the user as a passive observer of a promotional experience in his or her metaverse surroundings. In more aggressive examples, the controller will actively engage the user in targeted promotional experiences.

For example, consider the situation in which an AI-controlled avatar that looks and sounds like any other user in an environment engages the target user in agenda-driven promotional conversation. In an unregulated metaverse, the user may be entirely unaware that he or she has been approached by a targeted advertisement, but instead might believe he or she is in a conversation with another user. The conversation could start out very casual but could aim towards a prescribed agenda.

In addition, the controller will likely have access to a wealth of data about the target user, including their interests, values, hobbies, education, political affiliation, etc. – and will use this to craft dialog that optimizes engagement. In addition, the controller will have access to real-time information about the user, including facial expressions, vocal inflections, body posture, eye motions, pupil dilation, facial blood patterns, and potentially blood pressure, heartrate, and respiration rate. The controller will adjust its conversational tactics in real-time based on the overt verbal responses of the target user in combination with subtle and potentially subconscious micro-expressions and vital signs.

It is well known that AI systems can outplay the best human competitors at chess, go, poker, and a wealth of other games of strategy. From that perspective, what chance does an average consumer have when engaged in promotional conversation with an AI agent that has access to that user's personal background and interests, and can adapt its conversational tactics in real-time based on subtle changes in pupil dilation in blood pressure? The potential for violating a user's cognitive liberty through this type of feedback-control in the metaverse is so significant it likely borders on outright mind control.

To complete the diagram for metaverse-based feedback control, we can replace the generic word *controller* with AI-based software that alters the environment or injects conversational avatars that impart optimized influence on target users. This is expressed using the phrase AI AGENTS below.

Figure 4. Rosenberg's Scenario for Metaverse-based Mind Control (Source: Rosenberg, 2022)

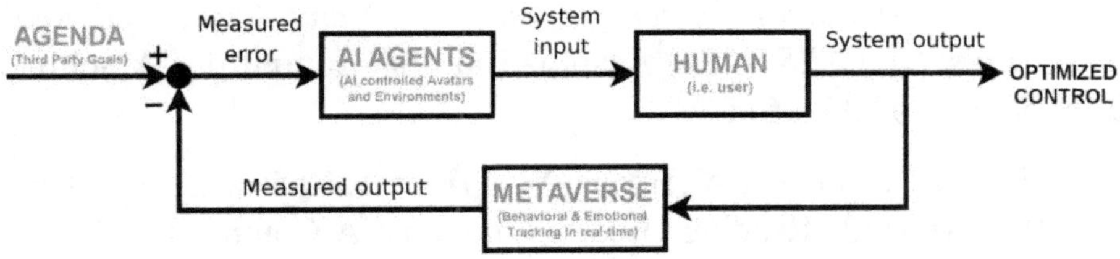

As described above, the metaverse could be used to create feedback-control systems that monitor user activities (behaviors and emotions) in real-time and employ AI technologies to modify their surroundings (i.e., their sights, sounds, and interactive experiences) to maximize persuasion. This means that large and powerful metaverse platforms could track billions of people and impart influence on select individuals by altering the world around them in targeted and adaptive ways. This scenario is frightening but not farfetched. For these reasons, policymakers should consider meaningful guardrails aimed at protecting populations from abuse or misuse of metaverse technologies (The XRSI Privacy and Safety Framework, 2022; Rosenberg, 2022).

REFERENCES

Benitez-Quiroz, C. F., Srinivasan, R., & Martinez, A. M. (2018, April 3). Facial color is an efficient mechanism to visually transmit emotion. *Proceedings of the National Academy of Sciences of the United States of America, 115*(14), 3581–3586. doi:10.1073/pnas.1716084115 PMID:29555780

Breves, P. (2021). Biased by Being There: The Persuasive Impact of Spatial Presence on Cognitive Processing. *Computers in Human Behavior, 119*, 106723. doi:10.1016/j.chb.2021.106723

Jacobs, S. (2022, October 12). Abnormality of Gait as a Predictor of Non-Alzheimer's Dementia. *New England Journal of Medicine*. https://www.nejm.org/doi/full/10.1056/NEJMoa020441

Johnson, K. (2022, October 13). Metas VR Headset Harvests Personal Data Right Off Your Face. *WIRED*. https://www.wired.com/story/metas-vr-headset-quest-pro-personal-data-face/

Rosenberg, L. 2022. Regulation of the Metaverse: A Roadmap: The risks and regulatory solutions for largescale consumer platforms. In *Proceedings of the 6th International Conference on Virtual and Augmented Reality Simulations (ICVARS '22)*. Association for Computing Machinery. 10.1145/3546607.3546611

Li, X., Hong, X., Moilanen, A., Huang, Xi., Pfister, T., Zhao, G., & Pietikainen, M. (2017). Towards Reading Hidden Emotions: A Comparative Study of Spontaneous Micro-Expression Spotting and Recognition Methods. *IEEE Transactions on Affective Computing*. doi:10.1109/TAFFC.2017.2667642

Barry, R. L. (1994). Virtual Fixtures: Perceptual Overlays Enhance Operator Performance in Telepresence Tasks. *Stanford University U.M., I*, 19971994.

Robertson, D. (2022, September 14). *The most dangerous tool of persuasion*. POLITICO. https://www.politico.com/newsletters/digital-future-daily/2022/09/14/metaverse-most-dangerous-tool-persuasion-00056681

Rosenberg, L. (2022, August 30). How a parachute accident helped jump-start augmented reality. *IEEE Spectrum*. Retrieved October 1, 2022, from https://spectrum.ieee.org/history-of-augmented-reality

Rosenberg, L (2022). *Marketing in the Metaverse: A fundamental shift*. Future of Marketing Institute. doi:10.13140/RG.2.2.35340.80003

Rosenberg, L. (2022, August 21). *Deception vs authenticity: Why the metaverse will change marketing forever.* VentureBeat. https://venturebeat.com/ai/deception-vs-authenticity-why-the-metaverse-will-change-marketing-forever/

Rosenberg, L. B. (2022, October 30). The Metaverse: From Marketing to Mind Control. *Future of Marketing Magazine*. https://futureofmarketinginstitute.com/the-metaverse-from-marketing-to-mind-control/

Rosenberg, L. (2022, September 19). *The case for demanding "immersive rights" in the metaverse*. Big Think. https://bigthink.com/the-future/immersive-rights-metaverse/

Rosenberg, L. B. (2022). Regulating the Metaverse, a Blueprint for the Future. In L. T. De Paolis, P. Arpaia, & M. Sacco (Eds.), Lecture Notes in Computer Science: Vol. 13445. *Extended Reality. XR Salento 2022*. Springer. doi:10.1007/978-3-031-15546-8_23

Rosenberg, L. (2022). *Marketing in the Metaverse and the Need for Consumer Protections*. 2022 IEEE 13th Annual Ubiquitous Computing, Electronics & Mobile Communication Conference (UEMCON), New York, NY. doi:10.1109/UEMCON54665.2022.9965661

XRSI. (2022, February 16). *The XRSI Privacy and Safety Framework - XRSI – XR Safety Initiative*. Retrieved October 18, 2022, from https://xrsi.org/publication/the-xrsi-privacy-framework

United Nations. (n.d.). *A/HRC/51/L.3 vote item 3 - 40th meeting, 51st Regular Session Human Rights Council | UN web TV*. United Nations. https://media.un.org/en/asset/k1d/k1dcro5var

Wang, Y., Wang, J., Liu, X., & Zhu, T. (2021, May 7). Detecting Depression Through Gait Data: Examining the Contribution of Gait Features in Recognizing Depression. *Frontiers in Psychiatry, 12*, 661213. doi:10.3389/fpsyt.2021.661213 PMID:34025483

Winkler, A. (2022, September 20). *QuestSim: Human Motion Tracking from Sparse Sensors with Simulated Avatars*. doi:10.1145/3550469.3555411

Wikimedia Foundation. (2022, September 19). Control theory. In *Wikipedia*. Retrieved October 18, 2022, from https://en.wikipedia.org/wiki/Control_theory

Chapter 2
Metaverse Applications as a Tool in Urban Policy Design

Abidin Kemeç
https://orcid.org/0000-0001-9395-4118
Usak University, Turkey

ABSTRACT

The purpose of this chapter is to make assessments of the metaverse's utility in urban policies. Within the scope of the study, the role of the metaverse in increasing people's quality of life, increasing efficiency in business processes, and creating policies that will meet expectations by changing the understanding of service delivery in public administration will be discussed. A literature review was conducted in this context in order to develop a theoretical framework for the concept of the metaverse. In the literature review, articles, book chapters, proceedings papers, websites, and reports were used. In the application part, the projects carried out by the municipalities on the metaverse were examined in detail within the scope of city management.

DOI: 10.4018/978-1-6684-6097-9.ch002

Copyright © 2023, IGI Global. Copying or distributing in print or electronic forms without written permission of IGI Global is prohibited.

INTRODUCTION

In the period from the industrial revolution to the present, important changes and transformations have been experienced in the history of the city. With the transition to mass production, economic, social and spatial relations have undergone a radical change. The increase in demand for the workforce to work in the factories has also come to the fore. With the increase in the population in the cities, firstly in places close to the factory, then in different parts of the city, residential centers where the employees would stay and places where their daily needs would be met were established. In the following times, cities have become the centers of economic activities, development, competition, employment, social and cultural opportunities and innovation. Due to such opportunities, a migration flow from the countryside to the city has started, and with the entry of the 21st century, the urban population has outstripped the rural population.

In parallel with the concentration of the population in cities, a series of environmental, sociological, spatial, economic, administrative and psychological problems have emerged. New generation technologies have been considered as a tool in the production of urban policies in order to find solutions to these problems occurring in cities, as well as to increase the quality of life of citizens and to provide different experiences. Today, new generation technologies such as metaverse, artificial intelligence (AI), data mining, internet of things (IoT), augmented reality (XR), blockchain, big data, 5G, mobile applications, spatial technologies, robotics and gamification are used in policy design.

Digitization is used to increase the level of digital literacy in cities, to provide citizens with transparent access to information, to participate in artistic and cultural activities with augmented reality tools regardless of location, to offer health services online, to develop a new business model, to increase the orientation to solid infrastructure and renewable energy sources. New generation technologies are used to use resources efficiently, to experience a different socialization, to overcome complex and risky tasks, to modernize the traffic system, and to offer a comfortable and sustainable lifestyle to city residents. While performing these applications, metaverse technology was also used. The concept of metaverse has been one of the most discussed concepts in recent years, occupying the agenda quite a lot.

While technological developments cause changes in social life, there has been a rapid transition to the digital world with the emergence of the Covid-19 epidemic. Due to the epidemic, the functions performed in real places such as education, shopping, sports, socialization, etc. in virtual environments have changed. Changes in daily life, aimed at reducing physical contact from person to person, have led to the transfer of life activities to digital environments or their more active use. Before the epidemic, digital platforms and tools that were used frequently depending on the competencies or preferences of individuals have become the primary environments where daily needs such as shopping, banking, public citizenship affairs are carried out, which facilitates life from home due to incoming closures and quarantines. Online activities such as distance work and distance education have changed the relations between work, education-learning and socialization that take place in real physical places such as workplaces, schools and university campuses (Yüksel, and Yıldız 2022).

Metaverse is a created virtual world where users interact simultaneously and endlessly. This created virtual world is sometimes a copy (digital twin) connected to the real world. Sometimes it's completely imaginary. There is a wide range of application possibilities from economy to management, from health to games, from education to urban planning. In the first stage, obligatory tools such as museum visits, online meetings, and training seminars were developed in virtual universes to reduce the effects of the pandemic. In the following processes, original projects were signed in every field of daily life. In Metaverse, the same environment is created by imagination so that users can play games, collaborate, participate in artistic activities, buy digital assets (NFT), watch movies, shop, attend courses, chat, buy or rent real estate and benefit from the services offered by the municipality. In a virtual universe created, new living spaces have been expanded infinitely by establishing direct communication and interaction that exceeds the physical time and space of reality.

In the first part of the study, the concept of the metaverse is discussed, different definitions of the metaverse, the technologies used, and the necessary tools for the metaverse are examined. In addition, in the first chapter, the historical process related to the metaverse is discussed. In the second part of the study, the urban policies designed by the municipalities using a metaverse tool were examined.

THE CONCEPT OF THE METAVERSE

Metaverse application provides advantages in various fields. Aircraft maintenance (Siyaev, and Jo, 2021); education (Barry, et all, 2015; Akour et all, 2020; Kye et all, 2021; Lee et all, 2022; Yang, Ren, and Gu, 2022; Zhou, 2022); healthy living (Ko, and Jang, 2014); cultural events (Hazan, 2010); medicine (Yang, et all, 2022; Huh, 2022; Lu, et all, 2022); librarianship (Tang, 2021); retailing (Bourlakis, Papagiannidis, and Li, 2009); museology (Choi, and Kim, 2017); There are many application examples in the fields of commerce (Shen, et all, 2021); marketing (Barrera, and Shah, 2023); healthcare (Zhang, et all, 2023; Garavand, and Aslani, 2022; Lee, 2022); social sustainability (Arpaci, et all, 2022); digital forest recreation (Jaung, 2022); remote manufacturing (Lee, and Kundu, 2022); working (Choi, 2022); social media (Aytaç, 2022), and tourism (Çelikkol, 2022; Tayfun, et all, 2022; Wei, 2022).

Metaverse refers to the combination of all digital elements of new communication media and technologies. Because there is a fictional universe in a collective virtual living space created by combining all digital elements. Web 3.0 is expressed as the third revolution of the internet world and it has become a subject that is mentioned a lot with the metaverse phenomenon. As it is known, web 1.0, which provides operation over servers, and web 2.0, which is a state of existence after becoming a member through platforms, are the internet infrastructures we still use. The reason why Web 3.0 is being talked about these days is that metaverse-based digital environments express the state of "intermediary" existence on the Internet (Çelik, 2022).

The authors made definitions by referring to different aspects of the concept of metaverse. In their definitions, it is emphasized that the metaverse is a three-dimensional virtual universe, that reality is moved to a different dimension and that it offers unique experiences for users. Some of the authors' emphases are as follows; an open, disconnected, immersive environment that removes the barriers of time and space (Jaynes, et all, 2003); a human-centered virtual world (Duan, et all, 2021); immersive three-dimensional digital environment (Dionisio, Burns, and Gilbert, 2013); a permanent, synthetic, three-dimensional, non-game-centered space (Nevelsteen, 2018); virtual extension of the physical world (Schlemmer, Trein, and Oliveira, 2009; Siyaev, and Jo, 2021; Akour,et all, 2022; Zhao, et all, 2022; Mystakidis, 2022); an immersive internet vision (Lee, et all, 2021; Wang, et all, 2022; Xu, et all, 2021; Ning, et all, 2021; Gupta, 2022;Vidal-Tomás, 2022).

Thanks to mobile devices that can connect to the Internet, it is possible to easily access Metaverse anytime, anywhere. The Roblox gaming platform has 50 million games and 3 billion hours of monthly usage. People now spend more time on gaming platforms than on social media. Metaverse has a strong side as a service with more sustainable content and social meaning. It also has a scalable environment that can accommodate large numbers of people to strengthen social meaning (Park, and Kim, 2022).

Besides gaming platforms, it is available in environments where people have different experiences. For example, various universes have been created for the real estate sector. Decentraland, Axie Infinity, Blocktopia, Genesis City, nextearth, Dvision Network, myneighboralice, Lunacia, MatrixWorld Land Sale are among these universes. Decentraland is the most popular metaverse universe. In this universe, users can buy land, rent land, visit museums and shops. In addition, users can vote for the decisions taken for the city. Decentraland is a type of metaverse that uses blockchain infrastructure. Land and other items in Decentraland are purchased using the cryptocurrency MANA. In November 2021, a real estate located in "Fashion Street" was sold for 2,428,740 US dollars (Howcroft, 2021).

Metaverse is an old idea that circulated with the development of the internet and other technologies. The first building block of the timeline of metaverse development was the birth of the internet in 1991. In the following period, the first online virtual world was entered with Second Life. The metaverse experience, which started in the playground, has been experienced in different areas with the enriching content production. In 2009, cryptocurrency Bitcoin and Blockchain technologies strengthened the metaverse infrastructure. Significant progress was made in 2014 with virtual reality glasses. In recent years, unique virtual universes have been created with decentralized organizations. Global companies such as Microsoft, Facebook and Google are making huge investments.

In the 1990s, as a result of the rapid transformation in computing power and computer graphics, text-based interaction was insufficient for people. As a result of the expectations, virtual worlds equipped with 3D graphics and more open-ended socialization opportunities emerged. In the created virtual worlds, an online 3D virtual environment was created where users can log in with the content produced. Along with the progress, communication methods have been enriched both in writing and verbally so that people can better share their experiences. At the point reached today, it is thought that the metaverse significantly reflects the human-centered computing vision, which is very beneficial for society in terms of accessibility, diversity, equality and humanity (Duan, et all, 2021).

Figure 1. Metaverse Timeline
Source: (Huynh-The, et all, 2022).

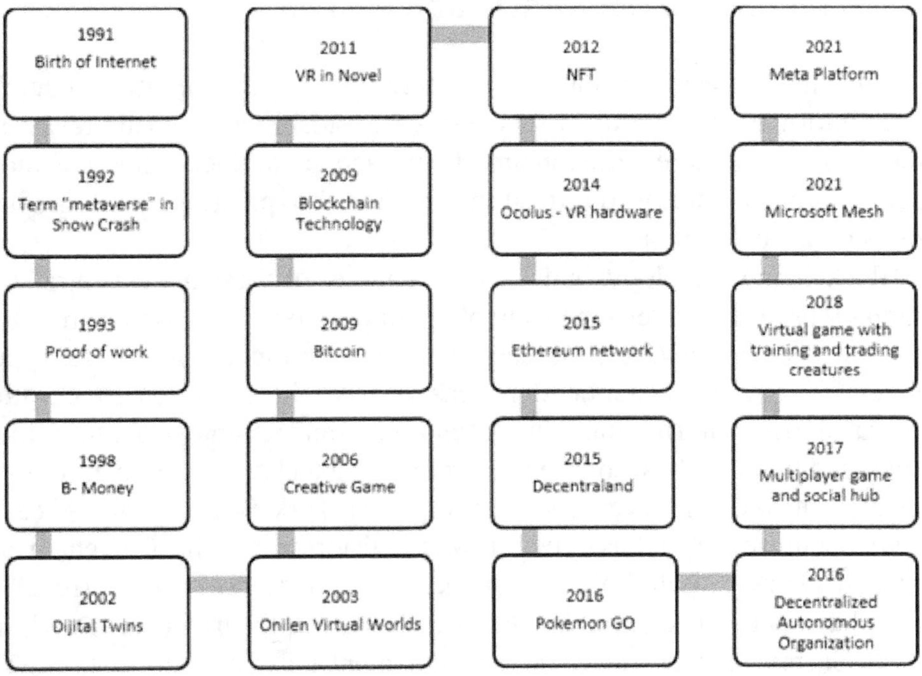

Internet, standards for open media, open programming language standards, extended reality hardware, decentralized ledger and smart contracts are needed to create the metaverse. The Internet is a major component as it provides a network independent of institutions, individuals or governments. Creating open standards for media such as audio, text and video in Metaverse applications is essential for an integrated system. Standards should govern the creation of media as well as combinations of creating new media formats. There may be a need for productive and clear programming language standards for programming languages. Extended reality hardware mainly focuses on creating an interface between world and the metadata store. Blockchain networks are necessary to provide better transparency in transactions and prevent outside interference (Geroni, 2021).

Technologies Related to Metaverse

New generation technologies such as blockchain, augmented reality and virtual reality, 3D graphics, artificial intelligence and the internet of things are used to make the Metaverse experience more immersive.

Blockchain, Cryptocurrency, and NFT

Blockchain is a shared database on a network of computers that securely stores information in digital blocks. NFTs are tradable rights to digital assets where ownership is recorded in smart contracts on a blockchain. The most used types of NFT are; are digitized characters such as paintings, photographs, works of art, collections.

Blockchain technology, built on open source software and decentralized foundations, is the underlying technology of cryptocurrencies that are often mentioned today. However, this technology, which cannot be limited to crypto money, has much wider application areas with its unique solution to recording and transferring information. This decentralized and reliable structure, which is planned to be the basis of the Metaverses, is a technology with enormous potential and is open to everyone's participation (Türk, Bayrakçı, and Akçay).

Ownership of an NFT asset begins with registering it on the blockchain in a crypto network. This digital asset can then be sold for more cryptocurrencies. NFTs have very different characteristics from cryptocurrencies (Dowling, 2022). Cryptocurrencies and coins are equivalent and interchangeable. NFTs, on the other hand, are defined as unique and unalterable digital assets. NFTs allow different items to show originality and ownership in different domains, which explains its rapid expansion over virtual events, digital collections (Vidal-Tomás, 2022).

NFT has attracted incredible interest from investors very recently and in a short period of time. NFTs are described by some as a craze and by others as the future of digital art. Despite questions about its comparative scarcity digitally, it is the code or object to which a buyer attributes "value". Investors have expressed interest in the diverse types of NFTs, some of which are auctioned for millions of dollars, although in basis they represent little more than code. Estimated sales of NFTs were $12 million in December 2020, rising to $340 million two months later (Chohan, 2021).

Smart contracts form the infrastructure of Blockchain technology. Smart contracts are programmable contract clauses that reliably automate and define rules in cross-party transactions without any intermediaries

(Szabo, 1996). Smart contracts allow unfamiliar parties and decentralized participants to trade safely and fairly without a third party. It also proposes a unified method for building applications in a wide variety of industries. Transparency is guaranteed in the execution of these instructions, as states containing instructions and parameters in smart contracts are shared by all participants (Wang, et all, 2021).

Smart contracts can manage tokens representing digital assets on blockchains. There are two types of these tokens, tradable and non-tradable. Fungible tokens can be split into smaller units (Hong, Noh, and Park, 2019). Interchangeable tokens differ from immutable tokens in terms of tradability, uniformity, and divisibility. Exchangeable tokens can be exchanged for other items containing one currency from the same currency to another. They are also identical to each other and can be divided into smaller units and do not affect its value. NFTs cannot be exchanged for another non-tradable token of a similar type; The immutable symbol of one work of art cannot be replaced by the immutable symbol of another work of art. An non- fungible coin cannot be split, e.g. a built property cannot be divided into different parts. Immutable tokens are unique in their distinctive information and attributes that make their exchange impossible. Each bounty is unique and completely different from the others. While some digital artworks have the same dimensions or artistic style, each has a different artist, creation date (Bal, and Ner, 2019).

Extended Reality (XR)

Extended reality technologies are a technology that helps everyone communicate in the virtual world using digital avatars. In the past, computers and mobile phones were based on a two-dimensional screen interface. That's why the Microsoft operating system is called "Windows". User interaction would be complete with mouse clicks and drags. Thanks to the developing technology today, Extended reality glasses provide a three-dimensional interface for viewing and interaction, allowing immersion in a virtual information world (Yang, et all, 2022).

Virtual reality; They are three-dimensional artificial universes produced outside of reality by interacting with real-time simulations of their users with the help of multi-sensory channels such as visual, touch, hearing, smell and taste, and special devices worn on the body. Enriching the real world with information from the computer and increasing its functionality is important for augmented reality. However, the important point here is that virtual objects can hide a part of the real world from the user. In other words, virtual and real objects in the same environment affect each other and move them away from the user's viewing distance (Orhan, and Karaman).

Virtual reality is technology that changes a person's view of the physical world with a virtual scene using software and hardware. Complete disconnection from the surrounding and real world when wearing full range headphones. A digitally created virtual environment is reflected by the screens inside the lenses of these devices, changing the perspective. Augmented reality is a technology that combines the virtual and real worlds. In this reality technology, real-world surfaces and objects are identified using technologies such as object recognition, plane detection, face recognition and motion tracking. It then places computer-generated data such as graphics, sounds, images and messages on these pre-recognized planes. Mixed reality, on the other hand, is expressed as a mixture of augmented reality and virtual reality (Mozumder, et all, 2022).

Technologies such as Metaverse have the potential to change users' connection and experience with the internet. Virtual reality technologies allow users to have a more realistic and memorable experience by simulating the operations in the virtual world with the real world. On the other hand, augmented reality/virtual reality integrates the physical world into the Metaverse by transforming the physical world into a virtual one. (Nalbant, and Uyanık, 2021). While creating a completely digital environment in virtual reality, augmented and mixed reality digital environment and real life are blended (Kemeç, 2022).

Virtual environments and digital objects created by virtual reality and augmented reality applications enable people to engage in multi-sensory interactions. Therefore, Metaverse can be defined as a network of interconnected social and networked immersive environments across persistent, multi-user platforms. Thanks to XR hardware, people interact in a fully or partially virtual digital environment. Users do not need to be stationary in these virtual environments. Also, users can activate their whole body and movements can be tracked by cameras and sensors (Mystakidis, 2022).

Artificial Intelligence (AI)

Metaverse practitioners take advantage of artificial intelligence technology to free them from tedious and demanding data analysis tasks such as monitoring, organizing, and planning (Lee, et all, 2021). Metaverse uses artificial intelligence technology so that anyone can safely and freely participate in social, cultural, artistic and economic activities that transcend the real world.

State-of-the-art artificial intelligence studies focus on machine learning, deep learning and reinforcement learning in areas such as computer vision, decision making, natural language process (Ynag, et all, 2022).

Technological developments have introduced social networks, then augmented reality experiences, and now the Metaverse experience to people's experience. As technology progressed, discussions of artificial intelligence emerged and intensified. While the debates on whether humanity will be able to establish a real communication between humans and machines, such as interpersonal communication in the future, or whether artificial intelligence will be conscious and manage humanity, have been going on for decades, dystopian scenarios are becoming more and more popular. With the Metaverse, human consciousness discussions, which are thought to surrender to artificial intelligence, have come to the fore again. The user activates his internal processes and gives intentional responses to the stimuli by means of stimuli sent to his brain in augmented reality (Türk, 2022).

Computers are improving in recognizing gestures, giving way to connect with them in a more natural way and ultimately to an understanding of emotion and body language. Photoreceptors in the eye are most concentrated in the region called the fovea, where the perception of highest resolution is located, and everything else is peripheral vision. Eye tracking is another important aspect of the immersion interface for virtual reality. Artificial intelligence is used to predict where the eye will look next, even when blinking, so that the best visualization can be prepared ahead of time. This is crucial to provide the most comprehensive experience and will be crucial for next-generation technologies such as holographic light fields that require it (Sivasankar, 2022).

3D Design

As a new media, Metaverse enables people to be in a 3D virtual world in different universes. It is expected that this technology will pave the way for dramatic changes in all human relations in societies, as it will offer unique communication facilities that were not previously available to humans. Metaverse, which aims to rebuild the world, is thought to go much further in transforming the existing relationship between people and cities. While in the past, cities were seen as a symbolic phenomenon reflecting real-world experiences, with the advent of the Metaverse, real cities seem to be able to evoke experiences from the virtual world (Hemmati, 2022).

3D virtual universes are supported by communication processes that allow fast and rich communication and any transformation of avatars. The first feature of 3D virtual environments is the 3D environment itself. All kinds of environments including parks, streets, residences, gymnasiums, libraries, museums and city designs are visualized in 3D. There is also the possibility of integrating different applications into the created virtual worlds. Additionally, 3D virtual environments offer the ability to drive 3D design for mission-related purposes (Van der Land, Schouten, and, Feldberg, 2011).

Internet of Things (IoT)

Metaverse requires the Internet of Things, providing fully connected, immersive and engaging online 3D virtual experiences through traditional personal computing as well as virtual and augmented reality devices. In Metaverse, users have their own avatars and can interact with virtual objects and other participants. One of the key building blocks of the metaverse are digital twins that are replicated in a virtual environment, reflecting the real-time physical world state. The connection between the virtual and physical world is linked to the data collected from IoT devices. Unified learning is a promising solution to enable collaboration between edge and server for better global performance and also to increase the security and privacy of the metaverse (Zhang, et all, 2021).

Metaverse is a computer-generated, multi-user, three-dimensional interface. To realize the Metaverse, the real world needs to be digitized. In the Metaverse, information measured in bits is the main entity. Both animate and inanimate entities in the physical world can be scanned and digitally reproduced in the Metaverse by drivers, roads, smart devices, e.g. IoT devices and sensors. This idea of digital duplication has recently been studied by many researchers around a concept called the digital twin. A key aspect of implementing a good digital twin is the constant data synchronization in the Metaverse. Digital copies of physical objects (digital twins) are essential enablers to make the human experience in virtual life more real. Virtual service providers offer a dynamic framework in which sensors and physical objects are encouraged to detect and collect state information to help synchronize digital twins (Han, et all, 2021).

METAVERSE EXPERIENCES IN URBAN POLICIES

Although many city administrators are hesitant to take part in a decentralized virtual world, this idea finds an intense response in urban policies. Embassies are opened in the virtual universe, municipalities offer different services, organize meetings, cultural events, artistic activities, entertainment programs and competitions.

In this section, practices for urban policies are discussed. Of these projects; The 'Metaverse Seoul' project, in which the Seoul Metropolitan Government aims to create a virtual communication ecosystem for all areas of municipal government; "CatVers" application, which creates an open, immersive digital universe developed by the government of Catalonia; Barbados administration's project to open an embassy in the virtual universe; The metaverse vision within the framework of Shanghai government's plan to become a globally influential digital hub; Sanya Municipality's idea of bringing games, music, e-commerce and online education to the virtual universe stands out. These projects will be examined in detail and a comprehensive evaluation will be made in terms of city management.

Seoul Metaverse Experience

The Seoul Metropolitan Government (SMG) has announced that it will be the first metropolitan city to enter the metaverse. Temporarily named 'Metaverse Seoul', the company aims to create a virtual communication ecosystem for all areas of municipal government. Approximately €2.8 billion has been invested in the project as part of the Seoul Vision 2030 plan. In line with its vision of a city of coexistence, a global leader, a safe city and an emotional city of the future, the citizens of Seoul will soon be able to wear VR headsets to meet with city officials for virtual consultation. They can even attend community events. Avatar public servants in the Metaverse will provide public service. It will also develop services for the socially vulnerable (Gaubert, 2021). Seoul's desire to become a metaverse city is considered as a new step in smart city evolution.

Many officials commented on the Metaverse Seoul plan, which is among the most concrete examples of the field. For example, metaverse researcher Kim Sangkyun warned policy makers against accessibility, security and affordability problems in metaverse projects in a bundle he gave to the Washington Post (Noor, 2022).

Catalonia Metaverse Experience

Catalonia, an autonomous region in Spain, launched the first Metaverse in Catalan, an application called CatVers. This application is a free access virtual platform. It is an open, immersive digital universe developed by the Catalan Blockchain Center (CBCat) with support from the government of Catalonia and the Barcelona Chamber of Commerce. According to Quirze Salomó, CatVers is "a 3D virtual reality world where several digital technologies merge and you can have immersive experiences". There are plans to create a virtual university campus within CatVers for use by Catalan universities. There are plans to create a virtual campus within CatVers this year to be used by Catalan universities as well as art exhibitions and festivals in the coming months. Organizers also aim to establish "decentralized management" of the metadata repository so that it can be run by enrolling groups (Iolov, 2022).

Shanghai Metaverse Experience

In Shanghai, the largest city of China, studies are carried out on the metaverse technology, which has attracted mass attention this year. In the Shanghai Municipal Economic and Information Technology Commission's five-year plan to develop the electronic information industry, it was argued that the metaverse is one of the four frontiers for exploration.

Calls were made for the development of metaverse projects in urban service delivery, entertainment environments, production, games, business meetings (Cheng, 2021). Shanghai has incorporated the concept into its development plan, hoping to gain an early advantage in the race for next-generation technology. In Shanghai, it is planned to encourage further use and study of research and development of core technologies, including sensors, real-time human-computer interaction, and blockchain. The inclusion of Metaverse in Shanghai's development strategy follows the city's long-term vision to transform itself into a "globally influential digital hub" with major information technology upgrades for a range of industries by 2035. Digital goals include building faster 5G and broadband networks, building smart factories and digital hospitals, developing artificial intelligence and data-driven services, and increasing applications for the elderly and disabled (Wei, 2022).

Barbados Metaverse Experience

The Caribbean nation of Barbados has signed a contract with blockchain metaverse platform Decentraland to open the world's first digital embassy. The embassy building to be established in Metaverse will serve various projects, determining and purchasing the land, creating the architecture of virtual embassies and consulates, and providing services such as e-visas. Barbados is not limited to the idea of a virtual embassy only to Decentraland. The government plans to make deals with Somnium Space, SuperWorld, and other Metaverse platforms (Loop Business, 2021).

There are ideas that virtual embassy service will fail in the metaverse universe. Skynews writer Martin Kimber noted that the new technology is unlikely to replace old diplomacy methods. Diplomacy will stubbornly cling to old ways of relating and while having a twitter account or a metaverse embassy is one way to complete that engagement, it certainly cannot replace it (Kimber, 2021).

Sanya Municipality Metaverse Experience

On december 25, 2021, NetEase, a Chinese internet technology enterprise, signed a strategic partnership agreement with the Sanya municipal government. NetEase plans to build a metaverse industrial foundation project in Sanya, with its headquarters in Hainan (Metanews, 2021).

It is expected that the technology base will become a global center where digital content is produced, internet technology is developed, legal ground for digital copyright is established and all services are integrated. In addition, the two sides will deepen their cooperation in interactive entertainment, e-sports, music culture, e-commerce, supply chain, live streaming and online education (Pandaily, 2021).

Uberlândia Municipality Metaverse Experience

The municipality of Uberlândia organized a chat at Horizon Workrooms to discuss agribusiness and technology perspectives in the city and Brazil. This metaverse initiative of the municipality of Uberlândia is the first in Brazil (Capelli, 2022). To attend the broadcast, Mayor Odelmo Leão, municipal secretary Ana Paula Junqueira, and Sapiens co-founder Maurício Lemos used virtual reality glasses to enter a chat room at Horizon Workrooms (Singh, 2022).

In the meeting, which created the first record of the official agenda of the municipal public authorities in the virtual and augmented reality environment in the country, the mayor Maurício Lemos said that the public service, which cannot keep up with modernity, will certainly not meet the wishes and needs of the people. He also stated that attention will be paid to the development and dissemination of equipment and services in the metaverse for the public good (Uberlândia Government, 2022).

CONCLUSION

Urban policymakers should take seriously the future opportunity represented by the metaverse. The Metaverse has the potential to offer entirely new ways, for example, to create jobs, provide education, provide healthcare and plan urban spaces. New organizations, products and services, everything from payment processing to authentication, recruitment, advertising content production and security will be taken care of in the virtual world. In order not to reduce the positive effects of the metaverse, which offers the opportunity to be applied in many areas, legal and administrative regulations are included in order to eliminate users' cyberbullying, abuse and security concerns. Care should be taken not to exclude groups that are in a disadvantaged position (children, young people, the elderly, the disabled, immigrants, women and the poor) while establishing the legal basis for the Metaverse.

For a successful urban policy design, an integrated urban governance is needed in which the urban problems that can be solved through the metaverse and the roadmap are well defined. Data analytics is an important tool in urban governance. Data collected from websites, mobile devices, mobile applications, social media shares, games and sensors are analyzed. In particular, it uses these data to implement applications related to the metaverse. For this purpose, steps are being taken to establish an urban big data analysis center in order to strengthen the data infrastructure and analysis capability.

It is presented in tools to strengthen participation in urban decisions through Metaverse projects. In urban policy making, users' right to vote is an important building block in the process leading to autonomous governance.

REFERENCES

Akour, I. A., Al-Maroof, R. S., Alfaisal, R., & Salloum, S. A. (2022). A conceptual framework for determining metaverse adoption in higher institutions of gulf area: An empirical study using hybrid SEM-ANN approach. *Computers and Education: Artificial Intelligence*, *3*, 100052. doi:10.1016/j.caeai.2022.100052

Alfaro, P. S. (2022). *Welcome to the Catalan metaverse that wants to replace zoom.* https://en.ara.cat/business/welcome-to-the-catalan-metaverse-that-wants-to-replace-zoom_1_4236566.html

Arpaci, I., Karatas, K., Kusci, I., & Al-Emran, M. (2022). Understanding the social sustainability of the Metaverse by integrating UTAUT2 and big five personality traits: A hybrid SEM-ANN approach. *Technology in Society*, *71*, 102120. doi:10.1016/j.techsoc.2022.102120

Aytaç, Z. (2022). Word Association and Thematic Distribution of Metaverse Application Areas: The Twitter Case. *Kastamonu University Journal of Faculty of Economics and Administrative Sciences*, *24*(1), 100–118.

Bal, M., & Ner, C. (2019). *NFTracer: a Non-Fungible token tracking proof-of-concept using Hyperledger Fabric.* arXiv preprint arXiv:1905.04795.

Barrera, K. G., & Shah, D. (2023). Marketing in the Metaverse: Conceptual understanding, framework, and research agenda. *Journal of Business Research*, *155*, 113420. doi:10.1016/j.jbusres.2022.113420

Barry, D. M., Ogawa, N., Dharmawansa, A., Kanematsu, H., Fukumura, Y., Shirai, T., Yajima, K., & Kobayashi, T. (2015). Evaluation for students' learning manner using eye blinking system in metaverse. *Procedia Computer Science*, *60*, 1195–1204. doi:10.1016/j.procs.2015.08.181

Bourlakis, M., Papagiannidis, S., & Li, F. (2009). Retail spatial evolution: Paving the way from traditional to metaverse retailing. *Electronic Commerce Research*, *9*(1), 135–148. doi:10.100710660-009-9030-8

Capelli, F. (2022). *Uberlândia MG is the first Brazilian municipality to hold a meeting in the metaverse.* https://programadoresbrasil.com.br/en/2022/02/uberlandia-mg-is-the-first-Brazilian-municipality-to-hold-a-meeting-in-the-metaverse/

Çelik, R. (2022). What is the metaverse? conceptual evaluation and overview. *Balkan and Near Eastern Journal of Social Sciences, 8*(1).

Çelikkol, Ş. (2022). Evaluation of Metaverse World In Terms of Consumer Purchasing Behaviors. *İstanbul Kent Üniversitesi İnsan ve Toplum Bilimleri Dergisi, 3*(1), 64-75.

Cheng, E. (2021). *Shanghai doubles down on the metaverse by including it in a development plan.* https://www.cnbc.com/2021/12/31/shanghai-releases-five-year-plans-for-metaverse-development.html

Chohan, U. W. (2021). *Non-fungible tokens: Blockchains, scarcity, and value.* Critical Blockchain Research Initiative (CBRI) Working Papers.

Choi, H. S., & Kim, S. H. (2017). A content service deployment plan for metaverse museum exhibitions—Centering on the combination of beacons and HMDs. *International Journal of Information Management, 37*(1), 1519–1527. doi:10.1016/j.ijinfomgt.2016.04.017

Choi, H. Y. (2022). Working in the Metaverse: Does Telework in a Metaverse Office Have the Potential to Reduce Population Pressure in Megacities? Evidence from Young Adults in Seoul, South Korea. *Sustainability, 14*(6), 3629. doi:10.3390u14063629

Dionisio, J. D. N., III, W. G. B., & Gilbert, R. (2013). 3D virtual worlds and the metaverse: Current status and future possibilities. *ACM Computing Surveys, 45*(3), 1-38.

Dowling, M. (2022). Is non-fungible token pricing driven by cryptocurrencies? *Finance Research Letters, 44*, 102097. doi:10.1016/j.frl.2021.102097

Duan, H., Li, J., Fan, S., Lin, Z., Wu, X., & Cai, W. (2021, October). Metaverse for social good: A university campus prototype. In *Proceedings of the 29th ACM International Conference on Multimedia* (pp. 153-161). 10.1145/3474085.3479238

Garavand, A., & Aslani, N. (2022). Metaverse phenomenon and its impact on health: A scoping review. *Informatics in Medicine Unlocked*, 101029.

Gaubert, J. (2021). *Seoul to become the first city to enter the metaverse. What will it look like?* https://www.euronews.com/next/2021/11/10/seoul-to-become-the-first-city-to-enter-the-metaverse-what-will-it-look-like

Geroni, D. (2021). *Know Everything About Blockchain Metaverse.* https://101blockchains.com/blockchain-metaverse/

Gupta, A. (2022). *What is a metaverse?*https://www.gartner.com/en/articles/what-is-a-metaverse

Han, Y., Niyato, D., Leung, C., Kim, D. I., Zhu, K., Feng, S., & Miao, C. (2022). A Dynamic Hierarchical Framework for IoT-assisted Metaverse Synchronization. *Journal of Latex Class Files, 14*(8). arXiv preprint arXiv:2203.03969.

Hazan, S. (2010). Musing the metaverse. Heritage in the Digital Era, Multi-Science Publishing.

Hemmati, M. (2022). The Metaverse: An Urban Revolution Effect of the Metaverse on the Perceptions of Urban Audience. *Tourism of Culture*, *2*(7), 53–60.

Hong, S., Noh, Y., & Park, C. (2019, December). Design of extensible non-fungible token model in hyperledger fabric. In *Proceedings of the 3rd Workshop on Scalable and Resilient Infrastructures for Distributed Ledgers* (pp. 1-2). 10.1145/3366611.3368142

Howcroft, E. (2021). *Virtual real estate plot sells for record $2.4 million.* https://www.reuters.com/markets/currencies/virtual-real-estate-plot-sells-record-24-million-2021-11-23/

Huh, S. (2022). Application of computer-based testing in the Korean Medical Licensing Examination, the emergence of the metaverse in medical education, journal metrics and statistics, and appreciation to reviewers and volunteers. *Journal of Educational Evaluation for Health Professions*, *19*, 19. doi:10.3352/jeehp.2022.19.2 PMID:35021317

Huynh-The, T., Pham, Q. V., Pham, X. Q., Nguyen, T. T., Han, Z., & Kim, D. S. (2022). *Artificial Intelligence for the Metaverse: A Survey.* arXiv preprint arXiv:2202.10336.

Iolov, T. V. (2022). *Catalonia has launched its own metaverse.* https://www.themayor.eu/en/a/view/catalonia-has-launched-its-own-metaverse-9744

Jaung, W. (2022). Digital forest recreation in the metaverse: Opportunities and challenges. *Technological Forecasting and Social Change*, *185*, 122090. doi:10.1016/j.techfore.2022.122090

Jaynes, C., Seales, W. B., Calvert, K., Fei, Z., & Griffioen, J. (2003). The Metaverse: a networked collection of inexpensive, self-configuring, immersive environments. In *Proceedings of the workshop on Virtual environments 2003* (pp. 115-124). 10.1145/769953.769967

Kemec, A. (2022). From Reality to Virtuality: Re-discussing Cities with the Concept of the Metaverse. *International Journal of Management Accounting*, *4*(1), 12–20.

Kimber, M. (2021). *Barbados to launch world's first virtual embassy in the metaverse.* https://news.sky.com/story/barbados-to-launch-worlds-first-virtual-embassy-in-the-metaverse-12470727

Ko, E., & Jang, J. (2014). The Virtual Device Managing Module of the Metaverse Assisted Living Support System. In *Proceedings of the International Conference on Modeling, Simulation and Visualization Methods (MSV).* The Steering Committee of The World Congress in Computer Science, Computer Engineering and Applied Computing (WorldComp).

Kye, B., Han, N., Kim, E., Park, Y., & Jo, S. (2021). Educational applications of metaverse: Possibilities and limitations. *Journal of Educational Evaluation for Health Professions*, *18*, 18. doi:10.3352/jeehp.2021.18.32 PMID:34897242

Lee, C. W. (2022). Application of Metaverse Service to Healthcare Industry: A Strategic Perspective. *International Journal of Environmental Research and Public Health*, *19*(20), 13038. doi:10.3390/ijerph192013038 PMID:36293609

Lee, J., & Kundu, P. (2022). Integrated cyber-physical systems and industrial metaverse for remote manufacturing. *Manufacturing Letters*, *34*, 12–15. doi:10.1016/j.mfglet.2022.08.012

Lee, J., Lee, T. S., Lee, S., Jang, J., Yoo, S., Choi, Y., & Park, Y. R. (2022). Development and Application of a Metaverse-Based Social Skills Training Program for Children With Autism Spectrum Disorder to Improve Social Interaction: Protocol for a Randomized Controlled Trial. *JMIR Research Protocols*, *11*(6), e35960. doi:10.2196/35960 PMID:35675112

Lee, L. H., Braud, T., Zhou, P., Wang, L., Xu, D., Lin, Z., . . . Hui, P. (2021). *All one needs to know about metaverse: A complete survey on technological singularity, virtual ecosystem, and research agenda.* arXiv preprint arXiv:2110.05352.

Loop Business. (2021). *Barbados to establish world's 1st Metaverse Embassy with Decentraland.* https://barbados.loopnews.com/content/barbados-establish-worlds-1st-metaverse-embassy-decentraland

Lu, Y., Yang, D., Yang, Y., & Bai, C. (2022). MIoT integrates health, MM benefits humans: Funding conference for International Association and Alliance of Metaverse in Medicine successfully held. *Clinical eHealth, 5*, 17-18.

Metanews. (2021). *NetEase to build a new metaverse industrial base in Sanya, China.* https://metanews.com/netease-to-build-a-new-metaverse-industrial-base-in-sanya-china/

Mozumder, M. A. I., Sheeraz, M. M., Athar, A., Aich, S., & Kim, H. C. (2022, February). Overview: Technology Roadmap of the Future Trend of Metaverse based on IoT, Blockchain, AI Technique, and Medical Domain Metaverse Activity. In *2022 24th International Conference on Advanced Communication Technology (ICACT)* (pp. 256-261). IEEE.

Mystakidis, S. (2022). Metaverse. *Encyclopedia*, *2*(1), 486–497. doi:10.3390/encyclopedia2010031

Nalbant, K. G., & Uyanık, Ş. (2021). Computer Vision in the Metaverse. *Journal of Metaverse*, *1*(1), 9–12. doi:10.57019/jmv.1148015

Nevelsteen, K. J. (2018). Virtual world, defined from a technological perspective and applied to video games, mixed reality, and the Metaverse. *Computer Animation and Virtual Worlds*, *29*(1), e1752. doi:10.1002/cav.1752

Ning, H., Wang, H., Lin, Y., Wang, W., Dhelim, S., Farha, F., . . . Daneshmand, M. (2021). A *Survey on Metaverse: the State-of-the-art, Technologies, Applications, and Challenges.* arXiv preprint arXiv:2111.09673.

Noor, M. (2022). *Urban life in the metaverse: Potential for utopia or wholly unnecessary?* https://www.theurbanist.org/2022/01/25/urban-life-in-the-metaverse-potential-for-utopia-or-wholly-unnecessary/

Orhan, S., & Karaman, M. K. (2011). *A new look at reality in education: Blended and extended reality.* XVI. *Internet Conference in Turkey*, *30*, 373–384.

Pandaily. (2021). *NetEase and Sanya Municipal Government Reach Cooperation to Build Metaverse Industrial Base.* https://pandaily.com/netease-and-sanya-municipal-government-reach-cooperation-to-build-metaverse-industrial-base/

Park, S. M., & Kim, Y. G. (2022). A Metaverse: Taxonomy, components, applications, and open challenges. *IEEE Access: Practical Innovations, Open Solutions*, *10*, 4209–4251. doi:10.1109/ACCESS.2021.3140175

Schlemmer, E., Trein, D., & Oliveira, C. (2009). The metaverse: Telepresence in 3D avatar-driven digital-virtual worlds. *@ tic. revista d'innovació educativa*, (2), 26-32.

Shen, B., Tan, W., Guo, J., Zhao, L., & Qin, P. (2021). How to Promote User Purchase in Metaverse? A Systematic Literature Review on Consumer Behavior Research and Virtual Commerce Application Design. *Applied Sciences (Basel, Switzerland)*, *11*(23), 11087. doi:10.3390/app112311087

Singh, Y. (2022). *Uberlândia city hall holds first meeting in the metaverse.* https://playcrazygame.com/2022/02/02/uberlandia-city-hall-holds-first-meeting-in-the-metaverse/

Siyaev, A., & Jo, G. S. (2021). Towards aircraft maintenance metaverse using speech interactions with virtual objects in mixed reality. *Sensors (Basel)*, *21*(6), 2066. doi:10.339021062066 PMID:33804253

Sivasankar, G. A. (2022). Study Of Blockchain Technology, AI and Digital Networking in Metaverse. *IRE Journals, 5*(8).

Susmitha, K., & Jayaprada, S. (2017). Smart Cities Using Big Data Analytics. *International Research Journal of Engineering and Technology*, *4*(8), 1615–1620.

Szabo, N. (1996). Smart contracts: building blocks for digital markets. *Extropy: The Journal of Transhumanist Thought, 18*(2), 28.

Tang, Y. (2021). Help first-year college students to learn their library through an augmented reality game. *Journal of Academic Librarianship*, *47*(1), 102294. doi:10.1016/j.acalib.2020.102294

Tayfun, A., Silik, C. E., Şimşek, E., & Dülger, A. S. (2022). Metaverse: An Opportunity For Tourism? Or is it a Threat? (Metaverse: An Opportunity). *Journal of Tourism and Gastronomy Studies*, *10*(2), 818-836.

Türk, G. D. (2022). An evaluation on intentionality, artificial intelligence and metaverse relationship. *International Journal of Economic and Administrative Academic Research*, *2*(3), 19–39.

Türk, G. D., Bayrakcı, S., & Akçay, E. (2022). Metaverse and Self Presentation. *The Turkish Online Journal of Design Art and Communication*, *12*(2), 316–333. doi:10.7456/11202100/008

Uberlândia Government. (2022). *Prefeitura de Uberlândia é a primeira do Brasil a realizar reunião no metaverso.* https://www.uberlandia.mg.gov.br/2022/01/31/prefeitura-de-uberlandia-e-a-primeira-do-brasil-a-realizar-reuniao-de-trabalho-no-metaverso/

Van der Land, S., Schouten, A., & Feldberg, F. (2011). Modeling the metaverse: A theoretical model of effective team collaboration in 3D virtual environments. *Journal of Virtual Worlds Research*, *4*(3). Advance online publication. doi:10.4101/jvwr.v4i3.6126

Vidal-Tomás, D. (2022). The new crypto niche: NFTs, play-to-earn, and metaverse tokens. *Finance Research Letters*, *47*, 102742. doi:10.1016/j.frl.2022.102742

Wang, Q., Li, R., Wang, Q., & Chen, S. (2021). *Non-fungible token (NFT): Overview, evaluation, opportunities and challenges.* arXiv preprint arXiv:2105.07447.

Wang, Y., Su, Z., Zhang, N., Liu, D., Xing, R., Luan, T. H., & Shen, X. (2022). *A Survey on Metaverse: Fundamentals, Security, and Privacy.* doi:10.36227/techrxiv.19255058.v2

Wei, D. (2022). Gemiverse: The blockchain-based professional certification and tourism platform with its own ecosystem in the metaverse. *International Journal of Geoheritage and Parks*, *10*(2), 322–336. doi:10.1016/j.ijgeop.2022.05.004

Wei, H. (2022). *Future of internet virtually in sight.* https://global.chinadaily.com.cn/a/202202/11/WS6205c99fa310cdd39bc860e0.html

Xu, M., Niyato, D., Kang, J., Xiong, Z., Miao, C., & Kim, D. I. (2021). *Wireless Edge-Empowered Metaverse: A Learning-Based Incentive Mechanism for Virtual Reality.* arXiv preprint arXiv:2111.03776.

Yang, D., Zhou, J., Chen, R., Song, Y., Song, Z., Zhang, X., ... Bai, C. (2022). Expert consensus on the metaverse in medicine. *Clinical eHealth*, *5*, 1-9.

Yang, F., Ren, L., & Gu, C. (2022). A study of college students' intention to use metaverse technology for basketball learning based on UTAUT2. *Heliyon*, *8*(9), e10562. doi:10.1016/j.heliyon.2022.e10562 PMID:36132173

Ynag, Q., Zhao, Y., Huang, H., & Zheng, Z. (2022). *Fusing Blockchain and AI with Metaverse: A Survey.* arXiv preprint arXiv:2201.03201.

Yüksel, S., & Yıldız, S. (2022). Changing virtual-real places in the metaverse world and the role of the designer. *7th International Zeugma Scientific Research Congress*, Turkey.

Zhang, T., Gao, L., He, C., Zhang, M., Krishnamachari, B., & Avestimehr, S. (2021). *Federated Learning for Internet of Things: Applications, Challenges, and Opportunities.* arXiv preprint arXiv:2111.07494.

Zhang, T., Shen, J., Lai, C. F., Ji, S., & Ren, Y. (2023). Multi-server assisted data sharing supporting secure deduplication for metaverse healthcare systems. *Future Generation Computer Systems*, *140*, 299–310. doi:10.1016/j.future.2022.10.031

Zhao, R., Zhang, Y., Zhu, Y., Lan, R., & Hua, Z. (2022). *Metaverse: Security and Privacy Concerns.* arXiv preprint arXiv:2203.03854.

Zhou, B. (2022). *Building a Smart Education Ecosystem from a Metaverse Perspective*. Mobile Information Systems. doi:10.1155/2022/1938329

Chapter 3
Ethical Concerns in the Metaverse Business

Muhammad Anshari
https://orcid.org/0000-0002-8160-6682
Universiti Brunei Darussalam, Brunei

Muhammad Syafrudin
https://orcid.org/0000-0002-5640-4413
Sejong University, South Korea

Norma Latif Fitriyani
https://orcid.org/0000-0002-1133-3965
Sejong University, South Korea

Abdullah Al-Mudimigh
Dar Al Uloom Univesity, Saudi Arabia

ABSTRACT

Companies are beginning to utilize the metaverse to broaden their service network and create new co-creation value for their clients. To better understand how the metaverse phenomena could impact corporate sustainability, investigative research should be conducted. In this chapter, the authors looked at the moral issues raised by businesses using metaverse to gain a competitive advantage. An exploratory evaluation of business ethics and a metaverse business model were used. Users, the general public, and consumers have a right to be fully informed of and understand that their data cannot be used by a third party for any reason in accordance with the consequentialist utilitarian principle and the notion of moral unity. Finally, those working in the disciplines of technology and public policy, including academics, entrepreneurs, and legislators, are expected to use the study.

DOI: 10.4018/978-1-6684-6097-9.ch003

Copyright © 2023, IGI Global. Copying or distributing in print or electronic forms without written permission of IGI Global is prohibited.

INTRODUCTION

New technologies like Metaverse are revolutionizing how businesses operate. According to 71% of respondents to an Accenture survey, the move to the Metaverse will have a positive business impact and be a breakthrough in the next years (Madeline Lewis, 2022). It has significant advantages to both individuals and businesses, such as cutting overhead expenses by doing away with the need for furniture and other upkeep. Metaverse will also be very strong because the platform can produce enormous volumes of data. Businesses will be able to gather enormous volumes of data in various types, including text, audio, video, object movement, 3D social media, and more, thanks to the existence and use of the Metaverse (Anshari et al., 2022).

While, historically, businesses have relied on data to guarantee their survival. Business organizations can obtain data from a variety of sources with the help of Metaverse. Big data can be produced by Metaverse as a digital platform, which helps organizations acquire, capture, and process both data sources into their databases for effective and efficient data analysis (Wu et al., 2014). The metaverse has emerged as a new location for monetizing massive amounts of data generation. Big data is often characterized as massive data sets with great volume, velocity, variety, variability, and value extracted for analysis (Katal et al., 2013). The organization would be able to gather insight and, more importantly, remain competitive in the market and outperform its rivals by implementing big data analytics from the Metaverse platform (Mayer-Schönberger & Cukier, 2013; Anshari et al., 2019).

In the Metaverse, big data is quickly gathered, created, and processed to produce new value co-creations for enterprises that will increase competition, productivity, innovation, and creativity (Anshari & Lim, 2017; Crane & Matten, 2016). There is, however, a moral issue concerning who owns the data on any digital network. It does not imply that firms can utilize data to generate profits without adhering to necessary ethical compliance just because it is available, particularly in Metaverse, one of the large data sources. The corporate ethics implications of the research domain have not received much attention because the metaverse is a relatively young field of study (Ahad et al., 2017; Razzaq et al., 2018)

Business ethics, as opposed to social right and wrong, is mainly the study of social situations, behaviors, and decisions that deal with morally right and wrong issues (Crane & Matten, 2016). It is just understanding what is good and wrong when pursuing society's goals, to put it simply (Hasmawati et al., 2020). The subject has gained prominence over the past ten years among a variety of community members, including public figures, lawmakers, corporate executives, shareholders, workers, clients, and researchers. If one chooses to be decent, learning about business ethics can show businesses how to conduct themselves, especially those in the customer service sector (Hooker, 2003). As a result, corporate ethics can influence behavior by educating organizations about the potential repercussions of their actions. This chapter looked into the potential for a data breach in Metaverse at a time when companies are embracing digital platforms swiftly to increase their position in the upcoming wave of Internet services.

METAVERSE AND BUSINESS ETHICS

The words "meta" and "universe" (Ball, 2022) were combined to form the phrase "metaverse" for the first time in the science fiction book Snow Crash from 1992 (Stephenson, 1992). Virtual reality technology progress is typically linked to growing immersion requirements (Brown, 2021; Antin, 2020; Neiger, 2021). It is a fictitious representation of the Internet that utilizes virtual reality (VR) and augmented reality (AR) headsets to create a single, pervasive, and immersive virtual world (O'Brian & Chan, 2021; Newton, 2021). The metaverse, in general, is a network of socially conscious 3D virtual worlds (Robertson, 2021; Clark, 2021). The way that businesses and their customers interact with goods and services may undergo a significant change as a result of the metaverse. Businesses give by developing a new method for interacting and communicating with customers from any location using technology like VR. Although the use of Metaverse as a new digital platform continues to follow the path that guarantees the safety, security, and comfort of customers, especially in light of the use of their data, here are some summaries of the literature on the business model for the Metaverse and the idea of business ethics.

The Metaverse is essentially a collection of virtual living, interactive, 3D settings that support identity continuity and enable user interaction through gaming, socializing, buying digital goods, learning in 3D, attending virtual events, etc. It is a multi-user environment that mixes physical reality with digital platforms and is eternal and persistent. The setting is the post-reality era. It is based on the fusion of technologies that enable multimodal interactions with digital items, virtual environments, and people, such as VR and AR (Mystakidis, 2022).

The entrances to the metaverse are provided through augmented and virtual reality. Nevertheless, it incorporates a multitude of next-generation technologies, including digital twins, blockchain, cryptocurrencies, cloud computing, big data, the Internet of Things, artificial intelligence (AI), VR, AR, and XR. The actors are users, service providers, and platform providers. Service providers on the Metaverse platform could be organizations or people who offer users digital services or digital assets, just like in the real world. In addition, people can buy digital assets from companies or other persons. Users of Metaverse are involved in social contact, news reading, playing games together, and other aspects of virtual life in addition to participating in digital commerce.

The interaction process changes users from two dimensions to three virtual dimensions, which is the only difference. Users will thus have a more engaging experience than they do with current 2D social media interactions. The 3D virtual environment offered by Metaverse has various advantages, including Big Data, an immersive user experience, an improvement in CRM for enterprises, interactive learning opportunities, virtual work productivity without 2D boundaries, and improved cross-cultural work collaboration. The main difference is that during an engagement, users go from two to three virtual dimensions. As a result, users will experience social media interactions more actively than they do now with 2D interactions. Big Data, an immersive user experience, an improvement in CRM for businesses, interactive learning opportunities, virtual work productivity without 2D boundaries, and increased cross-cultural work cooperation are just a few benefits of the 3D virtual environment provided by Metaverse.

The idea of ethics is challenging to define and understand. Ethics must first be defined to understand the crucial role they play in business. Merriam-Webster (2018) defines ethics as the study of right and wrong, as well as moral duty and obligation. People's views on what is good and evil, or what is right and wrong, vary widely. Because of this, it is difficult to comprehend and uphold ethical standards (De Cremer and de Bettignies, 2013). Oates and Dalmau (2013) define ethics as the body of knowledge concerned with the investigation of fundamental moral principles that set right from wrong.

Racelis (2010) claimed that ethics vary from morality in that ethics focuses on the widely accepted behavioral standards of a big population, whereas morality focuses primarily on the concepts of right and wrong. Therefore, it is critical to understand that moral behavior puts the welfare of others before one's own. The explanation was furthered by Mihelic et al. (2010) by stating that morally and legally permissible behavior falls within the category of ethical behavior. As a result, business ethics is a branch of applied ethics that deals with a wide variety of human business operations (Keller-Krawczyk, 2010). The capacity to comprehend and apply morally sound principles in business is one method to create an ethically sound corporate culture.

The idea of business ethics is interpreted differently by different people. Business ethics is generally the study of what is morally right and wrong (Velasquez, 2009). The relationship between the goals and purposes of an organization and its normative pressure is another way to explain it (Garret, 1970). According to Weihrich and Koontz (Jalil, Azam, and Rahman, 2010), business ethics is about establishing a standard of justice and integrity in all areas of a company's operations, both domestically and internationally. Christensen (2014) divided ethics into two categories: consequentialism and non-consequentialism, which are two different approaches to examining how the morality of individuals in business decisions.

ETHICAL METAVERSE BUSINESS SCENARIOS

The examination of a business scenario that will allow it to be considered concerning ethical compliance is provided below.

On the Metaverse platform, every time a user engages with the system, Big Data is produced. It is critical in this situation to track who will make use of or profit from the enormous amounts of data provided by users. Who will ensure that no digital personality mining or user profiling is carried out to learn the specifics of user behavior for marketing or promotional purposes? Because the information provided by Metaverse is significantly more valuable than the traditional 2D social media data collection methods now in use.

A moral conundrum arises from the possibility of privacy violations in the Metaverse; in this case, privacy intervention will be the main issue that needs to be resolved. Data privacy for users and customers requires a high level of security. Despite the platform provider's efforts to guarantee the privacy and security of users' data, concerns might arise regarding whether it uses artificial intelligence to track users' personalities, mines users' behavior without their knowledge, or has the potential for third parties to collect users' data without their consent. Data mining to maximize profits should not be allowed, even with the user's consent. Because it can be used to justify a lack of understanding of the procedure's purpose. It is unethical to invade someone's privacy or interfere with their other human rights without that person's agreement (Finn & Wright, 2012).

Potential proposals and application of ethical theories In the third step, different suggestions for resolving the issue on behalf of Metaverse service providers will be put up using ethical theories and principles. Below are some viewpoints on the two corporate ethics theories. First, in line with consequentialism theory, the utilitarian theory may be applied to understand why service providers would pick Metaverse as a practical substitute for their commercial endeavors despite the potential for unethical risk. According to utilitarian moral theory, a measure of an action's morality is calculated by adding up the happiness or well-being it results in. If participating in the Metaverse-adopting action leads to more enjoyment than pain and suffering, it is considered suitable. The benefit of utilitarianism is that actions' effects are thoroughly considered; nevertheless, the disadvantage is that the emphasis on overall happiness ignores the importance of the individual, who, although being a minority, may merit support. Additionally, according to Beauchamp et al. (2012), the utilitarian concept in business is based on how a moral corporate activity would benefit the most people possible. The ability to use Metaverse benefits both the business and the customers, who can have immersive 3D experiences while consulting with doctors or purchasing digital goods in e-commerce, therefore it makes sense from a utilitarian perspective why many businesses would assume the ethical risk of doing so.

The ethics of responsibilities, or deontology, is founded on moral principles that place a premium on doing what is right regardless of the repercussions. Deontology, often known as the ethics of obligations, is founded on moral principles that place a focus on acting morally, regardless of the repercussions. The deontological theory of the business's use of the Metaverse has a variety of duty ethics in terms of its internal shareholders. There must be matching obligations for claiming a right to data privacy when using this ethical framework to analyze data privacy. As a result, requirements must be established and imposed in accordance with the sources of this right to safeguard data privacy. Businesses that regard the Metaverse as the future of their industry have made large investments to take advantage of the possibilities for growing their clientele. The company's use of the Metaverse satisfies its ethical duty to its stakeholders by maximizing profit. The use of Metaverse will protect the well-being of their employees because the systems are sustainable and reduce the dangers of potential loss for organizations. Profit maximization was not the only moral purpose of Metaverse. But as was already mentioned, it is up to the users of Metaverse to decide how best to use it, which may not always be beneficial for consumers.

Making the "right" ethical option entails making the ethical choice that will produce the best possible result for all parties involved, particularly users. Businesses must create a strategy to deal with these ethical issues after assessing ethical theories such as consequentialist theories in connection to utilitarian principles and deontologist ethics. The aforementioned ethical issues need to be resolved to use the Metaverse's potential to its fullest potential. To retain user confidence and guard against data privacy violations, Metaverse should adopt a utilitarian stance while making decisions. However, reducing concerns about data privacy is greatly helped by transparency. To gain benefits or services, customers must trust the company with their data. Users should be given adequate and open assurances that their data won't be sold to uneducated third parties when it comes to consent. Businesses are not permitted to share user information with other parties for any reason, including direct and indirect information like personality profiles gleaned from data mining.

This is due to the fact that a company must give customers power over their personal data to be seen as ethical, such as by offering an opt-out option for data collecting. Additionally, if the company's privacy policy is open and transparent, explaining how users' data will be used and giving them the option to change their data profile while assuring that their data remains anonymous when sent to third parties, privacy infractions could be dealt with. In other words, if businesses using Metaverse refuse to disclose customer data, there is no utilitarian way to decide in this circumstance. Therefore, companies may avoid bigger losses like compensatory payments in legal proceedings and the loss of consumers' faith and trust if they took into account the cost of these effects and did not violate the privacy of their users' data. For controlling privacy infringement damages, on the other hand, a deontology-based technique should be taken into consideration. Businesses have a moral responsibility to maintain their customers' privacy and make sure that doing so is easy for them. Utilizing user data while limiting data privacy concerns must be done in a balanced manner. Businesses have a moral duty to protect customer data, regardless of how these choices may affect their performance.

The study concludes by looking at how the deployment of Metaverse should be justified in light of the arguments put forth in two widely accepted ethical frameworks. The morality of a particular action is emphasized by both utilitarianism and deontology. However, they have different viewpoints and beliefs about what constitutes good or bad behavior, leading to varying ratings. However, these compelling ethical theories can help clarify the issues raised above about the use of the Metaverse by enterprises.

METAVERSE AND SOCIAL RESPONSIBILITY

According to Friedman, a company's sole social responsibility is to boost profits for its owners (stockholders), so long as doing so does not result in dishonesty or fraud. When Friedman made a specific statement regarding deception or fraud, he insisted that businesses have a responsibility to consider all of the stakeholders. The responsibility involves ensuring that all stakeholders' rights are upheld and (ii) ensuring that the interests of all stakeholders are balanced in each action or decision that is made (Friedman, 2009). It is against the rules of ethics to seek to violate users' privacy to increase revenues. The moral debate should not be overlooked, even though it might result in greater consumer pleasure and growth. In this situation, businesses frequently face pressure on how to resolve issues to resolve the ethical conundrum. They must reassure users that both their personal information and safety are protected. The fundamental moral condition calls for firms to act carefully and guarantee that the choices they make will result in better benefits for everyone. Businesses have a responsibility to secure user data by ensuring that it is not exposed to hackers or used for deceptive marketing and advertising campaigns to preserve the privacy and rights of its users. Additionally, enterprises, especially those engaged in customer relationship management (CRM), must notify users of any use of customer data and secure their consent. The decision to use users' data without getting their permission is regarded as morally immoral. Users should be treated equitably in accordance with universal rules, and those rules should also be applied to others (Ferrell et al., 2015).

It is essential to overcome the aforementioned ethical issues if one is to effectively utilize the Metaverse for business initiatives. Several decisions were made to lessen the ethical difficulties and moral impasses that the Metaverse presents. The company should take a utilitarian stance when making decisions to avoid data privacy violations and preserve consumer confidence. In this situation, transparency is essential for reducing data privacy concerns. Users must trust a company with their data when they make a purchase or use a service, but typically very little information is provided about the data gathered, how it is used, and who has access to it. The privacy of the user may be threatened by the integration and dissemination of many datasets that were not previously thought to have privacy implications. If users are not fully informed about the intended purposes for the data collected and the involvement of unauthorized third parties, consent issues may also develop. Transparency must be implemented at all stages of data collection and processing to prevent these problems. Such accurate and timely disclosure will increase user awareness. To keep users' identities hidden and to notify them about the collection and intended use of their data, a privacy and disclosure policy may also be necessary. On the other hand, a deontology-based strategy ought to be taken into account for repairing the harm brought on by privacy infractions. The company owes it to its customers morals to safeguard their privacy and make sure they feel secure disclosing personal information. The usage of user data and the degree to which their privacy is violated must be balanced.

There should be no distinctions made between people when it comes to discrimination, allowing everyone to exercise their rights regardless of their sex, ethnicity, language, religion, socioeconomic status, etc. Human discrimination based on data correlation continues to be a contributing factor in the Metaverse's challenges. However, the algorithms are what may be programmed by someone to produce bias based on some links that may be false and unethical, not the data, which does not contribute to this form of discrimination. The work of locating discrimination in algorithms is essential. Algorithms must be audited to prove their legitimacy and remove any biases, notwithstanding their complexity. As well as adhering to all pertinent laws, including the Human Rights Act, and being culturally acceptable, which contributes to the development of a society in which people's rights and obligations are balanced and protect them from any violations, Metaverse must be ethical to be considered ethical. Following the implementation of this step, both of the aforementioned frameworks are applicable. According to utilitarianism, when there is no longer any discrimination, it is morally acceptable because it benefits society the most and makes the business's underlying incentive to maximize profits easier to understand.

Deontologists contend that it is the duty of business to eliminate bias and treat everyone equally; as a result, this action is ethically right. Stakeholder theory, which investigates relationships between a business and the people and groups who could influence or be influenced by its decisions, should generally be implemented by all organizations. All stakeholders must be treated fairly, according to the stakeholder theory. As a result, this theory would handle concerns like comprehending the potential negative effects and positive effects for groups or individuals, managing stakeholder relationships effectively so that they support the survival or growth of the organization, creating value, and preventing moral failure. Additionally, organizations and corporations ought to implement strong governance since it would guarantee transparency, equity, accountability, and responsibility in their operations and decision-making processes. Therefore, it is possible to prevent the company from failing because people no longer trust it, which would harm shareholder value and make it difficult for the company to remain competitive.

CONCLUSION

To fulfill the needs of the new Internet era, it was necessary to swiftly regulate data privacy laws and their core procedures in response to the concerns raised by the Metaverse. The obtained data must be used in the best interests of the users since ethical and responsible data usage is necessary for successful and efficient data use. It is possible to potentially reduce ethical and ethical concerns by being aware of and in control of data gathering and intended usage. All stakeholders are also crucial to the success of any organization since they are essential to running a structure where justice, trust, and social responsibility should exist. Strong new Internet experiences are possible if the issues surrounding the Metaverse's moral and responsible use are appropriately addressed.

REFERENCES

Ahad, A. D., Anshari, M., & Razzaq, A. (2017). Domestication of smartphones among adolescents in Brunei Darussalam. *International Journal of Cyber Behavior, Psychology and Learning*, *7*(4), 26–39. doi:10.4018/IJCBPL.2017100103

Anshari, M., Almunawar, M. N., Lim, S. A., & Al-Mudimigh, A. (2019). Customer relationship management and big data enabled: Personalization & customization of services. *Applied Computing and Informatics*, *15*(2), 94–101. doi:10.1016/j.aci.2018.05.004

Anshari, M., Hamdan, M., Ahmad, N., Ali, E., & Haidi, H. (2022). COVID-19, artificial intelligence, ethical challenges and policy implications. *AI & Society*, 1–14. doi:10.100700146-022-01471-6 PMID:35607368

Anshari, M., & Lim, S. A. (2017). E-Government with Big Data Enabled through Smartphone for Public Services: Possibilities and Challenges. *International Journal of Public Administration*, *40*(13), 1143–1158. doi:10.1080/01900692.2016.1242619

Anshari, M., Syafrudin, M., Fitriyani, N. L., & Razzaq, A. (2022). Ethical Responsibility and Sustainability (ERS) Development in a Metaverse Business Model. *Sustainability*, *14*(23), 15805. doi:10.3390u142315805

Antin, D. (2020). The Technology of the Metaverse, It's Not Just VR. *The Startup*.

Ball, M. (2022). *The Metaverse: And How it Will Revolutionize Everything*. Liveright. doi:10.15358/9783800669400

Beauchamp, T. L., Bowie, N. E., & Arnold, D. G. (Eds.). (2004). *Ethical theory and business*. Pearson Education.

Brown, D. (2021). What is the 'metaverse'? Facebook says it's the future of the Internet. *Washington Post*.

Christensen, L. (2014). Ethics and Manipulative Marketing. Academic Press.

Crane, A., & Matten, D. (2016). *Business ethics: Managing corporate citizenship and sustainability in the age of globalization*. Oxford University Press.

Stephenson, N. (1992). *Snow Crash*. Bantam Books.

De Cremer, D., & de Bettignies, H. C. (2013). Pragmatic Business Ethics. *Business Strategy Review*, *24*(2), 64–67. doi:10.1111/j.1467-8616.2013.00950.x

Ferrell, O. C., Fraedrich, J., & Ferrell, L. (2015). *Business ethics: Ethical decision making and cases* (10th ed.). Cengage Learning.

Finn, R. L., & Wright, D. (2012). Unmanned aircraft systems: Surveillance, ethics and privacy in civil applications. *Computer Law & Security Review*, *28*(2), 184–194. doi:10.1016/j.clsr.2012.01.005

Friedman, A. (2009). Intransitive ethics. *Journal of Moral Philosophy*, *6*(3), 277–297. doi:10.1163/174552409X433391

Garret, T. (1970). *Business ethics*. Prentice Hall.

Hasmawati, F., Samiha, Y. T., Razzaq, A., & Anshari, M. (2020). Understanding nomophobia among digital natives: Characteristics and challenges. *Journal of Critical Reviews*, *7*(13), 122–131.

Hooker, J. (2003). *Why Business Ethics?* Retrieved from http://web. tepper. cmu. edu/ethics/whybizethics. pdf

Jalil, M., Azam, F., & Rahman, M. K. (2010). Implementation Mechanism of ethics in Business organizations. *International Business Research*, *3*(4), 145–155. doi:10.5539/ibr.v3n4p145

Katal, A., Wazid, M., & Goudar, R. H. (2013, August). Big data: issues, challenges, tools and good practices. In *Contemporary Computing (IC3), 2013 Sixth International Conference on* (pp. 404-409). IEEE. 10.1109/IC3.2013.6612229

Keller-Krawczyk, L. (2010). Is Business Ethics Possible and Necessary? *Economia e Sociologia*, *3*(1), 133–142.

Lewis, M. (2022). *Why the metaverse is a big gamechanger for defence*. https://www.accenture.com/us-en/blogs/voices-public-service/why-the-metaverse-is-a-big-gamechanger-for-defence

Mayer-Schönberger, V., & Cukier, K. (2013). *Big data: A revolution that will transform how we live, work, and think*. Houghton Mifflin Harcourt.

Merriam-Webster Dictionary. (2018). Retrieved on 27th August 2018 from https://www.merriam-webster.com/dictionary/ethics

Mihelic, K. K., Lipicnik, B., & Tekavcic, M. (2010). Ethical Leadership. *International Journal of Management and Information Systems*, *14*(5), 31–41.

Mystakidis, S. (2022). Metaverse. *Metaverse. Encyclopedia*, *2*(1), 486–497. doi:10.3390/encyclopedia2010031

Neiger, C. (2021, Oct. 25). Virtual reality is too expensive for most people — but that's about to change. *Business Insider*.

Newton, C. (2021, July 22). Mark Zuckerberg is betting Facebook's future on the metaverse. *The Verge*.

O'Brian, M., & Chan, K. (2021, Oct. 28). EXPLAINER: What is the metaverse and how will it work? *ABC News*.

Oates, V., & Dalmau, T. (2013). Ethical Leadership: A Legacy For A Stronger Future. *Performance*, *5*(2), 18–33.

Racelis, A. D. (2010). The Influence of Organisational Culture on Performance of Philippine Banks. *Social Science*, *6*(2), 29–49.

Razzaq, A., Samiha, Y. T., & Anshari, M. (2018). Smartphone habits and behaviors in supporting students self-efficacy. *International Journal of Emerging Technologies in Learning*, *13*(2), 94. doi:10.3991/ijet.v13i02.7685

Robertson, A. (2021, Oct. 4). What is the metaverse, and do I have to care? *The Verge*.

Velasquez, M. G. (2009). *Business ethics: Concept and cases*. Prentice Hall.

Wu, X., Zhu, X., Wu, G. Q., & Ding, W. (2014). Data mining with big data. *IEEE Transactions on Knowledge and Data Engineering*, *26*(1), 97–107. doi:10.1109/TKDE.2013.109

Chapter 4
Islamic Compliant Frameworks for the Metaverse:
An Opportunity for More Equitable Finance in the Metaverse

Klemens Katterbauer
Euclid University, Central African Republic

Hassan Syed
Euclid University, Central African Republic

Laurent Cleenewerck de Kiev
Euclid University, Central African Republic

Sema Yilmaz Genc
https://orcid.org/0000-0002-3138-1622
Yildiz Technical University, Turkey

ABSTRACT

The metaverse has become of paramount importance within the last several years, being a virtual universe where individuals and companies can interact. While the metaverses are still in their nascent stage, there has been increasing interest and capital inflow into these universes. For Shariah-compliant focused financial investors and participants, this represents a considerable challenge given the existing lack of Islamic financing frameworks for the metaverses. This chapter outlines options for providing Shariah-compliant financing in the metaverse, outlining the challenges and aspects that have to be taken into account for creating Shariah-compliant financing forms

DOI: 10.4018/978-1-6684-6097-9.ch004

Copyright © 2023, IGI Global. Copying or distributing in print or electronic forms without written permission of IGI Global is prohibited.

in the metaverse. The framework adapts conventional Islamic financing options, such as Murabaha and Sukuk, to the metaverse, ensuring that both the contracting and crypto-payments are Shariah-compliant and supportive in the metaverse. The framework provides an important step towards the development of Shariah-compliant financing forms within the metaverse.

INTRODUCTION

The word "metaverse" has been encountered everywhere in recent years, with Facebook changing its name officially to Meta (Park & Kim, 2022). Non-fungible tokens (NFT) have become one of the major words of the year, where these tokens form a key part of the virtual universe. This has also led gamers and developers to move into this space, making it more and more attractive to conventional consumers. While there has been considerable attention around the virtual universe, understanding the environment behind the virtual universe and what value it creates is of critical importance. The land prices related to digital land have been on the rise, with Republic Real Estate launching a fund for investors to purchase virtual land (Narin, 2021). The fund will purchase virtual land across various online metaverses and transform them into hotels, stores, and other uses. This shall lead to an increase in the value of these properties amongst consumers.

While virtual land has, due to its connotation with physical land, attracted considerable interest, the art sector related to NFTs has experienced an even more significant rise, and there is the expectation that equities and bonds will be hosted on a digital asset platform that is built around blockchain technology. Another key area of the metaverse is the gradual online-only shopping and experience, which implies that individuals purchase assets that are entirely virtual. There are several stores that sell clothing and accessories entirely online, which only exist in the metaverse. Furthermore, there are virtual fashion shoes solely for the virtual world, which has attracted considerable investment amounts. The growing remote work operational model, in addition to the growing utilization of artificial intelligence and virtual technologies, has opened up new business models providing customers with different experiences in the virtual world. Another key change is the move towards remote work, where the metaverse can make remote work more permanent and immersive in order to maximize efficiency and interaction. This will enable stronger interaction and engagement of the employees (Wilson, Karg, & Ghaderi, 2021).

Given the growing importance of the metaverse, the financial industry has been looking into how to create value within the metaverse space and how fintech solutions can deliver financial services in this new environment. Furthermore, metaverse technology creates new business model opportunities that may strengthen the utilization of crypto-technology as an alternative financial system.

The technologies behind the metaverse combine technologies such as virtual reality (VR) and augmented reality (AR). This leads to an interactive, immersive and collaborative virtual 3D universe. The idea is that these individual universes may be integrated with each other as well as allow to connect across the world in various environments. This may be in the form of games but also in terms of real estate, commercial transactions, and other associated environments (Wohlgenannt, Simons, & Stieglitz, 2020).

As outlined by Facebook's transformation into Meta, financial data and transaction management will become key parts of the metaverse enabling individuals and corporations to transact and operate within these universes. For example, there are digital assets for purchase, such as the World of Warcraft and the Habbo Hotel, and these assets may be even moved from one universe into the other (Park & Kim, 2022).

The current metaverse is a composition of the capabilities of various social media and video game enterprises that build upon their user base and platform in order to connect these individuals. While this first glance may give the impression that the metaverse is solely about gaming, it has become more of another virtual world where individuals may be fully immersed and conduct most of their life within the metaverse. This may range from dating to having their social interactions within the metaverse, but also conduct business across it. This may be in the form of leading a real enterprise or a digital enterprise within the metaverse. Overall, this will lead to someone being completely immersed in the metaverse and living their daily lives within this universe.

Given these enormous opportunities, questions arise what kind of financial services may be provided within the metaverse. Providing management of finance and transactions is critical to provide the level of interaction and services that consumers require. As the metaverse will be a virtual version of everyday life, where one can work, earn salaries, spend on assets, such as furniture, clothing, cars, and also purchase and rent out land, this requires necessarily the financial infrastructure but also the financial regulatory environment. Furthermore, the integration of various financial services and technologies may lead to the creation of a finverse.

Substantial questions arise in terms of how financial services will be provided in such an environment and how these services differ from conventional financial services that are provided. Furthermore, questions arise on how artificial intelligence and blockchain play a critical role in strengthening the finverse and making it compatible with Shariah law. This chapter will provide an overview of Islamic financial options and opportunities in the metaverse.

Islamic Finance Options in the Metaverse

The metaverse has been a key component of the new digital economy representing a new virtual environment of life. Given the virtual nature of the metaverse, various financing structures that are applicable for conventional Islamic finance have to be analyzed how they can be applied to the metaverse. The first form of Islamic financing is the utilization of a financial lease, Ijara, that a Shariah-compliant version of a conventional lease. The terms of the ijara indicate that the maintenance responsibilities of the asset are separated into the major and minor maintenance of the asset. The major maintenance of the asset belongs to the lessor, while the minor maintenance belongs to the lessee. Furthermore, the lessor is likewise responsible for the insurance of the asset, which may be, in practice, challenging. Additionally, the special purpose vehicle (SPV) has limited operational functionality, which requires separate servicing agency arrangements. Additionally, the lessee is not liable for repaying if the asset is lost or destroyed. This is the responsibility of the SPV, and if the lessee wants to own the asset after the end of the maturity date, then a separate purchase contract is required.

In the case of the metaverse, the Ijara would involve a digital asset. This may be in the form of various digital assets such as virtual clothing or means of transportation. The main question is whether these digital assets incorporate components of Gharar, which would make them not permissible for investment. Gharar in Islamic finance relates to uncertainty, deception, and risk that may be associated with assets. In another context, it may be considered similar to the situation of an asset or service that is not present nor determinable. In a conventional sense, this relates to crops that are not harvested or fishes that are not yet netted. The concept of Gharar is critical in Islamic finance as it provides a measure of the legitimacy of a risky investment. Especially, this relates to short-selling, gambling, and selling goods and assets of uncertain quality. Furthermore, any contract that may not be drawn out in clear terms can be considered Gharar.

Necessarily, the term is rather broad and subject to interpretation. Therefore, sales or financial transactions are considered as gharar depending on the level of misunderstanding between the parties and the degree of uncertainty that exists in terms of the delivery of goods and payments. The main objective is to avoid situations that cause injustice or deceit against one of the parties and is generally considered a form of cheating.

The main source for Gharar can be found in the hadiths, where the prophet Muhammed outlined that one shall avoid selling birds in the sky, fish in the water, and unborn calf's in a mother's womb (Brown, 2017). Specifically, the prophet emphasized "Sell not what is not with you" (Sunan Ibn Majah, Hadith 2187). Specifically, gharar arises when the claim to ownership is either unclear or suspicious. Furthermore, the Quran states "And do not eat up your property among yourselves for vanities." which outlines the prohibition of predatory business practices.

In determining whether a specific asset class is classified as gharar, it is important to perform a comparative approach to analyzing whether an asset or transaction is to be considered gharar. Derivative transactions, such as forwards, futures, and options, are mostly forbidden as they involve significant uncertainty related to the future delivery of the underlying asset.

A critical differentiation is between minor and substantial gharar. Speculative forwards, such as betting on exchange rates, are clearly substantial gharar and forbidden. On the other hand, commercial insurance is generally permitted provided it adheres to Islamic principles, and the short-selling of fungible items, such as wheat and other commodities, where the items are delivered at a later time is also permissible.

Conventional comparisons are performed with cryptocurrencies, whose permissibility has been intensively discussed. Generally speaking, cryptocurrencies have been heavily associated with gambling and uncertainty, making them impermissible. However, they have an inherent nature of being a medium of exchange similar to gold and conventional currencies and solely utilize blockchain technology as their underlying technology. One of the major supporting declarations in Islamic law was the permissibility statement of Bitcoin by the Shariah advisor Mufti Muhammad Abu-Bakar (Alam, Gupta, & Zameni, 2019). The reasoning was that cryptocurrencies by themselves contain an element of speculation, but this is a common feature in any currency and does not automatically make it haram. Another supportive argument is that blockchain and cryptocurrencies are, by their design, not associated with any interest (Abu-Bakar, 2017). While there are staking options for these cryptocurrencies, this is not a form of riba but rather utilizing one's cryptocurrencies for transactions and the creation of value within the network. Another key aspect is that the decentralized nature of the blockchain allows reducing potential manipulation and greater transparency. Another key parameter is contracting, as Islamic contract rules state that there needs to be a form of Mal within the contract. This refers to the possession or effective storage of the asset underlying the contract (Bouheraoua, Mohamad, Kasri, & Abdullah, 2015). Cryptocurrencies can be possessed and stored and have a commercial value (Mutaqawwam). The main feature of cryptocurrencies is that they are real and viable digital assets. The worth is determined within an open market and is traded commercially (Asif, 2018).

Another key focus in evaluating cryptocurrencies is whether the income derived from an investment into these products satisfies Shariah law. Crypto investments comply in general with social justice, accountability, and ethics that transcend from the financial transaction. Therefore, the underlying transaction and not the cryptocurrency itself determines the compliance. This implies that just because cryptocurrencies can be used for illegal activities does not make them by themselves illegal, as the same applies to conventional currencies. Even though crypto is not backed by any central government, except for those issued by governments such as e-CNY, this does not make them an unlawful means of exchange (Yao, 2018). Furthermore, the owning of cryptocurrencies as a means of exchange and as a form of money, which may make its storage subject to Zakat.

Furthermore, there is the general view that as a medium of exchange and its widespread availability, it may make it more accessible to people in need. Especially when it comes to impoverished people, their access to the conventional banking system is typically limited, making a solution utilizing blockchain an attractive alternative to empower and support them (Howson & de Vries, 2022). When it comes to contracting, these contracts are based on smart contracts utilizing blockchain technology, which is both secure and automated. This implies that they reduce both administrative complexities, but also confusion and errors. Given that several cryptocurrency agencies are already operating in Dubai and Malaysia, cryptocurrencies can be, in most instances, considered permissible in Shariah law (Wilson C., 2019; McDevitt, 2021).

Given the general permissibility of cryptocurrencies, the cryptocurrencies within the metaverse can be considered a permissible medium of exchange, which assists in the execution of transactions and supports the ecosystem.

The next challenge is how assets in the metaverse are assessed in terms of their Shariah compliance. Virtual land may be considered similar to physical land as an asset within the metaverse, mimicking the evaluation of physical land (Sait & Lim, 2006). In comparison, this equality may, in its current form, be subject to debate since the perception is that the virtual land is more akin to software or intangible asset rather than a tangible asset.

We will outline for the metaverse framework several forms of Islamic financing options that are adapted to fit the needs of the metaverse.

META-MURABAHA FINANCING

One of the major forms of Islamic financing is based on Murabaha. Obviously, Murabaha financing is a form of financing where the financier will purchase the asset and sell it to an entity for an amount consisting of the asset price in addition to a profit margin. Murabaha financing needs to be adapted for the metaverse and is outlined in Figure 1. Henceforth, it will be denoted as Meta-Murabaha. The first main parties are the metafinancier and the metaentity. The metaentity may be an avatar or digital company that engages in a transaction with the metafinancier. The metafinancier may be a digital financial service provider, such as individuals or a lending company, or a digital bank within the metaverse. The metafinancier and metaentity then engage in a sale and purchase agreement for the digital asset, which requires the metafinancier to purchase the digital asset on a spot basis. The digital asset may be in various forms, such as digital clothes, equipment, avatars, and others. The metafinancier purchases the asset from a 3rd party, and then the metaentity either pays the metafinancier within a single payment or a series of phased payments. All these payments are conducted with the metaverse's cryptocurrencies. The overall agreement is a smart contract that is supported by the metaverse's contract blockchain. This, in general, secures the asset's ownership as well as contractual terms of the asset. Furthermore, the immutability of the blockchain framework makes the cybersecurity of the contractual terms strong.

The utilization of meta-Murabaha financing faces several challenges as it is not suitable for long-term financing. This is due to the fact that the price will be pre-set at the time of the purchase, which does not account for changes in the cost of funds. For the metaverse, the cost of funds may increase considerably within a short period of time if there is significant demand for the services within the metaverse. Hence meta-Murabaha is best suited for spot digital asset purchases that are paid off within a relatively limited period of time.

Figure 1. Meta-Murabaha structure in the metaverse

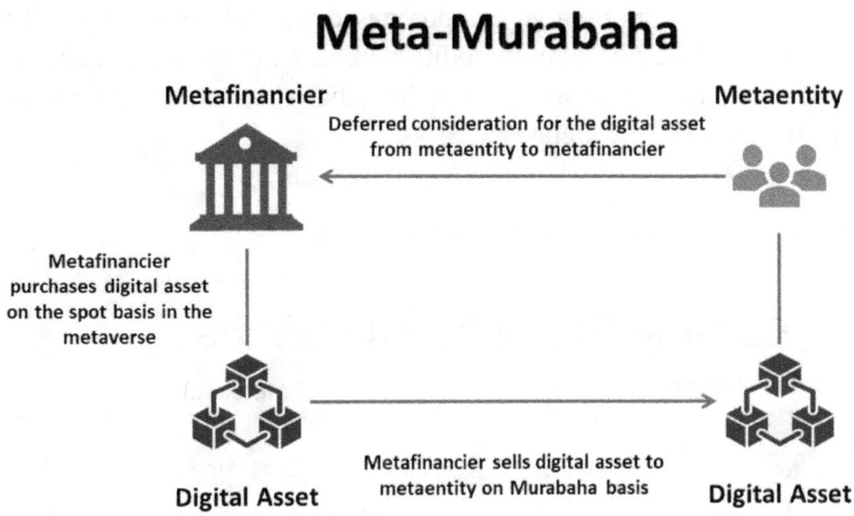

Another Islamic financing form in the metaverse is the commodity meta-Murabaha, as outlined in Figure 2. Virtual commodities may be in the form of various shapes, but non-fungible tokens (NFTs) have been amongst the most valuable commodities in the metaverse. Furthermore, land in metaverses is a significant commodity and has experienced considerable value increases. The commodity meta-Murabaha financing framework provides a Shariah-compliant financing option for commodities in the metaverse. In this instance, the metafinancier purchases the virtual commodity, such as NFT or virtual, which then forms the basis of the master meta-Murabaha agreement (MMAA). This provides long-term meta-financing without the necessity to acquire the virtual asset and the risks associated with it. The metaentity will serve an e-notice to the metafinancier in the agreement that the metafinancier will sell a virtual commodity to the metaentity. The metafinancier will purchase the commodity on the spot from a 3rd party within the metaverse. The virtual commodities are then immediately sold to the metaentity on the Murabaha contract, and the metaentity acquires the title of it. However, the crypto-consideration is deferred for a certain period of time. This may be in general three months but can be agreed on by the parties. The crypto-consideration is composed of the cost of the commodity in addition to the profit amount that is agreed in the e-agreement. The metaentity will immediately sell it to a 3rd party in the metaverse based on the market value. The resulting crypto-funds can be utilized by the metaentity for other purposes, such as the acquisition of an asset. At the end of the meta-Murabaha period, a new agreement is then set up where virtual commodities are purchased and sold on the spot. This recurring nature of the virtual commodity purchase brings some security to the metafinancier to engage in the meta-Murabaha agreement and provide consistent financing in the metaverse.

Figure 2. Commodity Meta-Murabaha process outline

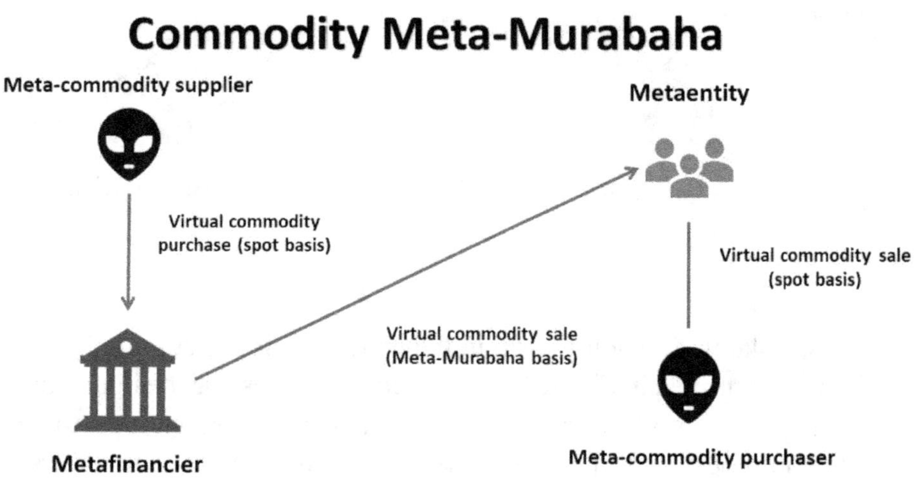

The parallel commodity meta-Murabaha structure is another financing format where a crypto interest-bearing facility agreement together with a special purpose vehicle (SPV) structure. The metaentity provides an e-notice to the SPV within the master meta-Murabaha agreement to sell the virtual commodity to the metaentity. The digital SPV takes out the loan within the facility agreement, and then the SPV purchases the commodities from a 3rd party. The SPV then sells the digital commodity on the basis of the meta-Murabaha agreement. The metaentity then sells the virtual commodity in order to perform another purchase with the received funds. In the end, the metaentity will then repay the cost in addition to a profit margin to the SPV that will cover the repayment of the crypto-loan.

Figure 3. Parallel meta-Murabaha

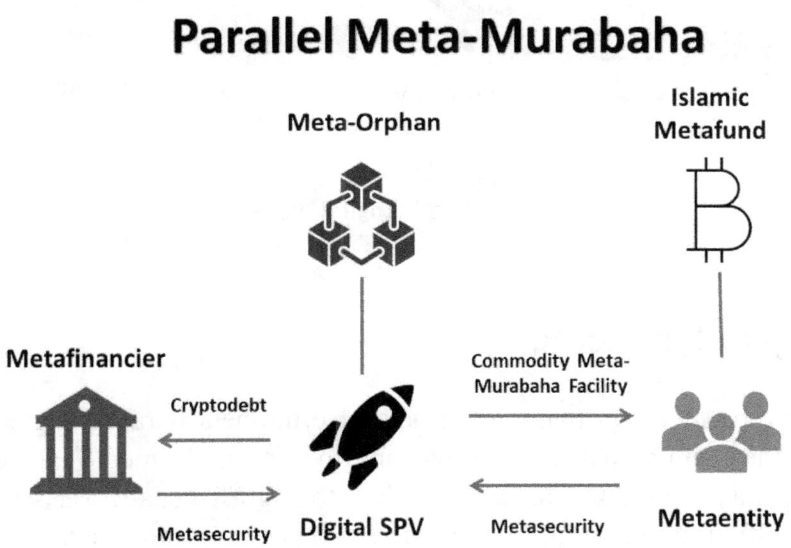

Another financing format is the equity Meta-Murabaha in the metaverse (Figure 4). This form of meta-Murabaha overcomes the concerns with respect to the security of the asset. The equity Meta-Murabaha has two parallel structures that are adjacent to each other. One of the structures is based on a crypto-interest bearing facility, and the other is Shariah-compliant. The main difference to the parallel meta-Murabaha agreement is that the income is utilized to service the interest within the crypto-facility agreement.

Figure 4. Equity Meta-Murabaha

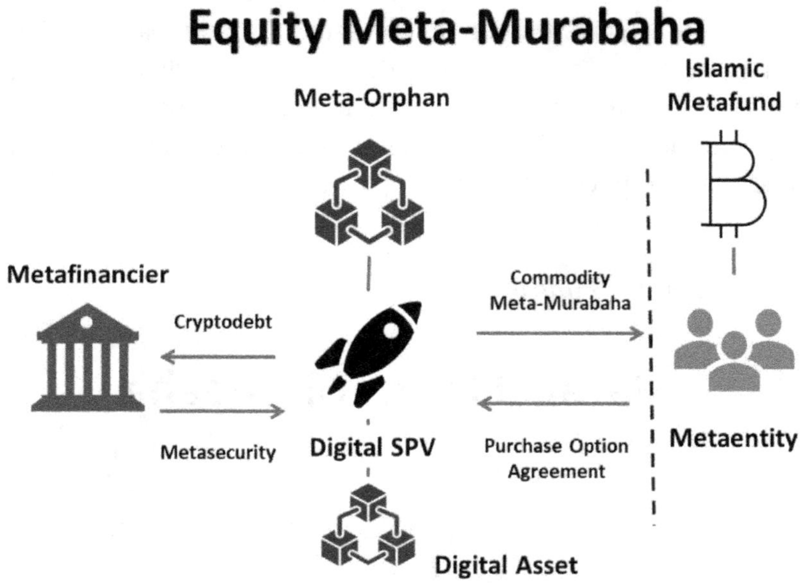

Meta-Ijara Financing

In order to provide lease options in the metaverse, the meta-Ijara lease agreement is one of the Islamic finance forms available to parties. The metafinancier and the metaentity engage in an agreement where the right to use an asset is granted for a specified time period. The rental crypto payments are predetermined, and this may work well for digital asset financing, as it allows, for example, to rent virtual land within the metaverse. Likewise, virtual dresses may be rented for special occasions for avatars in the metaverse. The lease process is initiated by the metaentity that specifies the asset it wants to acquire, and the metafinancier purchases the digital asset. The metaentity then enters into a meta-Ijara lease agreement with the metafinancier, where the metaentity leases the digital asset from the metafinancier. The periodic crypto-rental payments represent the cost of the asset in addition to a mark-up payment. Finally, the metaentity is responsible for the maintenance and insurance of the digital asset. Maintenance and insurance of the digital asset

Figure 5. Meta-Ijara lease

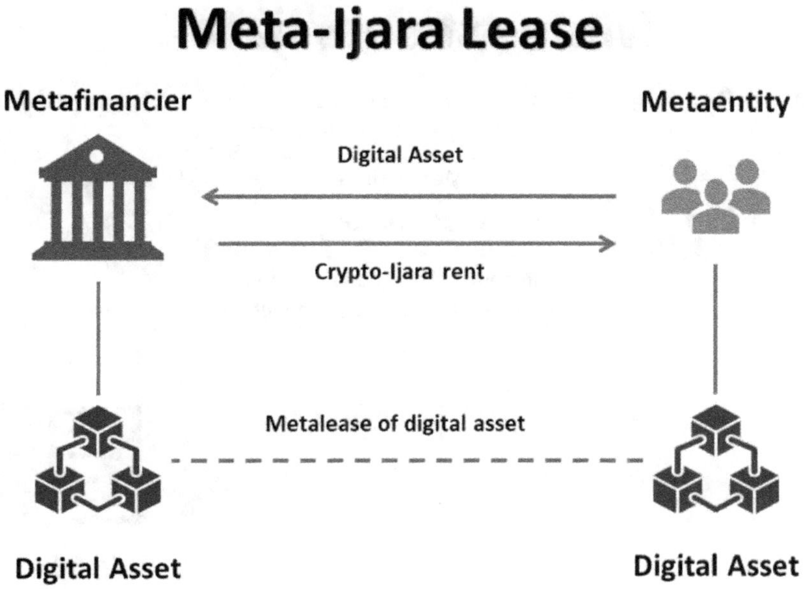

Another form of contract is the Meta-Istisna - Ijara, which is a contract that specifies an item to be manufactured or constructed, and the contractor is required to deliver the item upon completion (Figure 6). While the metaverse and assets seem to be created within an instance, there are several projects that require longer time periods for construction. Specifically, when it comes to the creation of new environments or features within the metaverse, these projects require substantial resources and are constructed over longer time horizons. The Meta-Istisna – Ijara contract provides an Islamic principles compliant project financing framework within the metaverse. The metafinancier and the metaentity enter into a meta-istisna agreement where the metaentity will deliver a project to the metafinancier within a specified timeframe. The metafinancier makes scheduled crypto payments to the metaentity that may mirror conventional payment advances in projects. The metafinancier will then assume the title of the digital project upon completion, after which the meta-Ijara lease is then started, where the metaentity will lease back and operate the project from the metafinancier. Furthermore, the metaentity may purchase the digital project for the in the Meta-Istisna/Ijara agreement outlined crypto-amount.

Figure 6. Meta-Istisna/Ijara process

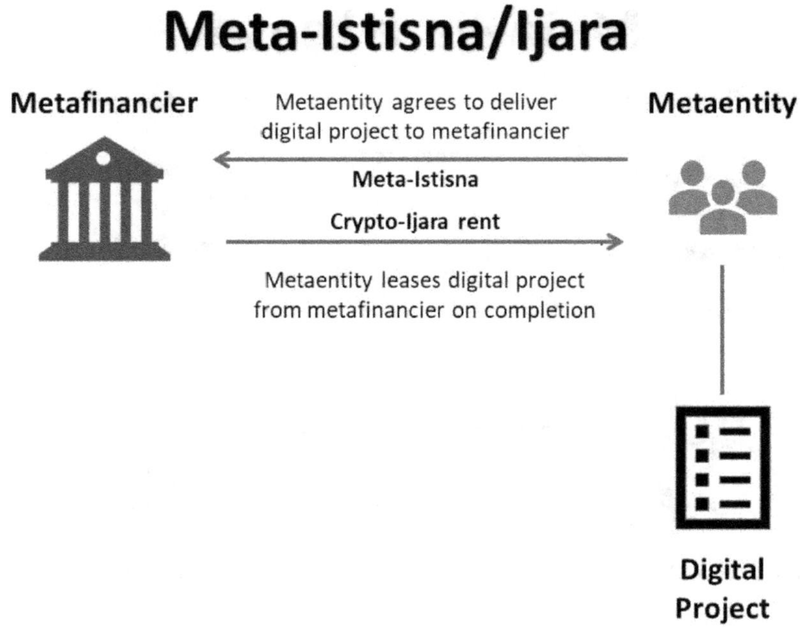

Meta-Sukuk

The metaverse Sukuk market is still in its nascent stage but will experience with the growth of the metaverse significant growth in the coming years. The first step in the Meta-Sukuk Al Ijara is the establishment of a meta SPV issuer that will issue the e-Sukuk in the metaverse. The Meta SPV issuer will issue an e-Sukuk in the form of trust certificates that either represent an undivided ownership interest in certain digital assets or a usufruct of assets. The e-Sukuk holders also obtain the right to the income that is generated by the meta SPV from the assets. The e-Sukuk holders then subscribe to the meta-Sukuk and pay the proceeds to the meta SPV issuer. The meta SPV issuer then declares its trust in the proceeds and the digital asset it has acquired for the e-Sukuk holder. The Meta SPV issuer then purchases the digital assets from the metaentity or a 3rd party with the proceeds of the Sukuk issuance. The meta SPV issuer then leases the digital assets to the metaentity under the meta-Ijara lease. The term of this meta-Ijara lease may be similar to the term of the Sukuk. The metaentity is required to pay periodic rental payments to the meta-SPV issuer that may be done at a fixed or variable rate. The meta-SPV issuer receives the periodic payments and will make periodic distribution payments to the e-Sukuk holders. There will be guarantees such that at maturity or in the case of a default, the meta SPV issuer will sell, and the metaentity will buy the digital asset at a prescribed price. The amount will be equal to what is owed by the metaentity to the meta SPV issuer. The funds are then distributed to the e-Sukuk holders. If there is maintenance and insurance required, the metaentity will engage in an agreement with the meta SPV issuer to service the digital asset.

Figure 7. Meta-Sukuk Al Ijara

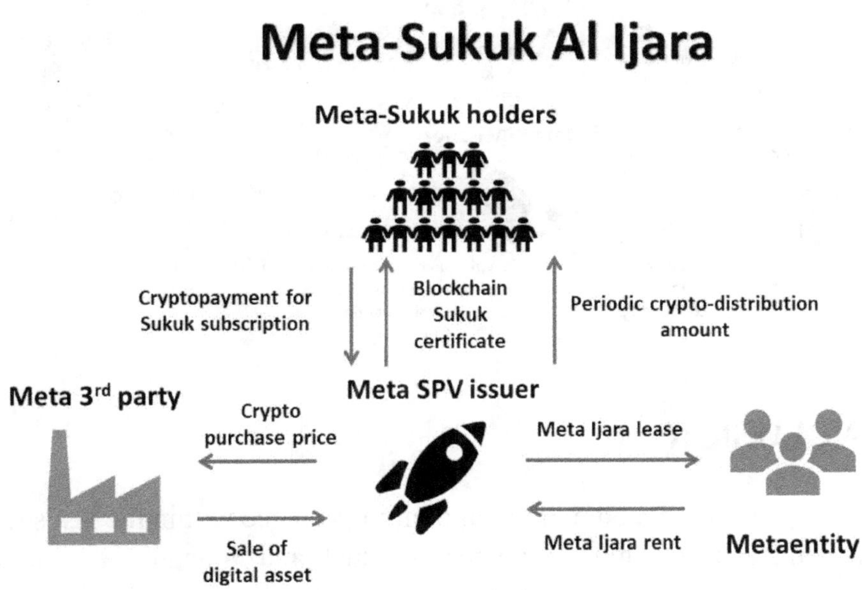

The final meta-sukuk option for the metaverse is the meta-sukuk al muarabaha (Figure 8). The metaentity will establish a meta SPV issuer in order to issue the Sukuk. The process regarding the Sukuk issuance and the retrieval of funds is similar to the meta-Sukuk al Ijara. The main difference is that the Meta SPV issuer purchases the meta-commodity on the spot basis, and the metaentity purchases the meta-commodity and makes a deferred crypto-payment. The meta-entity then immediately sells the meta-commodity and may utilize it for the purchase of other digital assets. After a specified period of time, the metaentity will then conduct a deferred crypto-payment, and a new Meta-Murabaha contract will be created. The metaentity will solely pay the meta SPV issuer the profit margin, which will be subsequently distributed to the e-Sukuk holders.

Figure 8. Meta-Sukuk Murabaha

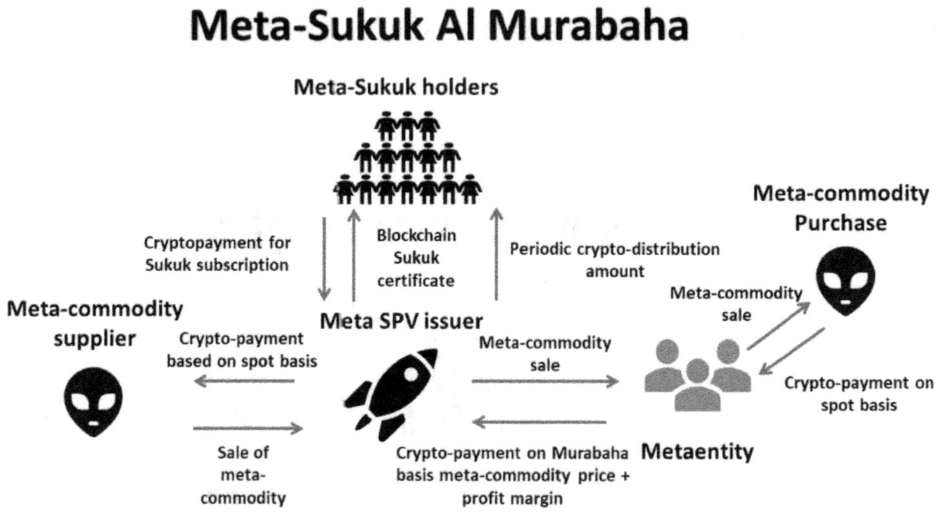

CONCLUSION

The metaverse has become of paramount importance within the last several years, being a virtual universe where individuals and companies can interact. While the metaverses are still in their nascent stage, there has been increasing interest and capital inflow into these universes. For Shariah-compliant focused financial investors and participants, this represents a considerable challenge given the existing lack of Islamic financing frameworks for the metaverses. We have outlined new frameworks for providing Shariah-compliant financing in the metaverse, outlining the challenges and aspects that have to be taken into account for creating Shariah-compliant financing forms in the metaverse.

REFERENCES

Abu-Bakar, M. M. (2017). *Shariah Analysis of Bitcoin, Cryptocurrency and Blockchain*. Blossom.

Alam, N., Gupta, L., & Zameni, A. (2019). *Fintech and Islamic Finance: Digitalization, Development and Disruption*. Palgrave MacMillan. doi:10.1007/978-3-030-24666-2

Asif, S. (2018). The halal and haram aspect of cryptocurrencies in Islam. *Journal of Islamic Banking and Finance*, 91-101.

Bouheraoua, S., Mohamad, S., Kasri, N. S., & Abdullah, S. (2015). Shariah Issues in Intangible Assets. *Jurnal Syariah*, 287-324.

Brown, J. (2017). *Hadith: Muhammad's legacy in the medieval and modern world*. Simon and Schuster.

Howson, P., & de Vries, A. (2022). Preying on the poor? Opportunities and challenges for tackling the social and environmental threats of cryptocurrencies for vulnerable and low-income communities. *Energy Research & Social Science*, *84*, 102394. doi:10.1016/j.erss.2021.102394

McDevitt, C. (2021, October 27). *The Future of Crypto Assets Regulation in the UAE*. Retrieved from Hadef & Partners: https://www.lexology.com/library/detail.aspx?g=88c0f35c-7ea5-439b-90d7-df3fe4f70586

Narin, N. G. (2021). A Content Analysis of the Metaverse Articles. *Journal of Metaverse*, 17-24.

Park, S.-M., & Kim, Y.-G. (2022). A Metaverse: Taxonomy, components, applications, and open challenges. *IEEE Access: Practical Innovations, Open Solutions*, *10*, 4209–4251. doi:10.1109/ACCESS.2021.3140175

Sait, S., & Lim, H. (2006). *Land, Law and Islam*. Zed Books. doi:10.5040/9781350221017

Wilson, C. (2019). Cryptocurrencies: The Future of Finance? *Contemporary Issues in International Political Economy*, 359-394.

Wilson, K. B., Karg, A., & Ghaderi, H. (2021). Prospecting non-fungible tokens in the digital economy: Stakeholders and ecosystem, risk and opportunity. *Business Horizons*.

Wohlgenannt, I., Simons, A., & Stieglitz, S. (2020). Virtual reality. *Business & Information Systems Engineering*, *62*(5), 455–461. doi:10.100712599-020-00658-9

Yao, Q. (2018). A systematic framework to understand central bank digital currency. *Science China. Information Sciences*, *61*(3), 1–8. doi:10.100711432-017-9294-5

Chapter 5
The Acceptance of the Metaverse as a Platform for Knowledge Creation and Sharing in the Workplace

Abdul Hafiiz Idris
Universiti Brunei Darussalam, Brunei

ABSTRACT

Innovation has always been a driving force for change in the social norm and increasing efficiency in the workplace. This study attempts to understand the acceptance of the metaverse today with predictions of the future whereby the integration of the metaverse has always been the next big thing since the existence of the internet. The technology acceptance model is a framework that is used to investigate whether a new technology will be accepted or rejected by the users. The metaverse is an alternate world through the use of hardware where immersion is improved in comparison to other devices. In a sense, it is the virtual world or a simulation of reality. However, the technology itself is still considered to be new and therefore has room for improvement before it can be a social norm or a tool to be used by companies. This would therefore build a platform to study the acceptance of this technology using technology acceptance model.

DOI: 10.4018/978-1-6684-6097-9.ch005

Copyright © 2023, IGI Global. Copying or distributing in print or electronic forms without written permission of IGI Global is prohibited.

INTRODUCTION

Technological advancements have always been the driving force of change in the lives of the world population. It can also be agreed upon those technological advancements in terms of computer science have improved human lives in various ways. The next big innovation expected to be a norm in our lives would be immersive technologies such as Virtual Reality and Augmented Reality, (Mystakidis, 2022). The technology itself is expected to be integrated into education, organizations, and entertainment. Today, the technology has been seen to show an increase in interest. Whilst not necessarily with the offerings from Meta, Virtual Reality is continued to be developed to increase immersion by both companies and indie creators. Kamenov (2017) mentioned that these technologies are the main drivers for the computing innovations of the fourth wave today.

With the lockdown from the COVID-19 pandemic, people have had experience with working from home globally (Anshari et al., 2022a; Juna et al., 2022). This has helped people to realize the potential of remote working and the convenience or efficiency it brings along. With the global lockdown, people understand the possibility of remote working is not as impossible as once thought. As such, it also triggers the possibility or the positive outlook on using VR/AR technology to be integrated into their workplace, (Taylor and Soneji, 2022; Anshari et al., 2022b). The increase in favor of technology has indeed made the platform to be more active than ever before. This may be since during this time, technology is heavily being depended on by companies for the use of geo-tracking, attendance, and remote activities. As such, Metaverse did surprise the world as they have taken the opportunity to announce such a project during the pandemic where people have seen the potential the project could bring. In addition, the aforementioned digital transformation has made VR/AR technology to be a part of the new normal whereby digital life and reality are being merged together, (Bibri and Allam, 2022). The merging of VR/AR to reality is further proven by the fact that the popular Social Virtual Reality Chat known as VRChat has seen a record-breaking number of online users during the pandemic whereby, on PC, the number of users online at a time was as much as 20,000 users, (Lang, 2020).

As such, the need to study the acceptance of this technology arises and with the proven change in perception, it is important to see the progress of the technology in the eyes of the public to help measure their potential. In addition, the use of Metaverse as a platform for knowledge creation and sharing also arises from the understanding of TAM. This is as the acceptance of Metaverse would be needed prior to validating the use of Metaverse for such a goal.

LITERATURE REVIEW

Hardware Comfort

Virtual Reality was a luxury that used to be limited and was often deemed to be inaccessible in the past. Fortunately, the hardware today has become affordable and accessible and is more recognizable by the public. With the introduction of Oculus Quest and Oculus Quest 2 (now known as Meta Quest 2), most of the public can now access Virtual Reality as the hardware provided a low-price entry point of USD299 formerly (now USD399 due to inflation). The ease of use of the hardware means that any non-tech savvy users can easily use the hardware in addition to it having the ability to function without the use of a computer. However, the low price comes with a cost whereby the comfort of the hardware is heavily sacrificed. As a result, the use of the hardware is often limited due to neck pain and headaches over prolonged use. In order to improve comfort, a user has reported having spent an extra USD83 in order to buy an aftermarket strap and cushion. Whilst improvements were seen, the hardware was still considered to be uncomfortable as the weight is heavily focused in the front of the head whilst the rear of the head has minimal weight. Such imbalance contributes to neck pain over prolonged use even if it is reduced. This would mean that to be accepted in every sector including entertainment and remote work, comfort would be needed to have a significant improvement before the integration of Virtual Reality technology in offices and the public is considered a norm. This is further reported in research by Yan et al (2018) whereby multiple designs of Virtual Reality headset were investigated and is associated with discomfort. The research found that there is a relationship between the weight of Virtual Reality headsets to discomfort and pressure load on the head. The research also found that a Virtual Reality headset similar to the stock form of the Meta Quest 2 provides discomfort to the user followed by a "halo-strap" type of Virtual Reality headset which is often needed to be bought separately from third-party suppliers to follow suit. Although the halo-strap provided less discomfort, the weight perception was seen to have changed after a slight increase in weight. In the Virtual Reality community, the battery is often seen to be a limitation with the Meta

Quest 2 and therefore a portable battery is often added to the headset. As such, this would also provide severe discomfort in accordance with Yan et al (2018) with the aftermarket "halo-strap". In conclusion, the chance of Virtual Reality technology becoming a norm in various aspects might still be far off. However, companies are now racing to provide better experiences with VR/AR hardware and therefore there is still a slight chance for it to become a norm in the next few years.

Metaverse Project

The reason for the race to provide the best VR/AR headset in the market might be due to the Metaverse Project among other things. The technology itself can be used for various purposes such as virtual training, simulations, and entertainment. But Metaverse is one of the biggest announcements that has been created within the Virtual Reality community. This is a project made by Mark Zuckerberg that costs billions of dollars. This has also become a driver of the development of the technology further with companies racing to provide the best hardware for such projects. This might be comparable to Android OS whereby smartphone providers are always trying to provide the best hardware to function with Android OS despite Google having its own offerings like the Google Pixel phone. Mystakidis (2022) defines the Metaverse as a post-reality universe whereby the merging of physical reality and digital virtuality occurs. It was also mentioned that multisensory interactions occur with the use of technologies and hardware through virtual reality and augmented reality. It was also stated the Metaverse is considered to be Web 3.0 in the world of Virtual Reality. The Metaverse itself has been in existence for quite a while, but only recently have gotten traction with the mass. With Metaverse, it can act as a platform for different types of sectors that exists in reality. In other words, it can act as a bridge to reality with many possibilities. When it comes to Metaverse, the common definition that is often thought of is Virtual Reality. However, Virtual Reality itself is not Metaverse. Metaverse is simply an extension of Virtual Reality and Augmented Reality with the inclusion of the workplace, social platforms, art, entertainment, and many others, (Meta, 2021). This is the main reason why these physical products or hardware is needed to be accepted and adopted by the community to ensure the advancement of Metaverse possible, (Isaac, 2021).

Virtual Reality and Augmented Reality

With the advancement of the internet and portability of powerful devices such as smartphones with strong computing power, it is no surprise that Virtual Reality and Augmented Reality hardware saw innovations over the year. This hardware is considered to be the next-generation interactive display that provides an immersive experience simulating real life in the virtual world. In a sense, Virtual Reality is considered a totally immersive experience, transforming the visual sight into a totally different world whilst Augmented Reality is the mixture of reality perception and virtual images whereby there is a see-through capability, (Xiong et al., 2021).

Meta Quest 2

Meta Quest 2, formerly known as Oculus Quest 2 prior to the acquisition of Oculus by Meta, is a beginner and one of the most popular Virtual Reality headsets available in the market. This might be due to their low price and user-friendly UI, (Smith, 2022). Despite that, it also has the capability of being an XR headset due to the feature of a hand tracking system and is accurate by most users, (AbdlKarim and Holland, n.d). Due to most new users having experience with Virtual Reality through Meta Quest 2, the existence of Meta Quest 2 has been deemed to be significant in the Virtual Reality Community with continuous support from indie creators and developers. However, it has also become clear that the low entry cost of the headset comes with the sacrifice of comfort. As mentioned by Yan et al (2018), the headset design is the second most uncomfortable design available in the market. However, Smith (2022) also mentioned that the existence of the Meta Quest 2 has bridged affordability and high quality together in the Virtual Reality headset market. The introduction of the headset proves that there is still the endless possibility of the balance of price and quality to be improved further as the technology continues to develop.

METHODOLOGY

This research will use a critical review of the existing data available on the internet and literature. As time, resources, information, and literature are limited, the chosen methodology will provide the best in-depth data that can be provided at this current stage in a newly formed topic of interest.

Data Collection Method

This study utilizes the review of currently available literature, information, and reliable internet sources as the method of data collection. This is due to the topic being in the infant stage whereby data is limited and considerably inaccessible in Brunei Darussalam whereby this study was made. As such, global views and information will be used to form an overview of the topic of interest and will be applied to form opinion-based data as well as evidence-based data.

DISCUSSION AND ANALYSIS

Technology Acceptance Model

Figure 1. Technology Acceptance Model by Davis (1986)

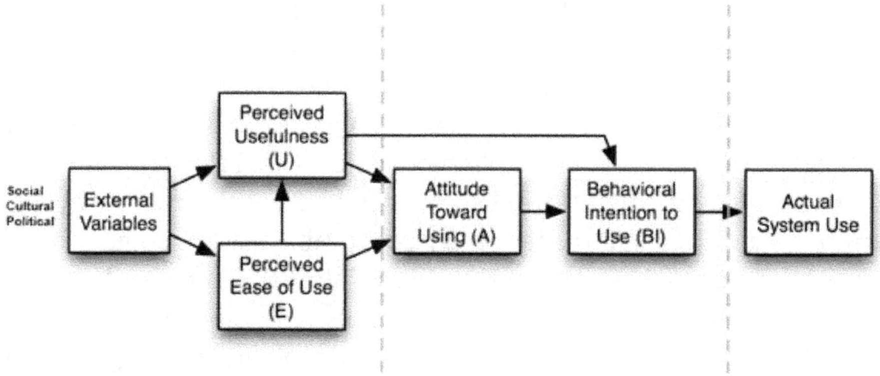

Technology Acceptance Model, created by Fred Davis in 1986, is a model for determining whether a technology will be welcomed by a user. Technology Acceptance Model is employed as a generic framework for examining the variables that affect individuals' intentions to use new technology. Perceived usefulness and perceived ease of use are the primary factors in the Technology Acceptance Model, (Dadayan and Ferro, n.d).

According to Davis (1989), perceived usefulness is the subjective likelihood that one will use a particular application system to improve their performance at work or in other areas of their lives, while perceived ease of use can be interpreted as the degree to which a user expects a system to be easy to use or effort-free. Davis (1989) asserts that these characteristics are influenced by extraneous variables, such as social, cultural, or political considerations. Language and skill are social and cultural elements. Political considerations are political issues that influence whether a target technology should be used (Surendran, 2012). Shaw (2018) claims that taxation, political stability, rules governing foreign trade, and employment laws are all political issues that can have an impact on businesses.

Due to the technology and the platform of Metaverse gaining traction only recently, the availability of literature was limited. Despite that, TAM was already implemented by Aburbeian et al, (2022) for Metaverse Prospects. Through their research, it was found that the most interested group of gender to be interested in Metaverse are males. In terms of age demographics, the majority of the interested party are below 20 in age. It was also seen that perceived ease of use was found to be impacted by perceived curiosity, perceived pleasure, and self-efficiency. Social norm was found to impact perceived usefulness positively. They have also found that the opinions of others would highly impact the perception of the usefulness of Metaverse. In addition, Metaverse is required to have a low cost and does not betray the expectations of users in order to gain favor from the participants. Overall, the research is essential before the analysis using SECI is done. This is because it provides a reason to perform such analysis on something that has a chance of being accepted rather than rejected. However, due to limitations of the literature, some factors are being overlooked such as the comfort, features, and availability of the hardware in the market. For example, the entry-level Virtual Reality hardware would be the Meta Quest 2 which causes neck strain and can be nauseating over prolonged use. This would negatively impact the user especially when it is used for remote working where the use of the hardware would last a long duration.

CATWOE

CATWOE is a method that offers a framework for defining and analyzing the views of business stakeholders. Customer, Actor, Transformation, Worldview, Owner, and Environment are the letters that make up the mnemonic. It's crucial to look at the perspectives of the numerous stakeholders in any change endeavor. Stakeholders frequently hold divergent opinions on the nature of the issues and opportunities, as well as the most effective strategies for solving them. A crucial component of every change project is managing the stakeholders, and the information gathered which the information obtained will be able to be used for such. With references from the Technology Acceptance Model of Virtual Reality, we can conclude that there is a strong future for the technology and therefore also Metaverse.

The elements of CATWOE include;

- **C** – Customer
- **A** – Actor
- **T** – Transformation
- **W** – Worldview
- **O** – Owner
- **E** – Environment

Using CATWOE helps in identifying the perspectives of business stakeholders and thus also help in analyzing such views towards Metaverse. This is crucial at this stage as Metaverse is a new project that has been announced and such framework would be able to assist in investigating the perspectives of stakeholders along with the problems and opportunities including the solutions that may come with it.

Customer

From the Technology Acceptance Model, it was seen that the most interested party in the technology are males under the age of 20 years old. As such, the data would suggest that the Metaverse project would gain more traction with people of the next generation. This would suggest that the users of Metaverse are the current population under 20 years old which may be the current and future workforce in the industry. With the current rate of innovation, there may be a possibility that this demographic group of people will be the ones to have access to stable and more suitable hardware to fully utilize Metaverse. The benefits will be able to be reaped by these groups of people and may mean that the future of Metaverse is still solid in terms of reception.

Actors

The main actors would be Meta or formerly known as Facebook whereby they are the company that announced the Metaverse Project. With Oculus being a well-known hardware provider for Virtual Reality now being owned by Meta, such case would also suggest the seriousness of the project with the inclusion of the billions of dollars spent. However, there are other hardware and software providers that can be used for the project. These include Playstation, HTC, Samsung, Nvidia, Microsoft, and many others. These suppliers may not be limited to the actual headset themselves but also the software, operating system, technology, and accessories of the technology that may improve the experience or immersion. For example, Bhaptics is a company that provides haptic feedback to the users and is often used in conjunction with Virtual Reality headsets. This is achieved using a suit and therefore improves the immersion level of the Virtual Reality headsets. This has been used by customers for games and social platforms such as VRChat whereby they are able to feel the sensation of touch from other users on their bodies.

Transformation

Metaverse provides a platform whereby people can live in the virtual world. This may be viewed as the second world of users whereby there are endless possibilities that can exist. The platform provides a simulation of the real world and therefore may increase efficiency in terms of work or increase the experience of education and meetings. By providing a 3D environment, the metaverse aspires to serve as the virtual setting for these interpersonal interactions. There will be the possibility for global employees of the same organization to get together in the metaverse to address problems through highly creative brainstorming, (Bloomberg, 2021). By donning a VR headset or AR glasses, they will be transported to a "virtual office" where they may interact with their coworkers without ever leaving the comfort of their homes. In terms of education, students will have the option to attend university classes in the metaverse or, if they want, they may choose not to do so (Hamdan et al., 2020; Anshari & Hamdan, 2022b). Teachers and students could connect in a virtual area via the virtual reality headset, regardless of where they were physically (Anshari & Hamdan, 2022a; Mulyani et al., 2019; Razzaq et al., 2018). Despite the distance between them, the teacher and students can still meet thanks to the metaverse (Anshari & Almunawar, 2021). The ability of the metaverse to display an immersive 3D world in addition to music makes it a more intriguing feature. This innovative function creates a calm, virtual academic environment, which not only aids in teaching but also enhances assimilation (CityAM, 2022). In essence, buying and selling are simply buying something, and getting something in return. When purchasing an item in the virtual 3D world that can be used in the virtual world, there is a possibility of paying with another virtual good of comparable value, such as NFTs or cryptocurrencies. Additionally, there is no need to make the lengthy trip and deal with any potential stress associated with having to be present in person at the store (Jaman & Anshari, 2021; Anshari et al., 2021). Additionally, when shopping in the metaverse, users' avatars may try on clothing, buy it, and have it delivered right to their real-world location. During the pandemic, the entertainment industry faced a huge loss of potential profits. For example, concerts were canceled, and cinemas were closed. As such, these companies had to find new ways of generating profit. Concerts were able to be held online by Travis Scott and it has attracted 27 million people which may be impossible when held physically instead of online due to logistics limitations, (Gestalt, 2022).

Worldview

In reference to the aforementioned technology acceptance model by Aburbeian et.al (2022), the perception of the virtual headsets shows the ease of use and convenience to be positive. With metaverse, this is something that promises to improve such experience further. As such, this would mean that Metaverse itself is viewed as something that is interesting, innovative, and useful in the future. Looking back at the transformation, the limitation is endless. This may mean that whatever can be done in the real world may provide a better experience in Metaverse. However, at this current stage, the limitation may be the cost, accessibility, and comfort of the hardware itself. The virtual/ augmented reality hardware is still at its developing stage and therefore will get better in solving these issues. In the future, whereby these issues have been overcome, the world of Metaverse may become a norm in society and in the workplace.

Owner

The residents of Metaverse themselves will be the future of the project. This is because they may have a second life in the virtual world whereby, they will be owners of shops, organizations, and many others. However, Meta will have the biggest stake and with Mark Zuckerberg being the head, his decisions will have the greatest power in the Metaverse world.

Environment

The environmental constraints would primarily come from government intervention. Political issues will certainly arise from the existence of the Metaverse as the governmental power of a country will be limited in the Metaverse. In addition, industries will face the negative impact that arises from the Metaverse. Unions will certainly have complaints in the future. For example, just as Uber had complaints from the Taxi drivers union, they will also complain about the less demand that may arise due to people having the option to work from home. In addition to that, the currency will also be an issue such is the case with cryptocurrency when first introduced (Anshari et al., 2019a). With less power from the government, there will be difficulties in controlling the currency and therefore there will be efforts to control the digital currency in the Metaverse. There is also a possibility of the Metaverse currency having better demand than real-world currency. U.S Dollars may fall in power in comparison.

SECI

Ikujiro Nonaka has arguably made the most significant contribution to this topic. He spent a lot of time experimenting with the ideas of explicit knowledge and tacit knowledge, calling attention to how Western businesses often place an excessive amount of emphasis on the former (Nonaka & Takeuchi 1996). The model developed by Nonaka and his colleagues, particularly the SECI matrix of knowledge conversion, is being referenced more frequently by authors in a wider range of disciplines, indicating that it has, in some ways, attained a paradigmatic status, (Gourlay, n.d.). Studies of information development in innovative organizations served as the foundation for the theory of organizational knowledge creation that Nonaka and his colleagues developed (Nonaka 1994; Nonaka & Takeuchi 1995; Nonaka et. al. 2000; 2001a; Nonaka & Toyama 2003).

The SECI matrix has no doubt left an imprint in knowledge creation and transfer theory in which four ways were proposed as a method whereby knowledge types can be combined and converted. It also helps in terms of knowing how knowledge is shared and created in the organization. The SECI matrix consists of:

- Socialization
- Externalization

- Combination
- Internalization

Figure 2. taken from Sandkuhl and Kurt (2015) showing the SECI Matrix

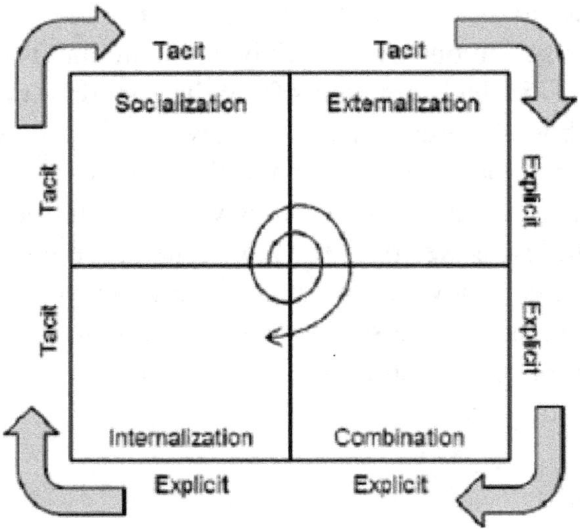

The model above is the visualization of the SECI matrix which also involves **Tacit** and **Explicit** Knowledge. Tacit knowledge refers to the ideas that still exist within the personal mind of people whilst Explicit knowledge refers to the documented knowledge that can be accessed by others (Anshari et al., 2019b). SECI helps identify how the transfer of tacit knowledge to explicit knowledge happens. With the promises of Metaverse, the SECI matrix is referred in order to help understand the potential of knowledge creation and transfer that could happen through Metaverse.

Through literature, it can be understood that Metaverse is simply a copy of reality in the virtual world. It is also found that there is a positive acceptance rate with Virtual Reality headsets and therefore would also suggest it is positive for Metaverse as the project itself is an addition to the current technology. The analysis through CATWOE also suggests that there is endless potential with Metaverse and therefore making the SECI matrix for Metaverse a viable option to investigate.

In terms of socialization, the option to socialize in the metaverse is similar to reality. This is whereby socialization would occur at a rapid pace and therefore the sharing of knowledge between each other would also occur. In terms of virtual workspace, it is similar to that of sharing an office together. In fact, in might be more efficient to share knowledge through the Metaverse over reality. This is as the technology that currently exists and potentially exists would suggest that there are multiple ways to contact and socialize with each other through the Metaverse. However, at this stage, it is still considered to be tacit knowledge whereby documentations are yet to occur.

Externalization in the Metaverse would happen from the socialization stage with documentation of information and knowledge being shared (Anshari, 2020). With the knowledge gained from the previous stage, reviews and reports are possible to be made especially since documentation in the Metaverse is much easier to have than in reality. This is as Metaverse works with a server and history interactions would leave an imprint. This opens the possibility of replay functions from previous interactions when a company chooses to have the option open.

The combination stage would then be possible as explicit knowledge has already been obtained. As mentioned before, Metaverse is simply a copy of reality with endless possibilities of features. With the possibility of having a replay function for daily interactions, the sorting and compiling of knowledge would then be easier (Almunawar & Anshari, 2021). This is as replays would be able to be played and refer to and thus provide much more accurate data obtained. The information gained at this stage would then be more complex and can be done systematically. As this stage requires the use of technology and communication; by comparison, the Metaverse would be superior in this stage in comparison to reality (Anshari et al., 2020).

The final stage of internalization would then occur. At this stage, the explicit knowledge is transferred to tacit knowledge. With previous explicit knowledge, there will be lessons learned to be improved and opinions made. As such, people would then have their own ideas and knowledge from experience that would then repeat the cycle from the SECI matrix.

CONCLUSION

Metaverse is a project that opens many possibilities in the workplace and in other sectors of industry. With promises of being a copy of reality, the use of Metaverse would be endless and may provide efficiency in the workplace and ease to the users. From the literature, it can be seen that the demographic groups of people highly interested in the technology are the ones who will most likely reap their full potential. Whilst Metaverse may not be at its peak stage anytime soon, the progress has been seen to be significant and promising. With continuous reception and support from the population and companies, there is high confidence attached to the Metaverse project. With the CATWOE model, the views were investigated further than it was from the technology acceptance model with a more in-depth focus on the Metaverse specifically over the Virtual Reality technology. Through this, potentials were analyzed and were found to be limitless with proofs of functions found from the past such as the Travis Scott concert during the pandemic. SECI matrix on the Metaverse also found that the transference and creation of knowledge through the use of the Metaverse will be easy and useful. By using the matrix, it can be seen that the Metaverse might be the most useful and innovative technology to create and transfer knowledge as of today.

REFERENCES

Abdlkarim, D., & Holland, P. (n.d.). *A Methodological Framework to Assess the Accuracy of Virtual Reality Hand-Tracking Systems: A case study with the Oculus Quest 2*. doi:10.1101/2022.02.18.481001

Almunawar, M. N., & Anshari, M. (2021). Digital enabler and value integration: Revealing the expansion engine of digital marketplace. *Technology Analysis and Strategic Management*, 1–11.

Anshari, M. (2020, March). Workforce mapping of fourth industrial revolution: Optimization to identity. *Journal of Physics: Conference Series*, *1477*(7), 072023. doi:10.1088/1742-6596/1477/7/072023

Anshari, M., Syafrudin, M., Fitriyani, N. L., & Razzaq, A. (2022). Ethical Responsibility and Sustainability (ERS) Development in a Metaverse Business Model. *Sustainability*, *14*(23), 15805. doi:10.3390u142315805

Anshari, M., & Hamdan, M. (2022). Enhancing e-government with a digital twin for innovation management. *Journal of Science and Technology Policy Management*.

Anshari, M., Syafrudin, M., & Fitriyani, N. L. (2022). Fourth Industrial Revolution between Knowledge Management and Digital Humanities. *Information (Basel)*, *13*(6), 292. doi:10.3390/info13060292

Anshari, M., & Hamdan, M. (2022). Understanding knowledge management and upskilling in Fourth Industrial Revolution: Transformational shift and SECI model. *VINE Journal of Information and Knowledge Management Systems*. Advance online publication. doi:10.1108/VJIKMS-09-2021-0203

Anshari, M., & Almunawar, M. N. (2021). Adopting open innovation for SMEs and industrial revolution 4.0. *Journal of Science and Technology Policy Management*.

Anshari, M., Almunawar, M. N., & Razzaq, A. (2021). Developing talents vis-à-vis fourth industrial revolution. *International Journal of Asian Business and Information Management*, *12*(4), 20–32. doi:10.4018/IJABIM.20211001.oa2

Anshari, M., Almunawar, M. N., & Masri, M. (2020). An overview of financial technology in Indonesia. *Financial technology and disruptive innovation in ASEAN*, 216-224.

Anshari, M., Almunawar, M. N., Lim, S. A., & Al-Mudimigh, A. (2019). Customer relationship management and big data enabled: Personalization & customization of services. *Applied Computing and Informatics*, *15*(2), 94–101. doi:10.1016/j.aci.2018.05.004

Anshari, M., Alas, Y., & Sulaiman, E. (2019). Smartphone addictions and nomophobia among youth. *Vulnerable Children and Youth Studies*, *14*(3), 242–247. doi:10.1080/17450128.2019.1614709

Bloomberg - Are you a robot? (2021). Retrieved 30 September 2022, from https://www.bloomberg.com/professional/blog/metaverse-may-be-800-billion-market-next-tech-platform/

Bibri, S. E., & Allam, Z. (2022). The Metaverse as a Virtual Form of Data-Driven Smart Urbanism: On Post-Pandemic Governance through the Prism of the Logic of Surveillance Capitalism. *Smart Cities*, *5*(2), 715–727. doi:10.3390martcities5020037

City, A. M. (2022). *How the metaverse will change the world.* Retrieved 30 September 2022, from https://www.cityam.com/how-the-metaverse-will-change-the-world/#:~:text=The%20metaverse%2C%20by%20offering%20a,so%20as%20to%20solve%20problems

Dadayan, L., & Ferro, E. (n.d.). *When Technology Meets the Mind: A Comparative Study of the Technology Acceptance Model*. Academic Press.

Davis, F. (1989). Perceived Usefulness, Perceived Ease of Use, and User Acceptance of Information Technology. *Management Information Systems Quarterly*, *13*(3), 319. doi:10.2307/249008

Gestalt, A. (2022). *10 Ways the Metaverse Will Change the World - Listverse*. Retrieved 30 September 2022, from https://listverse.com/2022/04/30/10-ways-the-metaverse-will-change-the-world/

Gourlay, S. (n.d.). *The SECI model of knowledge creation: some empirical shortcomings*. Academic Press.

Hamdan, M., Jaidin, J. H., Fithriyah, M., & Anshari, M. (2020, December). E-learning in time of COVID-19 pandemic: Challenges & experiences. In *2020 Sixth International Conference on e-Learning (econf)* (pp. 12-16). IEEE. 10.1109/econf51404.2020.9385507

Isaac, M. (2021). *To Build the Metaverse, Meta First Wants to Build Stores*. Retrieved 30 September 2022, from https://www.nytimes.com/2021/11/05/technology/facebook-stores-meta-metaverse.html

Jaman, S. F. I., & Anshari, M. (2021). Facebook as marketing tools for organizations: Knowledge management analysis. In *Research Anthology on Strategies for Using Social Media as a Service and Tool in Business* (pp. 117–131). IGI Global. doi:10.4018/978-1-7998-9020-1.ch007

Juna, M. A., Anshari, M., Ahmad, N., & Hamdan, M. (2022). Working from home, COVID-19 and multi-dimensional model of well-being theory. *International Journal of Work Organisation and Emotion*, *13*(3), 230–259. doi:10.1504/IJWOE.2022.126957

Kamenov, K. (2017). *The 4th Wave in Technology | Part 1 | Accenture*. Retrieved 30 September 2022, from https://www.accenture.com/gb-en/blogs/blogs-immersive-experience-wave-learning-ropes

Lang, B. (2020). *Social VR App 'VRChat' is Seeing Record Usage Amidst the Pandemic*. Retrieved 30 September 2022, from https://www.roadtovr.com/vrchat-record-users-coronavirus/

Meta. (2021). *The Facebook Company Is Now Meta | Meta*. Retrieved 30 September 2022, from https://about.fb.com/news/2021/10/facebook-company-is-now-meta/

Mystakidis, S. (2022). Metaverse. *Encyclopedia*, *2*(1), 486–497. doi:10.3390/encyclopedia2010031

Mulyani, M. A., Razzaq, A., Sumardi, W. H., & Anshari, M. (2019, August). Smartphone adoption in mobile learning scenario. In *2019 International Conference on Information Management and Technology (ICIMTech)* (Vol. 1, pp. 208-211). IEEE. 10.1109/ICIMTech.2019.8843755

Razzaq, A., Samiha, Y. T., & Anshari, M. (2018). Smartphone habits and behaviors in supporting students self-efficacy. *International Journal of Emerging Technologies in Learning*, *13*(2), 94. doi:10.3991/ijet.v13i02.7685

Smith, S. (2022). *Meta Quest 2 review: The affordable VR headset we've been waiting for*. Retrieved 30 September 2022, from https://www.laptopmag.com/reviews/oculus-quest-2

Nonaka, I. (1994). *A Dynamic Theory of Organizational Knowledge Creation*. Academic Press.

Nonaka, I., & Takeuchi, H. (n.d.). *The Knowledge-Creating Company*. Academic Press.

Nonaka, I., Toyama, R., & Konno, N. (n.d.). *SECI, Ba and Leadership: A Unified Model of Dynamic Knowledge Creation*. www.elsevier.com/locate/lrp

Nonaka, I., & Toyama, R. (2003). The knowledge-creating theory revisited: Knowledge creation as a synthesizing process. *Knowledge Management Research and Practice*, *1*(1), 2–10. https://doi.org/10.1057/palgrave.kmrp.8500001

Sandkuhl, K. (2015). Knowledge Reuse: Survey of Existing Techniques and Classification Approach. *Lecture Notes in Business Information Processing*, *205*, 126–148. doi:10.1007/978-3-319-17551-5_5

Taylor, S., & Soneji, S. (2022). Bioinformatics and the Metaverse: Are We Ready? *Frontiers in Bioinformatics, 2*. doi:10.3389/fbinf.2022.863676

Xiong, J., Hsiang, E.-L., He, Z., Zhan, T., & Wu, S.-T. (2021). Augmented reality and virtual reality displays: Emerging technologies and future perspectives. *Light, Science & Applications*, *10*(1), 216. https://doi.org/10.1038/s41377-021-00658-8

Yan, Y., Chen, K., Xie, Y., Song, Y., & Liu, Y. (2019). The Effects of Weight on Comfort of Virtual Reality Devices. https://doi.org/10.1007/978-3-319-94706-8_27.

Chapter 6
The Development of a Metaverse App for a Blended Learning in Higher Education Institutions

Nurul Nabillah Masnadi
https://orcid.org/0000-0002-9690-1211
Universiti Brunei Darussalam, Brunei

ABSTRACT

COVID-19 has led to the rise of blended learning, and many innovations have been introduced worldwide. Metaverse in education is one of the innovations. The chapter aims to introduce students, lecturers, and people coming to a higher education institution in Brunei Darussalam to a metaverse app. The app's objectives are to solve the problems encountered in online learning and simultaneously allow physical learning in a safer environment. The chapter also includes the CATWOE framework that aims to provide an overview of how the various transformations taking place in the field of education affect how students learn. The road map in knowledge management implementation is also shared in this chapter to show the stages of implementation in developing the metaverse app. This chapter will also discuss the challenges and limitations of a metaverse app in education.

DOI: 10.4018/978-1-6684-6097-9.ch006

Copyright © 2023, IGI Global. Copying or distributing in print or electronic forms without written permission of IGI Global is prohibited.

INTRODUCTION

Students worldwide have gone through the online learning phase due to the outbreak of COVID-19. Many schools and universities in the world have been temporarily placed under lockdown. Online learning can help alleviate this issue by allowing students to complete their studies. Instead of traditional classrooms, online courses offer a safer environment (Almunawar & Anshari, 2022). They can help protect students and their families from the virus by allowing them to continue their studies.

Although education is essential for everyone, various factors go into choosing the right type of education for a child or a person. There are many debates about physical and online classrooms. Even though it is possible to adapt to the technological advancements in the field of education, there are still reasons to doubt the effectiveness of online learning. The lack of proper school equipment and resources will also impact the various groups affected by the pandemic, such as students and teachers. Although many fields require practical experience, the same teaching methods cannot be implemented in every discipline. This has led to the development of new opportunities for improving the quality of education (Hamdan et al., 2020a).

This paper then aims to develop a metaverse app and encourage blended learning for students from higher educational institutions in Brunei Darussalam. Although learning had already moved toward a blended and virtual environment before COVID-19, students can participate in immersive campus life, exploring, socialising, and interacting with others through the metaverse (Anshari et al., 2022a). For instance, virtual reality headsets allow students to access learning pods, meet counsellors, and browse libraries (Juna et al., 2022). The metaverse's storytelling and visualisation capabilities set it apart from other learning environments. This is necessary after the numerous boring Zoom experiences featured during COVID-19 (Jagannathan, n.d.; Fithriyah et al., 2022).

The metaverse also allows students to develop their soft skills in a safe and real-world environment. Virtual reality allows students to practice their skills without feeling anxious or overwhelmed (Anshari et al., 2022b). It can also help those with mobility issues improve their quality of life. Through the metaverse, organisations can collect data on the behaviour of their students to improve their learning experience. The data can then be used to identify areas of their operations that need to be improved. The metaverse is a term that means "life after the internet". Its early applications include gamified activities, virtual campus simulations, and 3D simulations. This technology is only the beginning, as there are many more innovations that can be used to transform education (Jagannathan, n.d.).

LITERATURE REVIEW

Challenges of Online Learning

The pandemic can be considered a once-in-a-generation opportunity to transform how we educate our children. It has the potential to bring together various educators and students to come up with a new education model. This new model could help us rethink the way we think about education. The pandemic demonstrated that educators all around the world could change. Due to the pandemic outbreak, schools and governments had to close, leaving teachers, students, and adults with no choice but to carry out education differently (Anshari et al., 2022c). During the school closures, various regulations and exams that were previously implemented were lifted. These included ending the traditional accountability tests and eliminating other high-stakes tests (Razzaq et al., 2018; Hamdan et al., 2020b). Education was allowed to adapt to the situation (Zhao & Watterston, 2021).

According to Alexander et al. (2012), the main advantages of taking online courses are avoiding paying attention to their clothes and getting to class on time. The researchers also added that the most desirable features of an online learning system are its flexibility and ability to work at its own pace and time. This is because most classroom teachers would expect this system to allow them to provide a more flexible and personalised learning experience. Another advantage many students consider is the ability to view and review lectures.

Besides the advantages of online learning, it has also been identified that there are still some disadvantages that need to be considered when implementing the technology. One of the disadvantages of online courses is the lack of face-to-face interaction and the likelihood of procrastination. Other common disadvantages of online classes include the lack of guidance and the ability to contact the instructor for help (Alexander et al., 2012). Without proper management and support, a network may fail in just a few minutes (Anshari et al., 2021). A network can cripple a whole school or even affect a lab. In addition, all devices, such as a computer, a modem, and a router, must be connected to the network. The user must have the necessary hardware and software to use the internet. In wireless connections, signal strength is often an issue (Yuhanna et al., 2020).

According to Firmansyah et al. (2021), one of the most significant disadvantages of online learning is the requirement that students complete their assignments and studies at home. This is because the mindset of many students has changed, as they previously believed that the house was not a place for them to do their homework. This will make them feel like they are not being supported properly. This will result in them experiencing learning shock and other psychological issues. The concept of learning shock refers to the various experiences students experience when they start using online learning. It can be caused by the lack of understanding of the teaching methods and instructions (Mulyani et al., 2021).

Although taking online classes is widely acknowledged, it is essential to note that these courses may not meet students' learning styles. The various challenges that face the world of education are not easy to overcome. However, universities and educational institutions worldwide can still succeed with the right resources and strategies.

Blended Learning in Higher Education Institutions

Several researchers define blended learning differently. Blending is an approach that aims to achieve an educational goal by intermixing various instructional methods. According to Singh (2003), blended learning is a type of teaching that combines multiple media to promote effective and meaningful learning (Mulyani et al., 2019). Instructors can use tools to implement this type of learning, including online classes, live chats, and social networking sites. Meanwhile, Garrison and Kanuka (2004) explained that blending is not about replacing traditional classroom learning with online learning. It is about integrating the two methods into one.

Despite the various challenges of implementing hybrid learning in higher education, Garrison and Kanuka (2004) research has shown that this approach can provide better learning outcomes. For instance, by combining face-to-face and online instruction, this type of learning can help improve student outcomes. Moreover, blended teaching can help facilitate collaborative and independent learning experiences. It creates a platform for interactive dialogue and free and independent inquiry. The increasing popularity of face-to-face interaction and asynchronous Internet technology has improved the quality of education (Bonk & Graham, 2004). Being digitally literate is also beneficial for students as it allows them to extend their conversations and lessons beyond the classroom (Kasraie & Alahmed, 2014).

Through live events and online discussions, instructors can provide their students with different educational content that can be accessed at their own pace. This type of learning can help them develop their social and cognitive skills simultaneously.

The Importance of Knowledge Management in Education

The increasing globalisation of educational institutions and the shift toward lifelong learning are some factors that have prompted the development of knowledge management. According to Dhamdhere (2015), this discipline is expected to help improve the efficiency of academic institutions and reduce the cost of collecting and managing massive amounts of data. It is tough to record the tacit knowledge that staff members have created in an institution. Many of them leave the institute, and their knowledge goes with them (Sait & Anshari, 2021). If knowledge management practices are carried out continuously in an institute, then only the generated knowledge would be preserved and used for future reference. While inspecting the academic development of a university, officers should regularly review the various aspects of the institution's operations and policies. This discipline can help them improve the efficiency of their work.

Through knowledge management, educational institutions could improve their capacity to collect and share information and develop effective problem-solving techniques (Anshari et al., 2022d). This discipline also helps them maintain their quality of teaching and learning. Information should be collected and disseminated at various levels to improve the professional knowledge of their staff members and their students' quality. Through knowledge management, educational institutions can also strengthen their capacity to transfer their ideas and methods to other institutions, and it is not limited to their institution. This discipline can help them create a network of interaction that will allow them to develop new ideas and improve their performance. The exchange of ideas and information in networks can also help improve the quality of teaching and learning (Dhamdhere, 2015).

Dhamdhere (2015) also explained that faculty experts, students, and researchers of educational institutions regularly contribute to the knowledge base by developing new concepts. The increasing globalisation of higher education has created the need to share organisational knowledge. Through knowledge management, techniques can capture and store hidden knowledge in individuals and organisations (Anshari & Hamdan, 2022). When the performance of an educational institution is gradually improved, all its past years' worth of explicit and tacit knowledge can be accessed in one place. This discipline can help transform the organisation's efficiency and effectiveness. Through advanced technology, data, and information, knowledge management can help improve the scope of operations and increase the institution's effectiveness. Through knowledge management, educational institutions can also enhance their capacity to collect and share information and develop effective problem-solving techniques. This discipline can help them maintain their quality of teaching and learning.

The Importance of Knowledge Management in Innovation

The importance of knowledge management is acknowledged as a vital part of the innovation process, as it can help reduce the complexity of the process and ensure that the resources are used effectively. This can be done by recognising and managing the various aspects of knowledge. Due to the complexity of the process, the available knowledge must be managed and recognised (Adams & Lamont, 2003; Shani et al., 2003; Darroch & McNaughton, 2002; Pyka, 2002; Cardinal et al., 2001). Tamer Cavusgil et al. (2003) acknowledged the importance of knowledge management as a vital part of the innovation process, as it can help reduce the complexity of the process and ensure that the resources are used effectively. This can be done by recognising and managing the various aspects of knowledge. Additionally, according to Tamer Cavusgil et al. (2003), organisations that can create and use knowledge effectively are more likely to be successful than those that do not. Pyka (2002) also stated that innovation networks are driven by knowledge management and create synergy (Anshari & Almunawar, 2021).

Integrating internal and external knowledge is one of the most critical factors when implementing knowledge management. This process can help make available timely insights used to make informed decisions. The concept of knowledge integration refers to the process of bringing together the various aspects of an organisation's knowledge to create a more compelling sense of purpose. This process can help make available timely insights used to make informed decisions. By integrating knowledge management platforms, processes, and tools, organisations can facilitate dialogue and reflection to allow their employees and customers to access and use knowledge effectively.

This process can also help make available timely insights that can be used to make informed decisions. Many organisations acknowledge the importance of having effective knowledge management as a vital part of their innovation strategy. Without this process, they could be left with a lack of innovative resources.

In conclusion, knowledge management systems can help companies develop a sustainable competitive advantage through innovation. Despite the importance of having a comprehensive knowledge management system, it is not enough to simply have one. Organisations must also have the necessary resources and core competencies to develop and maintain a competitive advantage. With the help of knowledge management systems, organisations can transform their core competencies and learning capabilities into sustainable advantages. This can be done through the development of effective resource management processes.

Development of the Metaverse in Education

The metaverse offers a wide variety of learning environments designed to provide a rich and engaging experience. These environments can be created using cognitive and emotional immersion. Jensen and Konradsen (2018) conducted a study investigating virtual reality's effects on individuals' learning and training. Their findings revealed that technology could help improve the cognitive abilities of students. Sirakaya (2018) analysed the effects of augmented reality on various aspects of seventh-grade students' academic performance, such as achievement and misconception. They found that the technology did not affect the students' engagement levels. Nevertheless, the study's results revealed that augmented reality helped improve students' academic performance. It also reduced the number of misconceptions about theoretical learning.

Denholm et al. (2013) conducted a study to evaluate the effects of mixed reality games on the collaboration skills of international students. The study's results revealed that 75% of the students believed that the games improved their team collaboration, while 60% stated that they were more beneficial than lectures. Cascales et al. (2013) conducted a study to analyse parents' perceptions about using augmented reality in their preschool programs. They categorised the parents' perceptions into five elements: knowledge, writing, reading, creativity, and degree of satisfaction. Despite the findings showing that the parents had varying perceptions about the technology, most believed it was beneficial.

Introducing a metaverse app can help enhance student motivation and develop new teaching methods. It can also extend traditional practices by allowing students to interact with each other in various ways. Numerous studies have shown that it can provide new opportunities to interact with students. The rise of the metaverse has been regarded as the next generation of social networking. It refers to a world where people can live under the rules set by the creator (Farjami et al., 2011). The metaverse can be described as a virtual reality if it is entirely virtual or augmented reality if it is a partially virtual world. In addition, in the metaverse, people can participate in various social activities such as playing games and discussing issues. They can also collaborate on projects and solve problems. Various events and activities can be carried out in the metaverse, just like in real life (Hwang & Chien, 2022).

The rise of the metaverse has started again due to the emergence of the COVID-19 pandemic. The four existing metaverse types, virtual reality, augmented reality, lifelogging, and mirror world are rapidly becoming more prevalent as they evolve into a new type of service. This concept shows how different types of metaverse can be affected by COVID-19. Due to the lack of face-to-face communication, activities previously only possible offline is now available in virtual reality. Some of these include medical care, education, fashion, and tourism (Kye et al., 2021).

Kye et al. (2021) also mentioned that due to the outbreak of the COVID-19 pandemic, it has been difficult for people to have private meetings or eat together in a restaurant. In the metaverse, people can gather to watch a concert or hold a festival. Virtual reality platforms such as Roblox and Zepeto have provided people with a new social space to meet and relax (Kye et al., 2021).

Metaverse can help students improve their learning by making it fun. It can also motivate them to complete tasks and focus on their studies. In addition to providing various activities, such as badges and quests, it can also introduce gamification features to help students stay focused. Despite the advantages of Metaverse, its actual efficiency can only be judged based on how well it can help students master their subjects. Teachers and parents can only accept this technology if it can help students improve their grades. The study examined whether immersive virtual reality learning could improve students' test scores. The results indicated that those who experienced the program scored higher than the control group. The study also concluded that VR learning could be an effective alternative to traditional educational storytelling (Ravi, 2022).

Additionally, according to Kye et al. (2021), although some may think that the metaverse is merely a gaming platform, this concept is an evolution of the concept. In online games, the users are expected to perform limited missions to meet the game's goals. In the metaverse, users can perform whatever they want without setting a specific goal. With the freedom of the metaverse, people can enjoy various activities in the real world, such as shopping, sightseeing, and exhibitions. They can also share experiences that are difficult to experience in the real world due to certain physical restrictions. People can also spend their time relaxing and getting away from their busy lives by going fishing, picking fruits, or exploring a friend's island. They do not have to solve the metaverse to enjoy these activities.

METHODS

There are various reasons why people should consider adopting the metaverse in their educational settings. Due to the rapid emergence and evolution of new technologies, such as wearable devices and high-speed computers, the metaverse is becoming more feasible.

The CATWOE Analysis

The CATWOE method is a framework that aims to provide an overview of the various transformations that are taking place in introducing a metaverse in education. CATWOE definitions can be seen in Table 1.

Table 1. CATWOE Analysis

CATWOE	Definitions
Customers	People in the surrounding area of the higher education institutions, such as students, lecturers, staff and the public Own alternative ways of learning or teaching
Actors	Institutions, Heads/Presidents of the Institutions, Designers, Developers/ Programmers The success will benefit the people inside and outside the institutions, which therefore may increase its reputations
Transformation Process	The development of metaverse app while using blended learning
World View	Attract students/people worldwide and introduce the institutions internationally
Owners	People with higher status in the institutions, The Ministry
Environmental Constraint	Cost, tools, support

Knowledge Management Implementation Road Map

In developing the metaverse app, stages of implementation will be applied in this paper. Figure 1 shows that there are five stages to successful knowledge management. The stages will be further elaborated on in this chapter.

Figure 1. Road Map to Knowledge Management Results

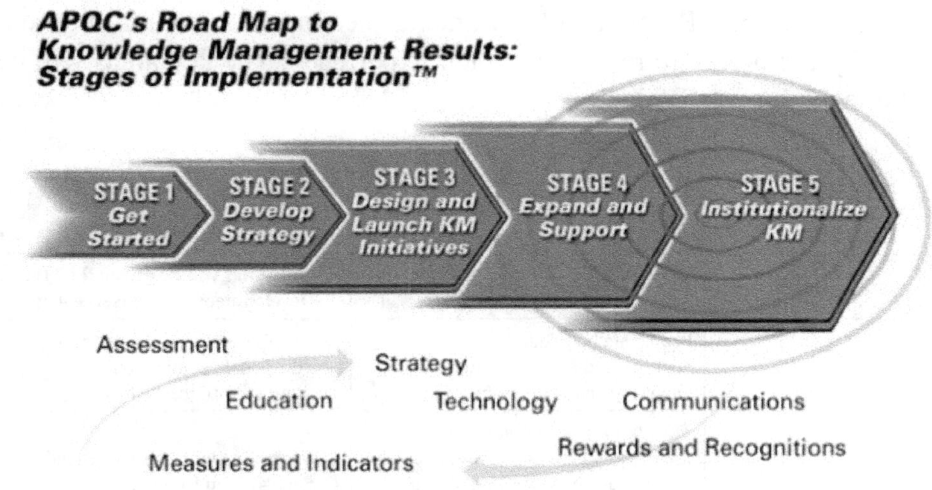

Stage 1: Get Started

This stage covers establishing objectives. As the paper aims to develop a metaverse app for students to offer a safer environment during the endemic phase in Brunei Darussalam, the innovation's objectives are introduced and explained in Table 2.

Table 2. The Objectives

Objectives	Details
Facilitate the activities of students	For blended learning and for the student's attendance
Easily locate themselves while being at the campus physically	To see if certain places have been occupied to reduce time in searching for places and encourage physical distancing
Introduce interesting features	To encourage and motivate students in both online and physical learning

Stage 2: Develop Strategy

When developing the strategy, it is essential to have the best practices. This paper will review various assessment tools and literature related to global health and knowledge management according to Ohkubo (2015). The article identified the key elements that will resonate with practitioners, which then mapped into five critical areas that practitioners commonly use. The key domains of People, Platform (Technology), and Process are all linked to a concept widely accepted by practitioners of various disciplines. The two remaining domains, Problem Solving and Partnership, are also informed and guided by the literature review and their experience. The key areas will be further explained in Table 3.

Table 3. Five Key Elements in Developing Strategy

Elements	Explanation	Who/What will be affected by the Development of Metaverse App
People	People are both individuals who contribute to an organisation's knowledge base and users	The app's developers or programmers, and the people coming to the institutions with metaverse
Platform (Technology)	The platform is an organisation's use of various tools and resources to automate and operationalise its knowledge management activities	3D modelling tools, such as Blender, Cinema 4D and Houdini
Process	The process discipline is a set of actions and steps an organisation can take to achieve its knowledge management goals	It involves implementing a strategy aligned to the development of metaverse apps in education
Problem-Solving	The most critical skills organisations need to develop to improve their knowledge management efforts	This discipline can help the users identify and resolve issues arising from environmental changes
Partnership	Through a partnership, organisations can improve their knowledge management efforts by working with other organisations and individuals	This discipline can also help them develop effective communication and collaboration strategies. Possible collaborations are between the institutions and the ministries

Source: Ohkubo (2015): People, Process, Platform, Partnership, and Problem Solving: The 5P.

Stage 3: Design and Launch KM Initiatives

As the development of the metaverse app aims to be used for blended learning, the app's design will be an augmented reality (AR). AR is most suitable for blended learning as it uses a real-world setting, while VR is entirely virtual. AR is a type of digital media that uses graphics, audio, and text to enhance the appearance and experience of objects. It can be used to enhance the digital experience by blending the real world with the virtual space. AR is ideal for technical training because it can provide a quick reference to specific technical details, such as how to repair or use machinery (Kumar, 2022).

It can also reduce distractions and enhance the learning experience. With the availability of smartphones, people can access AR without having to go to a computer. It allows users to transform their physical world into a colourful and interactive digital representation by displaying virtual characters and pictures through their phones' cameras. The following are two existing apps that can be applied in making the app:

(i) Zepeto

ZEPETO is the closest example. ZEPETO allows users to create and decorate their avatars using augmented reality and facial recognition functions. They can also use virtual currencies such as gems and coins to decorate their maps and create their own space. Although the platform does not support coding, users can still explore maps and build their creations. ZEPETO recommends various types of poses through their various avatars and other crews, which are designed to support crew classification. They also encourage users to share content through live streaming and My Photobooth features (Han et al., 2021).

(ii) Roblox

Roblox is where people can play and share games made by others using the online gaming platform. It features a variety of games and a game-development tool known as Roblox Studio, which allows users to create and share their creations. After signing up, users can play a wide range of games and chat with other users for free.

Stage 4: Expand and Support

In creating the app for the higher education institutions in Brunei Darussalam, the designers/developers need to work closely with the institutions themselves, with the permission of the Ministry of Education. They need to include maps of the institutions in the app with details on the interior, such as classrooms, staffrooms, libraries, and cafes.

As mentioned in Stage 1 earlier, the app would be an AR where it is downloadable to the users from their phones. Like Roblox, users can access the app and meet and chat with others. With the avatars' feature, the users can locate themselves throughout the maps while connected to the internet. This is to avoid clashes with other people coming to the institutions, when having the traditional face-to-face learning or whenever they need to come to the institutions, such as going to the library. As the development of the app focuses on blended learning, the app can also be used by the students as their attendance to ease their lecturers while having online classes. However, it is also necessary to ensure that the students download the app and sign up first.

Stage 5: Institutionalise KM

This stage is where structure and budget will be realigned, monitored and measured. However, as the app has not yet existed in Brunei Darussalam, here are some suggestions for creating the metaverse app.

As e-learning courses are being delivered through a new approach, it is also vital that the various groups are supported and have clear communication regarding the changes. This can help facilitate buy-in from the students and staff members. A continuous improvement program should also be maintained to ensure the learning experience is not disrupted. In addition to using technology, students and staff members may also require new skills to improve their knowledge and skills in various areas. These include information literacy, e-learning development, and time management. For trainers, these skills can develop their students' e-learning knowledge and improve efficiency (Harris et al., 2009).

According to Stewart (2002), due to the increasing number of e-learning courses being delivered through virtual learning environments, users must have the necessary skills to manage the various aspects of these courses. For instance, they should be able to multi-task in a virtual learning environment during a session. The expectations of the users, as well as their learning styles and motivations, should be considered to create a conducive buy-in environment. Meeting these expectations can help motivate them to continue participating in the blended learning program.

CHALLENGES

The main challenge in creating the metaverse app for blending learning is ensuring people come to the institutions to download the app. Active participation by all parties is significant to implement the environment effectively. Moreover, many factors still go into deciding on a system, such as the tools used, the cost, and the available support. Choosing a system that is right for the institution can be very challenging. Implementing an online learning system is often exacerbated by the financial considerations involved. If the institution decides to use a system that is not insubstantial, it will most likely face the obligation to either stick with it or spend the money on the development of new courses. One of the most significant factors affecting an institution's decision regarding an online learning system is the need to maintain its current product. This is because the latest innovations can help improve the system's performance. However, finding the right money to spend on new systems can also be very challenging (Liang & Chen, 2012).

Due to the increasing number of companies shifting to hybrid or remote workplaces, executives are becoming more aware of the need to develop and train their teams. This is why they are adopting new approaches to learning and development.

LIMITATIONS

Although this paper focuses on the use of AR, however, many metaverse platforms are designed for use with VR headsets. There is still much research to determine if they are safe for children. Additionally, the innovation may not apply to all levels of education. As it is necessary to download the app first, this innovation is only helpful for schools that allow phones.

CONCLUSION

As the evolution of technology continues, it is important that we continuously monitor the effectiveness of new learning tools and methods. The metaverse is the latest evolution of the internet. The metaverse is expected to impact the development of e-learning significantly. It will allow users to experience the world through a more realistic and engaging environment. Before implementing a new e-learning system, the organisation must choose the right learning modality that fits its business requirements and goals. Unfortunately, despite the positive effects of Metaverse, it can be hard for people to adapt to its concept in education due to its lack of human interaction. The rise of the metaverse is a step in the evolution of EdTech. It involves using various teaching aids and augmented reality (AR) for a more engaging experience. Metaverse is expected to have a huge impact on the field of education. Some schools have already started using it for immersive learning. As more schools start using it, it will become inevitable that one of their classes will be in it.

REFERENCES

Adams, G. L., & Lamont, B. (2003). Knowledge management systems and developing sustainable competitive advantage. *Journal of Knowledge Management*, *7*(2), 142–154. doi:10.1108/13673270310477342

Alexander, M. W., Truel, A. D., & Zhao, J. J. (2012). Expected advantages and disadvantages of online learning: Perceptions from college students who have not taken online courses. *Issues in Information Systems*, *13*(2), 193–200. doi:10.48009/2_iis_2012_193-200

Almunawar, M. N., & Anshari, M. (2022). Customer acceptance of online delivery platform during the COVID-19 pandemic: the case of Brunei Darussalam. *Journal of Science and Technology Policy Management*.

Anshari, M., & Almunawar, M. N. (2021). Adopting open innovation for SMEs and industrial revolution 4.0. *Journal of Science and Technology Policy Management*.

Anshari, M., Almunawar, M. N., & Razzaq, A. (2021). Developing talents vis-à-vis fourth industrial revolution. *International Journal of Asian Business and Information Management*, *12*(4), 20–32. doi:10.4018/IJABIM.20211001.oa2

Anshari, M., & Hamdan, M. (2022). Understanding knowledge management and upskilling in Fourth Industrial Revolution: Transformational shift and SECI model. *VINE Journal of Information and Knowledge Management Systems*. Advance online publication. doi:10.1108/VJIKMS-09-2021-0203

Anshari, M., Hamdan, M., Ahmad, N., Ali, E., & Haidi, H. (2022a). COVID-19, artificial intelligence, ethical challenges and policy implications. *AI & Society*, 1–14. doi:10.100700146-022-01471-6 PMID:35607368

Anshari, M., Sakalayen, Q., Fithriyah, M., & Lim, S. A. (2022c). Decision Aid in Logistics during COVID-19 Induced Disruption and Significance of a Digital Ecosystem. In *2022 International Conference on Decision Aid Sciences and Applications (DASA)* (pp. 1371-1377). IEEE. 10.1109/DASA54658.2022.9765144

Anshari, M., Syafrudin, M., & Fitriyani, N. L. (2022d). Fourth Industrial Revolution between Knowledge Management and Digital Humanities. *Information (Basel)*, *13*(6), 292. doi:10.3390/info13060292

Anshari, M., Syafrudin, M., Fitriyani, N. L., & Razzaq, A. (2022b). Ethical Responsibility and Sustainability (ERS) Development in a Metaverse Business Model. *Sustainability*, *14*(23), 15805. doi:10.3390u142315805

Bonk, C. J., & Graham, C. R. (Eds.). (in press). *Handbook of blended learning: Global Perspectives, local designs*. Pfeiffer Publishing.

Cardinal, L. B., Alessandri, T. M., & Turner, S. F. (2001). Knowledge codifiability, resources, and science-based innovation. *Journal of Knowledge Management*, *5*(2), 195–204. doi:10.1108/13673270110393266

Cascales, A., Pérez-López, D., & Contero, M. (2013). Study on parent's acceptance of the augmented reality use for preschool education. *Procedia Computer Science*, *25*, 420–427. doi:10.1016/j.procs.2013.11.053

Darroch, J., & McNaughton, R. (2002). Examining the link between knowledge management practices and types of innovation. *Journal of Intellectual Capital*, *3*(3), 210–222. doi:10.1108/14691930210435570

Denholm, J. A., Protopsaltis, A., & de Freitas, S. (2013). The value of Team-Based Mixed-Reality (TBMR) games in higher education. *International Journal of Game-Based Learning*, *3*(1), 18–33. doi:10.4018/ijgbl.2013010102

Dhamdere, S. N. (2015). Importance of knowledge management in the higher educational institutes. *Turkish Online Journal of Distance Education*, *16*(1), 162–183. doi:10.17718/tojde.34392

Farjami, S., Taguchi, R., Nakahira, K. T., Nunez Rattia, R., Fukumura, Y., & Kanematsu, H. (2011). Multilingual problem based learning in metaverse. *Knowledge-Based and Intelligent Information and Engineering Systems*, 499–509. doi:10.1007/978-3-642-23854-3_53

Firmansyah, R., Putri, D. M., Wicaksono, M. G. S., Putri, S. F., & Widianto, A. A. (2021). The university students' perspectives on the advantages and disadvantages of online learning due to COVID-19. *Proceedings of 2nd Annual Management, Business and Economic Conference (AMBEC 2020)*, 183. 10.2991/aebmr.k.210717.025

Fithriyah, M., Masri, M., Almunawar, M. N., & Anshari, M. (2022). Financial Inclusion and Mobile Payment to Empower Small and Medium-Sized Enterprises: Post-COVID-19 Business Strategy. In FinTech Development for Financial Inclusiveness (pp. 50-59). IGI Global.

Garrison, D., & Kanuka, H. (2004). Blended learning: Uncovering its transformative potential in higher education. *The Internet and Higher Education*, *7*(2), 95–105. doi:10.1016/j.iheduc.2004.02.001

Hamdan, M., Ahmad, N., Jaidin, J. H., & Anshari, M. (2020b). Internationalisation in Brunei's higher education and its policy implications: Case study of Universiti Brunei Darussalam. *TEST Engineering and Management*, *83*, 764–779.

Hamdan, M., Jaidin, J. H., Fithriyah, M., & Anshari, M. (2020a). E-learning in time of COVID-19 pandemic: Challenges & experiences. In *2020 Sixth International Conference on e-Learning (econf)* (pp. 12-16). IEEE. 10.1109/econf51404.2020.9385507

Han, J., Heo, J., & You, E. (2021, October). Analysis of metaverse platform as a new play culture: Focusing on roblox and zepeto. In *Proceedings of the 2nd International Conference on Human-centered Artificial Intelligence (Computing4Human 2021). CEUR Workshop Proceedings*. https://ceur-ws.org/Vol-3026/paper3.pdf

Harris, P., Connolly, J., & Feeney, L. (2009). Blended learning: Overview and recommendations for successful implementation. *Industrial and Commercial Training*, *41*(3), 155–163. doi:10.1108/00197850910950961

Hazari, S. (2021, February 19). *The Benefits Of Online Learning During The Pandemic*. London College of Contemporary Arts. https://www.lcca.org.uk/blog/student-life/the-benefits-of-online-learning-during-the-pandemic/

Hwang, G. J., & Chien, S. Y. (2022). Definition, roles, and potential research issues of the metaverse in education: An artificial intelligence perspective. *Computers and Education: Artificial Intelligence*, *3*, 100082. doi:10.1016/j.caeai.2022.100082

Jagannathan, S. (n.d.). *Education Meets The Metaverse: Reimagining The Future Of Learning*. World Bank Group. Retrieved September 20, 2022, from https://olc.worldbank.org/about-olc/education-meets-the-metaverse-reimagining-the-future-of-learning

Jensen, L., & Konradsen, F. (2017). A review of the use of virtual reality head-mounted displays in education and training. *Education and Information Technologies*, *23*(4), 1515–1529. doi:10.100710639-017-9676-0

Juna, M. A., Anshari, M., Ahmad, N., & Hamdan, M. (2022). Working from home, COVID-19 and multi-dimensional model of well-being theory. *International Journal of Work Organisation and Emotion*, *13*(3), 230–259. doi:10.1504/IJWOE.2022.126957

Kasraie, N., & Alahmad, A. (2014). Investigating the Reasons Institutions of Higher Education in the USA and Canada Utilize Blended Learning. *Mevlana International Journal of Education*, *4*(1), 67–81. doi:10.13054/mije.13.68.4.1

Kumar, A. (2022, July 10). *The Metaverse In eLearning*. eLearning Industry. https://elearningindustry.com/the-metaverse-in-elearning

Kye, B., Han, N., Kim, E., Park, Y., & Jo, S. (2021). Educational applications of metaverse: Possibilities and limitations. *Journal of Educational Evaluation for Health Professions*, *18*, 32. doi:10.3352/jeehp.2021.18.32 PMID:34897242

Liang, R., & Chen, D.-T. V. (2012). Online learning: Trends, potential and challenges. *Creative Education*, *03*(08), 1332–1335. doi:10.4236/ce.2012.38195

Mulyani, M. A., Razzaq, A., Sumardi, W. H., & Anshari, M. (2019, August). Smartphone adoption in mobile learning scenario. In *2019 International Conference on Information Management and Technology (ICIMTech)* (Vol. 1, pp. 208-211). IEEE. 10.1109/ICIMTech.2019.8843755

Mulyani, M. A., Yusuf, S., Siregar, P., Nurihsan, J., Razzaq, A., & Anshari, M. (2021, August). Fourth Industrial Revolution and Educational Challenges. In *2021 International Conference on Information Management and Technology (ICIMTech)* (Vol. 1, pp. 245-249). IEEE. 10.1109/ICIMTech53080.2021.9535057

Ohkubo, S. (2015, August 24). *People, Process, Platform, Partnership, and Problem Solving: The 5P Approach to Strengthening Knowledge Management Capacity and Culture*. Learning Lab. https://usaidlearninglab.org/community/blog/people-process-platform-partnership-and-problem-solving-5p-approach-strengthening

Pyka, A. (2002). Innovation networks in economics: From the incentive-based to the knowledge-based approaches. *European Journal of Innovation Management*, *5*(3), 152–163. doi:10.1108/14601060210436727

Ravi, P. (2022, April 24). *Metaverse — A Stepping-Stone To New-Gen Education*. Mindtree. https://www.mindtree.com/insights/blog/metaverse-stepping-stone-new-gen-education

Razzaq, A., Samiha, Y. T., & Anshari, M. (2018). Smartphone habits and behaviors in supporting students self-efficacy. *International Journal of Emerging Technologies in Learning*, *13*(2), 94. doi:10.3991/ijet.v13i02.7685

Sait, M. A., & Anshari, M. (2021). Industrial Revolution 4.0: A New Challenge to Brunei Darussalam's Unemployment Issue. *International Journal of Asian Business and Information Management*, *12*(4), 33–44. doi:10.4018/IJABIM.20211001.oa3

Shani, A. B. R., Sena, J. A., & Olin, T. (2003). Knowledge management and new product development: A study of two companies. *European Journal of Innovation Management*, *6*(3), 137–149. doi:10.1108/14601060310486217

Singh, H. (2003). Building effective blended learning programs. *Educational Technology*, *43*, 51–54.

Sirakaya, M., & Cakmak, E. K. (2018). The effect of augmented reality use on achievement, misconception and course engagement. *Contemporary Educational Technology*, *9*(3), 297–314. doi:10.30935/cet.444119

Stewart, J. M. (2002). A blended e-learning approach to intercultural training. *Industrial and Commercial Training*, *34*(7), 269–271. doi:10.1108/00197850210447264

Tamer Cavusgil, S., Calantone, R. J., & Zhao, Y. (2003). Tacit knowledge transfer and firm innovation capability. *Journal of Business and Industrial Marketing*, *18*(1), 6–21. doi:10.1108/08858620310458615

Yuhanna, I., Alexander, A., & Kachik, A. (2020). Advantages and disadvantages of online learning. *Journal Educational Verkenning*, *1*(2), 13–19. doi:10.48173/jev.v1i2.54

Zhao, Y., & Watterston, J. (2021). The changes we need: Education post COVID-19. *Journal of Educational Change*, *22*(1), 3–12. doi:10.100710833-021-09417-3

Chapter 7
Potential and Challenges of the Metaverse on Future Businesses

Dk Farhanah Izzati Pg Mohd Japar
University Brunei Darussalam, Brunei

Muhammad Anshari
https://orcid.org/0000-0002-8160-6682
Universiti Brunei Darussalam, Brunei

ABSTRACT

The term metaverse refers to a virtual environment that exists beyond the physical world we live in but, at the same time, is similar to the real world. This chapter intends to investigate the impact of the metaverse for future business scenarios and whether there are other uses for the metaverse besides for business and entertainment purposes. The research for this chapter explains the potential and challenges of the metaverse, ways to create and maintain a strategic information systems, and the role of big data analytics in Industry 4.0. The significant findings indicate that the metaverse creates business opportunities for both consumers and sellers due to the growth of digital commerce since shopping can become more immersive with the option to buy physical or digital goods. However, digital footprints may be tracked from the metaverse to disclose the real-world identity of the user and other private information, which can be an invasion of privacy.

DOI: 10.4018/978-1-6684-6097-9.ch007

Copyright © 2023, IGI Global. Copying or distributing in print or electronic forms without written permission of IGI Global is prohibited.

INTRODUCTION

Definition of the Metaverse

The *metaverse* is a virtual environment that consists of groups of people interacting with one another while managing virtual versions of themselves, also known as avatars. It combines virtual reality and the Internet (Kensinger, 2021). It also creates an economic system built on blockchain technology that closely combines the virtual world and real worlds into the economic, social, and identity systems, enabling every user to create content and alter reality (Dionsio, Burns & Gilbert, 2013). As far as we know, the metaverse is still a concept and does not fully exist yet; however, several platforms have metaverse-like features. For example, video games such as Minecraft and Fortnite.

Objective of this Chapter

This report aims to investigate the impact of the metaverse on future businesses as well as determining its potentials and challenges. The three main questions that are going to be explored are:

- What are the potentials of the metaverse for the future of business?
- What are the challenges of the metaverse for the future of business?
- Are there other uses for the metaverse besides for business and entertainment purposes?

To provide context for considering the impact of the metaverse, the report begins by presenting the potential and reasons why the metaverse matters for businesses.

LITERATURE REVIEWS

Potential and Reasons the Metaverse Matter for Businesses

Although the metaverse is still emerging, it would be a huge loss for businesses to ignore it. There are other major brands that have entered the metaverse besides the digital big players like Microsoft and Facebook. For example, the legendary fashion label, Gucci, recently launched a virtual gallery (Carrillo, 2022), while an American multinational investment bank called JP Morgan, becomes the first bank to launch in the metaverse (Birch, 2022).

As a virtual-reality environment, the metaverse has a lot of business potential. Every business should look into the following advantages of the metaverse for business:

Profits From Virtual Products

The virtual market is growing. Millions of dollars' worth of digital goods are sold on online platforms such as Decentraland, Fortnite, Roblox, and the Sandbox, which creates a profitable business opportunity. Brands might open up new revenue streams by designing digital replicas of their physical items for use by people of the metaverse (Awosika, 2022). Several businesses already have products available in the metaverse. For example, Ralph Lauren recently launched a line of wearables, and has successfully sold over 100,000 items (Swant, 2021). Gucci and Dolce & Gabbana are two other high-end designer brands that have started working on virtual apparel lines (Thomas, 2021).

Smaller businesses are also encouraged to join the trend. For example, eyeglasses manufacturer could encourage customers to buy the actual item while offering them a pair as an NFT. There will be a market for every real product that can be displayed in virtual reality (Anshari et al., 2022).

Greater Customer Experience

Over the years, the emergence of e-Commerce changed how customers purchase products. Some customers prefer the traditional shopping experience where they can feel, see, and touch the products before making a purchase (Zhang, Chang, & Neslin, 2022). However, others prefer online shopping (Rahman, 2016).

With metaverse, businesses may use augmented reality (AR) and virtual reality (VR) technologies to offer customers new ways to engage with their products or services (Awosika, 2022). Customers will be able to experience the products and rate their experiences instead of just looking at static photos (Anshari et al., 2019a). For example, a customer is more likely to purchase the actual product if they feel comfortable whilst trying it on the virtual glasses.

A few branded companies—such as Ferragamo, Harrods, and Burberry—have already created virtual stores where customers are able to browse branded goods (McDowell, 2021). This innovation will help shorten the journey of the customers to the brick-and-mortar store, reduce purchasing costs, and increase total revenue (Awosika, 2022).

Availability and Accessibility of Virtual Worlds Create Business Opportunities

The metaverse will achieve the same—but better—than the Internet did in removing geographical boundaries (Almunawar & Anshari, 2022). Anyone can explore and interact with businesses in the metaverse regardless of where they live (Almunawar et al., 2020). This makes it easier for businesses to create experiences available to their customers across the world (Awosika, 2022).

Recent Web applications and browsers are a software-side enabler toward virtual world availability due to their complete programmability, standardised networking, 3D, and media interfaces, and low setup or access methods (Anshari et al., 2019b). The widespread availability of e-commerce, social networking, and other applications has already involved modern Web designs and browsers. Virtual worlds may likely achieve this level of availability as Web standards combined with the applications on which they operate, begin to meet the requirements of a 3D virtual environment. The metaverse will open new opportunities for consumers and sellers to connect because of the growth of digital commerce. Shopping can become more immersive with the option to buy physical or digital things. Moreover, a mass-market platform allows brands to create digital goods that cross over between the actual and digital worlds and create new ways to sell their goods (Wong, 2022).

Better Employee Engagement and Collaboration

Meta showed a demo of a virtual reality space for teams to engage together called the Horizon Workspace (Germain, 2022). It shows how virtual worlds can change the current workplace and improve inter-employee communication in a post-COVID world where remote employment is the norm. Individuals can work together, brainstorm new ideas, and communicate in a shared, virtual workspace rather than spending hours looking at a Zoom screen. No matter where they are in the world, everyone will be able to engage with one another and exchange ideas due to the metaverse (Awosika, 2022).

Blockchain and Cryptocurrency Will Become Necessities

Blockchain or decentralised technology is essential for the widespread adoption of the metaverse in businesses. It is the technology behind cryptocurrencies such as Bitcoin, Ether, Dogecoin, and others. Also, it is used to support and sustain cryptography to function. It may be used to create non-fungible tokens (NFTs) and decentralised apps, as well as a distributed ledger for recording peer-to-peer asset transactions (Ramesh et al., 2022).

Moreover, the rapid growth of cryptocurrency has already seemed unstable for most investors. Nonetheless, it is safe to assume that since the announcement of the metaverse, it will just serve to prolong this chaotic-yet-profitable situation (Anshari, Syafrudin, Fitriyani, 2022). Since the metaverse is a digital environment, digital currencies will be the most natural form of payment. Block-chain based cryptocurrencies are well-positioned to meet that need. Existing digital tender, as well as countless future iterations, will have the possibility of becoming the main engine for financial transactions in the metaverse (Dixon, 2022).

Challenges and Issues of the Metaverse

Shifting Value of Crypto

Several business transactions in the metaverse will use blockchain, either through cryptocurrencies or non-fungible tokens (NFTs). However, the value of cryptocurrencies is known to fluctuate dramatically from day to day, which might lead to economic instability in the metaverse. Furthermore, significant investments made by NFTs might not be quite as dependable as real-world trading (Nichols & Patel, 2002). For example, the NFT consumer may be unable to change the work despite having purchased it legally. This may put off a lot of clients.

Side Effects on Health

VR-induced sickness is a significant side effect of this technology. It can include dizziness, nausea, headaches, eye strain, loss of limb and postural control, sensory loss, and the creation of responses that are unsuitable for the real world. VR should not be used on those who have seizures when watching television or playing video games (Nichols & Patel, 2002).

In addition, excessive use of the Internet causes a cyber syndrome—a physical, social, and mental issue. Electronic gadgets have shrunk in size and grown more portable as interactive technologies have advanced. People are spending more and more time on the Internet as technology becomes more efficient. At the same time, the metaverse is deeply linked to the physical world. The integration of virtual and real worlds, as well as the high level of immersion in the metaverse, add to the problem of cybersickness (Lee et al., 2021).

Social Privacy in the Metaverse

In the social metaverse, digital footprints may be tracked to disclose the real-world identity of the user as well as other private information like location, shopping habits, and even financial information. The importance of privacy has a significant impact on how the metaverse is shaped. Traditional social networks make it considerably easier to implement confidentiality strategies since users may choose whom they want to share their social media content with. Conversely, in the metaverse, such privacy protection is not possible since users cannot alter the virtual features of the created virtual environment, making confidentiality maintenance difficult (Lee et al., 2021).

Strategic Information System (SIS)

Strategic information system (SIS) refers to the goals, methods, products, or environmental factors that help a business achieve a competitive advantage. SIS often make extensive efforts to find the sources of a sustainable competitive advantage. However, it is important to differentiate between the two terms. Competitive advantage refers to the end-result whereas sustainability is a state that continues after efforts to duplicate that advantage which ended (Barney, 1991). As a result, a specific competitive advantage may be temporary, and this is becoming extremely common when analyzing IT-based advantage. Thus, what is necessary is to understand the mechanisms and processes that lead to a situation in which an organization frequently and consistently realizes outcomes that produce a competitive advantage in the market through the adoption of IS/IT (Peppard & Ward, 2004).

Creating and Maintaining a Strategic Information System

Strategic information systems (SIS) aim at creating a profitable and sustainable position against the competitive rivalry within that industry. Considering the advancements in system development, maintaining an advantage over a long period of time has become increasingly challenging. Experience has also shown that information systems, on their own, rarely offer a sustainable competitive advantage (Shanbhag, 2020).

The table below shows how SIS can offer businesses to gain a competitive advantage to maintain in an industry (Sousa & Oz, 2015).

Table 1. The eight basic ways to gain competitive advantage

No.	Initiative	Benefits (how can they gain competitive advantage?)
1.	Reduce cost	If the business can sell more units at a lower price while maintaining or expanding its profitability.
2.	Raise barriers to competitors' entry	If the business could prevent a potential competitor from entering the market, resulting in less competition and increased market potential.
3.	Establish high switching cost	The higher the switching costs, the less likely customers would be willing to switch to other brands, products, or businesses.
4.	Create new products/services	By offering a unique product or service—something that competitors have not done before.
5.	Differentiate products/services	If the business can attract customers by showing them how innovative their products or services are, and how it differs from their competitors.
6.	Enhance products/services	If the business created products or services that are better than their competitors.
7.	Establish alliances	Businesses from different industries can create a joint venture so they can help each other to gain a competitive advantage by offering combined packages of goods or services at a discounted price.
8.	Lock in suppliers/buyers	The business can benefit if it can lock in one or both of its suppliers or buyers, making it difficult for those parties to do business with rivals.

Role of Big Data Analytics in Industry 4.0

Big data, in general, refers to a massive complex amount of data that requires additional computation to extract, assess, and process in order to drive decision making. Big data is classified into three types; (1) **Structured**, (2) **Unstructured**, and (3) **Semi-structured** data. Structured data sets consist of well-defined data types, making them simple to search and arrange in relational databases (Anshari et al., 2021). Unstructured data cannot be easily searched or stored in a structured database format. This data may be textual, audible, or video, and both humans and machines could create it (Anshari & Hamdan, 2022). At the same timee, semi-structured data is a kind of data that cannot be arranged in relational databases and lacks a strict structural foundation. However, they do possess certain structural features (Chauhan & Sood, 2021).

Big data analytics is used in Industry 4.0 in a few settings, such as smart factories, where sensor data from manufacturing machinery is examined to foresee the need for service and repair activities (Anshari & Almunawar, 2021; Anshari, 2020). Manufacturers who use it gain production efficiency, real-time data analysis with self-service systems, predictive maintenance optimization, and automation of production management (Berawi, 2018).

How Businesses Use Big Data Analytics

Businesses use big data analytics to analyze massive amounts of customer information to understand their patterns and identify trends in order to make better business decisions. Mostly all businesses are now required to have the ability to collect, store, combine, and analyze data in order to extract information (Anshari & Sumardi, 2020). Successful businesses around the world such as Target, Walmart, and eBay, have found benefits from using big data. By embracing and managing the change, these businesses are excelling in an environment that is transforming the game. Big data analytics has been used by businesses to generate unique insights and provide new kinds of value (Zulkarnain et al., 2021). After all, big data is how big companies like Walmart discovered that consumers love to stock up on the sweet treat Pop Tarts after a hurricane; eBay discovered which online designs increases revenue; and Target discovered how to recognize pregnant customers (Sanders, 2016).

Moreover, applying analytics that can provide a strategic advantage can be found at every stage of the supply chain decision-making process, from targeted location-based marketing to streamlining supply chain inventory to facilitating thorough supplier risk analysis. Businesses may use analytics to convert the huge amounts of data generated by supply chains—from POS, GPS, and RFID to social media feeds—into information. There are several success examples of businesses that have tapped into the potential of big data analytics, like Amazon and Walmart. Conversely, most businesses have still not used big data analytics to alter their supply chain processes as they are not Walmarts and Amazons. For many, investing in new hardware and software is expensive and has a vague return on investment (Sanders, 2016).

METHODOLOGY

To identify relevant studies on the impact of the metaverse for future business scenarios, we conducted a broad literature search in databases from various disciplines, i.e., Google Scholar, ResearchGate, Emerald, JSTOR, using multiple groups of keywords. The first group of keywords used referred to the metaverse, namely; *meta, virtual reality, augmented reality, mixed reality, industry 4.0,* and *big data*. Searching for the aforementioned words were purposely broad so that we could collect all relevant information and lead to interesting results. The second group of keywords referred to potential findings that could link with the metaverse, namely, *potential, challenges, issues, health, consumer behavior,* and *future business.* The terms were searched in the following fields; title, abstract and keywords. The Google and Google Scholar websites were then used to conduct internet research on other relevant papers. Then, a secondary search was conducted by looking at the citations of the publications found in the initial broad database search. The abstracts of the publications that had been identified were then examined and filtered using specific inclusion and exclusion criteria. Papers that were chosen based on abstract information were then thoroughly inspected to ensure that they satisfied the inclusion criteria.

ANALYSIS AND DISCUSSION

The Metaverse and Future Businesses

The potential to market their metaverse-like services to a highly desirable demographic was the most prominent and early motivation for businesses to become engaged in virtual worlds. Still, the possibilities did not start with virtual types of brick-and-mortar businesses (Collins, 2008). It started with virtual goods as they were believed to be the next big business model back in 2011, where Screen Digest predicted that it would be a $1.5 billion industry. At the same time, Strategic Analytics predicted nearly one billion virtual world users and an $8 billion services market by 2018. The global virtual goods market size was already valued at USD 38 billion as of 2017 (as seen in *Figure 1*), which is higher than the initial predicted amount. The growth of this market is contributed mainly by social gaming amongst teenagers. The growing popularity of free-to-play games among players and game creators has boosted the purchase of virtual goods, resulting in the rapid growth of the market.

Figure 1. The global virtual market size 2015-2025. From Virtual Goods Market by Adroit Market Research, 2019

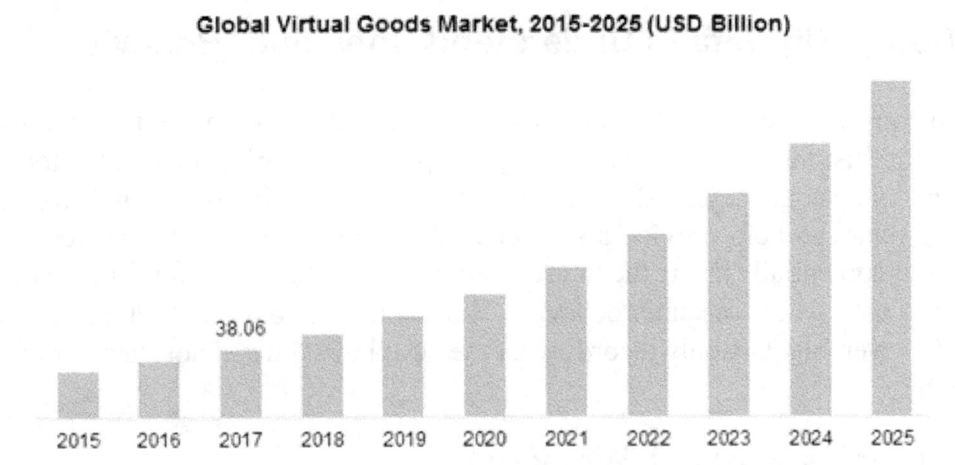

In addition to the marketing efforts and the buying and selling of virtual goods, other business uses of virtual worlds are also growing. For instance, the CEO of Facebook, Mark Zuckerberg, has rebranded the company name to *Meta* to focus the company onto the metaverse. Zuckerberg believes that the metaverse is the next evolution of social connection. Thus, the reason why he rebranded the company is to reflect their commitment to the future and the growth of the company and its goals to go beyond social media (Milmo, 2021).

How Businesses Prepare for the Metaverse

Meta, for example, is already planning for a future in which a traditional physical office is entirely augmented by a digital version. Many industry analysts are exploring the potential of virtual worlds to minimize travel for anything from day-to-day corporate activities to large-scale conferences and meetings as energy consumption, and global climate change becomes more pervasive challenges. Mitch Kapor, the founder of Lotus Development Corporation and designer of the discontinued Lotus 1-2-3, and a member of the Board of Directors for Linden Lab, spoke about the work being done to improve the "sense of presence" in virtual worlds through better gestures, avatar animations, and interfaces at the World Economic Forum in Davos, Switzerland back in early 2008 (Collins, 2008). He mentioned that the cost-savings of conducting virtual meetings in comparison to flying people off for physical meetings would save a massive amount of money.

Using Big Data to Understand Consumer Behavior

In consumer behavior, big data is used to analyze data points of the journey of the customer from search to purchase, providing marketers with the tools and knowledge they need to maximize their strategic efforts. In other words, big data can help provide a predictive description on what the customers would potentially buy in the future. Predictive analytics is the most frequently used data set in consumer behavior (Hofacker, Malthouse, & Sultan, 2016). However, big data only records what the customers did and not state reasons why.

Other Uses of the Metaverse

There are also other uses of the metaverse besides for business or entertainment purposes, such as for education and for health applications.

The Metaverse as an Educational Environment

Among the various types of the metaverse, VR is believed to be the most diverse and actively used technology in education. As of writing, it has been over two years since the COVID-19 pandemic started, which made face-to-face communication difficult due to how easy the virus could spread. Activities that were previously considered to be exclusively possible only offline are being transferred to virtual reality and are rapidly expanding into industries including education, medical care, fashion, and tourism. The metaverse has the potential to be a space for new social communication. Virtual reality metaverses like Roblox and Zepeto provided a new social space for gathering and relaxing for those that are unable to go out due to COVID-19 (Kye et al., 2021).

Due to the ability of the metaverse to take 360-degree panoramic images and volumetric spherical video, immersive journalism can correctly and objectively educate large consumers on unfamiliar circumstances and events in remote locations. Furthermore, new models of metaverse-powered remote education may arise in order to overcome the limits of 2D platforms. Meta-education can provide rich, hybrid formal and informal active learning experiences in permanent, alternative, online 3D virtual campuses where students co-own virtual environments and co-create liquid, individualized curricula (Kye et al., 2021)

Using Metaverse-Like Features in Psychology and for Health

VR has become a significant tool for psychiatric and medical studies due to its wide range of applications in the past two decades. Srivistava, Chaudhury and Das (2014) found that using VR for cognitive behavioural therapy and counselling for the treatment of addictions can be effective. It has also been used for the treatment of various other conditions such as social phobia, agoraphobia, and fear of driving. It can be utilised for cognitive rehabilitation. For individuals with psychosis, VR can help them improve their skills in identifying facial expressions and communicating with others.

Using the *big data* of social media for health applications—specifically in the mental health area—is still a growing area of research. Twitter has been used for population-level influenza surveillance, monitoring mass gatherings, understanding the opinions of the public towards vaccination, understanding public attitudes toward new and emerging tobacco products and e-cigarette marketing, and investigating pre-market research (Conway & Connor, 2016). Some countries such as Brunei and India use the instant messaging services app called *Telegram* to share official government information including press releases.

VR FOR DEPRESSION

Moreover, recent research conducted by the University College London and the University of Barcelona shows that an immersive VR might be a groundbreaking technique to treat users that suffer from depression. According to research published in the British Journal of Psychiatry Open in 2016, patients can learn to be less judgmental towards themselves and be more sympathetic by immersing in VR. In the mid-1960s, MIT was the first to use virtual reality to treat mental health problems. Patients with post-traumatic stress disorder (PTSD) and spider phobia have previously recovered from this treatment method. The Duke University Virtual Reality Treatment Program uses VR information to address anxiety problems including flying, public speaking, and heights.

In addition, VR techniques have been adapted and evolved into a more therapeutic and sophisticated approach to treating depression since the 1960s. VR technology is similar to that of a video game console. Patients will look at themselves via the eyes of a life-size avatar wearing a VR headset with a viewing screen (Freeman et al., 2008).

Before the existence of VR therapy, users who suffer from depression would use antidepressants to "feel better". However, despite their effectiveness, antidepressants have had some major side effects. One of the most dangerous side effects that might threaten a patient's health and life is an increase in suicidal thoughts. Nausea, sleeplessness, sleepiness, exhaustion, anxiety, agitation, and restlessness are all common harmful effects. VR therapy may be a safer therapeutic option than antidepressants since it does not have the same negative effects (Freeman et al., 2008).

CONCLUSION

This study aimed to investigate the impact of the metaverse on the future of businesses, the potential, or challenges of the metaverse for future business scenarios and whether there are other uses for the metaverse besides for business and entertainment purposes. Our research has shown that there are some potentials for the metaverse, especially in the business sector since it creates business opportunities for brands everywhere. Nowadays, users may use the metaverse to better understand and interact with one another, watch movies, play games, and gain a better understanding of the world everywhere. Users are also able to conduct virtual meetings and interact with each other similar to the physical environment instead of just staring at a Zoom screen. They would be able to explore freely, visualise and explore beyond the boundaries of the screen. As a result, the metaverse is perhaps the most essential to the internets of the upcoming generation. However, there are some limitations to the metaverse, such as its side effects on the health of the users. It could deteriorate the health of a user if they were to enter the metaverse for so long. Moreover, the metaverse could be an invasion of privacy for some users. At the same time, several findings were found that were not expected, such as the other uses of the metaverse. The metaverse can also be used as a virtual education environment and for health applications such as virtual therapy.

While a single, united metaverse is likely a long way off, we already can see developments that may lead to its creation. It looks to be yet another sci-fi use case for blockchain technology and cryptocurrencies. We will reach the point of a metaverse as it is inevitable since technology is already evolving; however, the duration to get to the metaverse is still unsure. Nevertheless, we may just participate in metaverse-like activities and continue to incorporate blockchain into our everyday lives.

REFERENCES

Almunawar, M. N., & Anshari, M. (2022). Customer acceptance of online delivery platform during the COVID-19 pandemic: the case of Brunei Darussalam. *Journal of Science and Technology Policy Management*.

Almunawar, M. N., Anshari, M., & Lim, S. A. (2020). Customer acceptance of ride-hailing in Indonesia. *Journal of Science and Technology Policy Management*.

Anshari, M. (2020, March). Workforce mapping of fourth industrial revolution: Optimization to identity. *Journal of Physics: Conference Series*, *1477*(7), 072023. doi:10.1088/1742-6596/1477/7/072023

Anshari, M., & Almunawar, M. N. (2021). Adopting open innovation for SMEs and industrial revolution 4.0. *Journal of Science and Technology Policy Management*.

Anshari, M., Almunawar, M. N., Lim, S. A., & Al-Mudimigh, A. (2019a). Customer relationship management and big data enabled: Personalization & customization of services. *Applied Computing and Informatics*, *15*(2), 94–101. doi:10.1016/j.aci.2018.05.004

Anshari, M., Almunawar, M. N., Masri, M., & Hamdan, M. (2019b). Digital marketplace and FinTech to support agriculture sustainability. *Energy Procedia*, *156*, 234–238. doi:10.1016/j.egypro.2018.11.134

Anshari, M., Almunawar, M. N., & Razzaq, A. (2021). Developing talents vis-à-vis fourth industrial revolution. *International Journal of Asian Business and Information Management*, *12*(4), 20–32. doi:10.4018/IJABIM.20211001.oa2

Anshari, M., & Hamdan, M. (2022). Understanding knowledge management and upskilling in Fourth Industrial Revolution: Transformational shift and SECI model. *VINE Journal of Information and Knowledge Management Systems*. Advance online publication. doi:10.1108/VJIKMS-09-2021-0203

Anshari, M., & Sumardi, W. H. (2020). Employing big data in business organisation and business ethics. *International Journal of Business Governance and Ethics*, *14*(2), 181–205. doi:10.1504/IJBGE.2020.106349

Anshari, M., Syafrudin, M., & Fitriyani, N. L. (2022). Fourth Industrial Revolution between Knowledge Management and Digital Humanities. *Information (Basel)*, *13*(6), 292. doi:10.3390/info13060292

Anshari, M., Syafrudin, M., Fitriyani, N. L., & Razzaq, A. (2022). Ethical Responsibility and Sustainability (ERS) Development in a Metaverse Business Model. *Sustainability*, *14*(23), 15805. doi:10.3390u142315805

Awosika, E. (2022, March 14). *Why Should Businesses Care About The Metaverse?* Retrieved from Business Tech Guides: https://businesstechguides.co/importance-of-metaverse-for-businesses

Barney, J. (1991). Firm resources and sustained competitive advantage. *Journal of Management*, *17*(1), 99–120. doi:10.1177/014920639101700108

Berawi, M. A. (2018). Utilizing Big Data In Industry 4.0: Managing Competitive Advantages And Business Ethics. *International Journal of Technology*, *3*(3), 430–433. doi:10.14716/ijtech.v9i3.1948

Birch, K. (2022, February 17). *JP Morgan is first leading bank to launch in the metaverse*. Retrieved from FinTech Magazine: https://fintechmagazine.com/banking/jp-morgan-becomes-the-first-bank-to-launch-in-the-metaverse

Carrillo, A. (2022, June 24). *Gucci unveils an NFT gallery with 'The Next 100 Years of Gucci'*. Retrieved from Input Magazine: https://www.inputmag.com/style/gucci-100-years-nft-gallery

Chauhan, P., & Sood, M. (2021). Big Data: Present and Future. *IEEE Computer Society*, *54*(4), 59–65. doi:10.1109/MC.2021.3057442

Collins, C. (2008). Looking to the future: Higher education in the Metaverse. *EDUCAUSE Review*, *43*(5), 51–63.

Conway, M., & O'Connor, D. (2016). Social media, big data, and mental health: Current advances and ethical implications. *Current Opinion in Psychology*, *9*, 77–82. doi:10.1016/j.copsyc.2016.01.004 PMID:27042689

Dionisio, J., Burns, W. III, & Gilbert, R. (2013). 3D Virtual Worlds and the Metaverse. *ACM Computing Surveys*, *45*(3), 1–38. doi:10.1145/2480741.2480751

Dixon, R. (2022). *What You Need to Know About How the Metaverse Will Affect Business*. Retrieved from https://www.entrepreneur.com/article/415480

Germain, J. (2022, March 17). *A Step Into Meta's VR Meeting World, Horizon Workrooms*. Retrieved from Tech News World: https://www.technewsworld.com/story/a-step-into-metas-vr-meeting-world-horizon-workrooms-87448.html

Hofacker, C. F., Malthouse, E. C., & Sultan, F. (2016). Big Data and consumer behavior: Imminent opportunities. *Journal of Consumer Marketing*, *33*(2), 89–97. doi:10.1108/JCM-04-2015-1399

Kensinger, R. (2021). *Metaverse*. doi:10.13140/RG.2.2.19971.22564

Kye, B., Han, N., Kim, E., Park, Y., & Jo, S. (2021). Educational applications of metaverse: Possibilities and limitations. *Journal of Educational Evaluation for Health Professions*, *18*, 32. doi:10.3352/jeehp.2021.18.32 PMID:34897242

Lee, L. H., Lin, Z., Hu, R., Gong, Z., Kumar, A., Li, T., ... Hui, P. (2021). *When Creators Meet the Metaverse: A Survey on Computational Arts*. Academic Press.

McDowell, M. (2021, November 24). *Virtual stores: Fashion's new mode of shopping*. Retrieved from Vogue Business: https://www.voguebusiness.com/technology/virtual-stores-fashions-new-mode-of-shopping

Milmo, D. (2021). Enter the metaverse: the digital future Mark Zuckerberg is steering us toward. *The Guardian*. Retrieved from https://www.theguardian.com/technology/2021/oct/28/facebook-mark-zuckerberg-meta-metaverse

Nichols, S., & Patel, H. (2002). Health and safety implications of virtual reality: A review of empirical evidence. *Applied Ergonomics*, *33*(3), 251–271. doi:10.1016/S0003-6870(02)00020-0 PMID:12164509

Peppard, J., & Ward, J. (2004). Beyond strategic information systems: Towards an IS capability. *The Journal of Strategic Information Systems*, *13*(2), 167–194. doi:10.1016/j.jsis.2004.02.002

Rahman, M. T. (2016, July 2). Customers' Attitude towards Online Shopping: The Case of Bangladesh. *World Journal of Social Sciences*, *6*(2), 82–91.

Ramesh, U. V., Harini, A., Gowri, C. S. D., Durga, K. V., Druvitha, P., & Kumar, K. S. (2022). Metaverse: Future of the Internet. *International Journal of Research Publication and Reviews*, *3*(2), 93–97.

Sanders, N. (2016). How to Use Big Data to Drive Your Supply Chain. *California Management Review*, *58*(3), 26–48. doi:10.1525/cmr.2016.58.3.26

Shanbhag, R. (2020). Maintaining Strategic Information Systems. *International Journal of IT & Knowledge Management*, *13*(2), 19–21.

Sousa, K., & Oz, E. (2015). *Management Information Systems*. Cengage Learning.

Srivastava, K., Chaudhury, S., & Das, R. (2014). Virtual reality applications in mental health: Challenges and perspectives. *Industrial Psychiatry Journal*, *23*(2), 83. doi:10.4103/0972-6748.151666 PMID:25788795

Swant, M. (2021, August 25). *Ralph Lauren Is Now Selling Digital Apparel For Avatars Inside Of Zepeto*. Retrieved from Forbes: https://www.forbes.com/sites/martyswant/2021/08/25/ralph-lauren-is-now-selling-digital-apparel-for-avatars-inside-of-zepeto

Thomas, D. (2021, August 27). *Dolce & Gabbana Is Bringing NFTs To The Traditional World Of Couture*. Retrieved from Vogue: https://www.vogue.co.uk/fashion/article/dolce-and-gabbana-nfts-couture

Wong, J. (2022). *How Will the Metaverse Impact Businesses in The Consumer Goods Sector?* from https://www.forbes.com/sites/forbestechcouncil/2022/01/19/how-will-the-metaverse-impact-businesses-in-the-consumer-goods-sector

Zhang, J. Z., Chang, C. W., & Neslin, S. A. (2022). How Physical Stores Enhance Customer Value: The Importance of Product Inspection Depth. *Journal of Marketing*, *86*(2), 166–185. doi:10.1177/00222429211012106

Zulkarnain, N., Anshari, M., Hamdan, M., & Fithriyah, M. (2021, August). Big data in business and ethical challenges. In *2021 International Conference on Information Management and Technology (ICIMTech)* (Vol. 1, pp. 298-303). IEEE. 10.1109/ICIMTech53080.2021.9534963

Chapter 8
Metaverse and Soft Skills Development Through Video Games

Mohd Abi Syarillizam Sabtu
Universiti Brunei Darussalam, Brunei

ABSTRACT

By offering both technical and nontechnical courses, educational systems have tried to prepare students. However, with video games, there is the opportunity to create specific metaverses that can assist in educating soft skills, including during informal pleasures. The research will provide a set of design approaches for metaverse and video games in order to foster soft skills. Although there are several soft talents that one may learn, this chapter will concentrate on a few, based on certain games and research. Some data will be gathered from the data to back up the model and justifications. The chapter will help game designers create inventive games, and users will learn soft skills that will help them in both their professional and social lives.

DOI: 10.4018/978-1-6684-6097-9.ch008

Copyright © 2023, IGI Global. Copying or distributing in print or electronic forms without written permission of IGI Global is prohibited.

INTRODUCTION

Even if the technical skills are required to complete any task, many organizations discovered that soft skills such as communication, teamwork and creativity are important as it provide a great opportunity in a workplace, yet it was found that many recent graduates were still lacking in these soft skills. Without these non-technical skills, it can lead to some unwanted issues or conflict in the workplace (Anshari, Almunawar, & Masri, 2022). For several years, there has been a shift in the needs for soft skills in the workplace. Many organizations had their own initiative to make their employees to identify their soft skills by using some method of soft skill training or giving course (Anshari & Hamdan, 2022). Other than that, gaming or playing video games also can develop the soft skills which are needed by the organizations. By playing video games, it helps to develop both technical and soft skills, which are becoming more and more important for them to perform routine tasks (Anshari, Syafrudin, & Fitriyani, 2022). The ability to think critically, creatively, emotionally, and solve complicated problems is enhanced by playing video games. it also educates the gamers to give or receive feedback very efficiently. Finding and developing these soft skills is quite challenging. According to the Manpower Group (2021), over 43% of employers claim that teaching soft skills is more challenging. The rise of Covid-19 pandemic over the 3 years has increased the need for soft skills such as teamwork, communication, and the ability to learn, and by playing video games it can address some of these skill gaps (Hamdan et al., 2020; Anshari et al., 2019). All regions saw double-digit increases in the amount of time spent playing video games during the COVID-19 epidemic as of June 2020. During the pandemic, the most popular games were Fortnite, Call of Duty, PUBG, and virtual reality games. The reasons why most of the people play games is because they were shown to feel less alone and generally happy while playing video games under lockdown and they had positive gaming experiences. Most video games need the gamers or players to think fast and logically in order to overcome issues. This requirement promotes decision-making and assists in the development of management skills. In some cases, video games and esports competitions is not always favorable to the younger generations. This is because most of the people thought playing video games is a waste of time. In 2016, the Royal Melbourne Institute of Technology conducted a study that discovered, students who play online games on a regular basis in high school earn much better in academic achievements (RMIT, 2017). According to a study conducted by the Michigan State University (2011), children were more imaginative in things like sketching or writing stories the more video games they played. One of the easiest ways to identify this non-technical skill is by exploring into the metaverse and video games where this can help most people to develop their soft skills. The term "metaverse" has gained popularity in the tech world. It is mentioned in the media every day, for the launch of new platforms and the entry of big businesses into the world of digital engagement (Anshari et al., 2022).

The virtual world is an interesting topic in the field of human-technology relationships since it is a computer-generated 3D environment (Almunawar & Anshari, 2021). The metaverse, according to MetaMandrill (2022), is the collaboration of the real and virtual worlds as a result of the use of various tools and software. In this definition, it is highlighted that the metaverse is a living universe that goes hand in hand with the real one. The metaverse is a persistent system, therefore it never shuts down. It consists of a variety of virtual worlds, each with its own special features, ecosystem, and social settings (Hasmawati et al., 2020). The Metaverse remains in its early stages, but several key parts have begun to emerge and are altering anything including e-commerce to media and entertainment and even real estate. However, themes regarding what the metaverse is and might be are starting to emerge. The fact that there are many virtual worlds developing to allow users to develop and extend social connections virtually is a crucial factor. This is accomplished by enhancing the web with a three-dimensional, immersive overlay to produce experiences that are more real and organic (Almunawar et al., 2021). Even from the convenience of one's own home, the metaverse has the potential to democratize access to important products, services, and experiences by dismantling barriers. The idea of metaverse is not new. This evolution is consistent in many aspects. Online multiplayer role-playing games like The Sims and Second Life have been available for almost 20 years, and gamers log in to these worlds for 20 hours a week on average. comparable modern examples like Roblox, Minecraft and Call of Duty which have huge number of users and supporting economies (Ahad et al., 2017). This conception of the metaverse is made possible by the convergence of several new technologies. AR and VR headsets have gotten more affordable and powerful, enhancing the user experience. NFTs and digital currencies are now possible thanks to blockchain. The new means of transacting and owning digital products enable producers to monetize their activity through tokens. Token holders can take part in the platform's governance in addition to using the platform for monetization and value exchange. From a social point of view, the creation of more online virtual reality (VR) experiences is assisting people in creating societies based on common values and in finding more authentic methods to express themselves (Jaman & Anshari, 2021). Some people may view the metaverse as nothing more than the newest buzzword in technology and assume it to be an improved kind of virtual reality. However, supporters see it as transformative. For instance, Meta (previously Facebook) aims to take use of the new possibility. In contrast, the phrase appears in the names or descriptions of over 550 smartphone apps. Although it's still uncertain what a fully developed metaverse would look like, there seems to be agreement that avatars on screen representations of people will be used by users to participate and interact in connected 3D worlds.

Video games have been around in some shape or another for almost 50 years. However, they did not completely enter popular culture only until 1970s and 1980s, once home systems became available. During this time, scientific curiosity on how playing video games affects many aspects of behavior increased, which was in line with the growing commercial success of video games at the time. Numerous researches have been undertaken over the last few decades to investigate the potential connection between gaming and aggressiveness. how using video games in educational environments can improve learning (Gee, 2003). Furthermore, video games have been looked into as potential tools in therapeutic contexts, such as the treatment of dyslexia (Franceschini et al. 2013). Early research on the impact of gaming on cognitive, attentional, and perceptual functioning identified a variety of advantages to playing video games. Regular video game players, for instance, fared better than non-players in a range of capabilities, such as split attention, spatial skills, and hand-eye coordination. Additionally, intervention studies showed that non-gamers who played particular video games were able to improve their ranges of cognitive, learning and memory, indicating that there was a causal link between gaming as well as improved performance. Green and Bavelier (2003) initially proved in a significant study that persons who enthusiastically played one specific action video games, excelled those who did not play that sub-genre of game on multiple distinct tasks of selective attention. Video games are becoming an integral part of everyday life across the world, and they are appreciated by a broad and diversified audience. The gaming industry offers a wide range of genres, game kinds, and hardware platforms to cater to client preferences. Its audience is as diverse as the industry itself. The games and players in today's video games are becoming more sociable and cooperative. Games encourage the imagination since they are engaging as opposed to passive kinds of entertainment. There is no single dominant genre; rather, the business provides a universe of entertainment and interaction channels to suit requirements as a broad as imagination allows. There are games devoted to social and scientific issues like exploring the universe, building cities, modeling societal change, and playing with evolutionary processes in addition to more popular gaming genre like racing or action-adventures. The COVID-19 epidemic had tremendous influence on people all around the world, raising the video game industry's already high visibility even further in the society and the economy. In addition to providing much-needed social connection through the networks of online games, the sector has served as a source of amusement, stress release, and escape for those who are socially isolated in their homes. Because video game and hardware demand offered one of the few opportunities for profitable financial development throughout the crisis, it has also served as a refuge for investors. There are also games that promote a greater understanding of epidemiology, the transmission of infectious illnesses, and methods to control them.

The metaverse and video games both have the power to change people's life on an individual basis. However, when both media are combined, they have the ability to go beyond and beyond their inherent limitations. Before spreading out into other areas, a large portion of the metaverses had its roots in massively multiplayer online role-playing games (MMORPGs). Additionally, there are fully created games that make use of the metaverse and have exciting potential that might further support the stability of this connection (Anshari, 2020). A lot of customers were pleased with the progress made by this collaborative effort, and devoted researchers found it to be useful. For example, many MMORPGs were created to meet social demands by giving players a place to make friends. Call of Duty Warzone (COD) was a hit because it combined this concept with "realistic" behaviors that generated a social presence. Meeting others who enjoyed the series and had similar interests resulted in an improvement in social interaction for those who played this game. There were other games that allowed players to explore a virtual area (Razzaq et al., 2018). Uncharted, in example, made advantage of the 3D environment to create puzzles that encourage creativity by utilizing the architecture to create areas for players to explore and visual signals to direct them as they come up with potential answers (Sait & Anshari, 2021). The Sims is perhaps the most well-known metaverse games. Although not precisely an online game, The Sims's virtual world functions like an MMORPG since many players may participate in a real-world event for participatory learning and inventive use of their area. These are just a few of instances when metaverses and games are used to introduce non-technical abilities.

LITERATURE REVIEW

The term "metaverse" is used to describe a hybrid of VR technology and mixed reality worlds that may be accessible by a website or headset and that enable real-time interactions and experiences amongst individuals who are geographically separated. According to Lik-Hang LEE, Tristan Braud and Pengyuan Zhou (2021), Metaverse, which combines the prefix "meta" with the term "universe," refers to a possible synthetic environment that is linked to the physical world. The first use of the term "metaverse" appeared in the science fiction novella Snow Crash. Most definitions of a metaverse include the elements of immersion, interaction, and a strong sense of community. Virtual reality or augmented reality, sometimes referred to as VR or AR, may or may not be necessary. It may also cover ownership and user-generated material. It can replicate systems and items seen in the real world and is industrial and collaborative (Hanish Patel, 2022). Metaverse in a simple term is an online progression that allows a user to go beyond surfing and inhabit and/or participate in a continuous shared experience that covers the spectrum of our actual world to the totally virtual and in between (Julie Sweet, 2022). Another definition of Metaverse by Jean Folger (2021), it is a kind of virtual interaction that mixes elements of social networking, online gaming, AR technology, VR technology, and cryptocurrency. In order to improve the user experience, augmented reality places visual components, audio, as well as other sensory input over real-world situations. Virtual reality, on the other hand, improves made-up worlds and is fully virtual. Further she explained the difference between Augmented Reality (AR) and Virtual Reality (VR). Augmented reality includes superimposing visual features, music, and other sensory cues onto a real-world scene to improve the user experience. Smartphones may be used to access augmented reality, and users can manage their presence there. Virtual reality, in contrast, enhances made-up worlds and is entirely virtual. Users are managed by the system, and VR calls for a headgear device.

Because of the kind of player interactions that are often used in each genre of video game, there is a correlation between those genres and particular families of soft skills. According to ManpowerGroup (2021), games like Pac-man and League of Legends games help to develop decision-making, planning, focus, and persistence. Action-based games such as Pokémon typically have an interest in developing abilities, working together, and participating in team competitions. Free roaming in open-world games such as Grand Theft Auto V and Red Dead Redemption encourages creativity and improves visual-spatial abilities. Lastly, team-playing games such as Call of Duty and FIFA help players improve their planning and strategy, teamwork and communication, overcoming obstacles, and spatial awareness abilities.

There is a growing interest in the metaverse. It happens at one time when businesses are more eager than ever to invest in value-creation projects that help them compete better and engage customers and staff members in fresh, more effective ways. According to Peter Bendor Samuel (2022), The fundamental reason of the rapidly expanding popularity in the metaverse is that businesses have realized that spending in the metaverse is a more appealing way of producing company growth than spending in technology to boost efficiency. Businesses perceive this metaverse as a fresh method to interact with customers and open up fresh business prospects. Further, companies now utilize the metaverse for marketing, to develop shopping platforms, to sell digital assets using NFTs, to create virtual locations for property transactions and events, and for other customer- or partner-related projects. Employers utilize technologies like Microsoft Teams to create virtual workspaces for regular collaborative sessions in the metaverse. Through avatars that represent them in the meeting or event, employees access the platform. For use cases including training, development, and upskilling, businesses also create virtual environments and offer virtual tools. As discussed by Jack Brassel (2022), there are three possible potential futures in the metaverse. The worst case is when the metaverse stays as a niche market and never develops into a broad market platform. Under this hypothetical situation, known as "low orbit," metaverse rules would constantly remain ambiguous as well as the platform would be mostly utilized for gaming, sports, and entertainment. The metaverse will always remain a brilliant curiosity used and appreciated by "fans" alone due to a lack of actual value for the mainstream and an inability to alter its methods or ingrained perceptions, despite attention from some disciplines and some courageous and intriguing new experiments. As for the second potential, there are usually several well-liked metaverses rather than a single interoperable metaverse. By providing exclusive content, each metaverse would successfully self-govern and strive for user loyalty. However, because of the lack of compatibility, consumers would probably have to choose only one metaverse. It functions quite similarly to the current console market. But most users will stick with only one option for having fun in the metaverse, spending practically all of their money and time there (Brassel. J, 2022). Lastly, the third potential, the technology known as "the metaverse" allows for complete interoperability between virtual and actual worlds. The exponentially more complicated world of the metaverse as well as its intersections with reality can function similarly to how there is single internet and all the numerous service providers surrounding it act fairly and by the same set of rules.

Virtual reality, augmented reality, and mixed reality (MR) technology and gadgets are currently very important to the metaverse. The majority of them are not portable, lightweight, or inexpensive, hence metaverse cannot be widely used. The difficulty is in having a very high and greater models that can reach the proper retina display and pixel resolution for a 3d virtual immersion, in addition to hardware accessibility. Everyone is discussing the many potential advantages of the metaverse. Ignoring the fact that there is darker aspect to everything. It has its own unique set of problems or challenges. Kajal Tharwani (2022) highlighted that one of the biggest problems in the metaverse is its impact on kids. Children suffer from the emergence of new technology. The issues of monitoring children's internet activity as working parents remain with the metaverse. Children's physical and virtual wellbeing may be in danger due to the metaverse. It can have a harmful effect on children and teenagers through video games addiction, sexual or abusive contents, and can result in psychological harm. According to IndustryTrends (2022), Obsession to the metaverse world may bring not only mental health issues such as sadness and anxiety, but also weight and cardiac problems due to sedentary lifestyle. Another problem of the metaverse is privacy and security. More than only passwords and email addresses are stored in Metaverse. It will also keep behaviors. A massive data mine requires technology that protects user confidentiality and personal data security. A new security approach will be needed (Rashmeet Kaur, 2022).

DISCUSSION

People may learn and apply a wide variety of soft talents. However, based on some research and the theoretical background, soft skills are divided into two categories for defining design practices: communication and creativity. The two groups will be further subdivided, and further help will be provided by referencing particular game studies and relating it to metaverse principles.

One of the most crucial abilities to develop is the capacity to communicate with both familiar and new individuals. The capacity to communicate along with other abilities like independence and frustration tolerance might be efficiently taught through games. As a result, players would be more socially present, which is necessary for avatar-interaction. Players would also continue to be engaged and conversate. Although this is a crucial element for any sector, it is required to remind people that it must be utilized during social gatherings, which may also lead to important employment. Using this reasoning, the subcategories of cooperation and socializing for game development and metaverse design were established.

Numerous video games provide wireless or local multiplayer options for numerous players. They are very quickly connected to competitive gaming. However, experts think that firmly integrating collaboration into the core gameplay is the greatest method to promote effective communication. Gamers will be encouraged to communicate with one another to do little tasks towards a greater goal of achieving an aim required the participation of more than just a person. A perfect example is Sand Box Games' cooperative local multiplayer adventure game Minecraft. To achieve objectives and move stages, the game demands nearly faultless coordination and communication among players, which is what distinguishes it from other competitive games. According to Roach and Utami (2017), Playing co-op games requires listening to one another and communicating with them. Games like Minecraft may be able to do this by giving players a range of activities that encourage them to multitask and switch roles, which in turn necessitates active interpersonal interaction. Shifting landscapes were designed to enhance this gaming and keep players engaged, which is consistent with the relationship between the metaverse's responsiveness and active data processing. To further improve the metaverse's ability to promote collaboration and communication, player interactions might be strengthened, and teamwork could be implemented into gaming.

Creativity is essential for innovation in any business that the typical employee works in. Most early video games have straightforward goals or straightforward routes to those goals. They gained depth throughout time as creators advanced in each genre and gamers got more creative in their approaches to the games. They may change the virtual places in the metaverse to suit their wants and creativity. This model's ability to incorporate creative thinking into actual life situations is a key component. The crafting system in Minecraft may be a source of inspiration for designers. Young children may learn how to create games with Roblox. The list could continue. Previous studies on certain games shown how players might use exploration and resourcefulness to apply their creative thinking.

Exploration in the virtual world results from the interactive nature of the metaverse. Giving players the opportunity to move about an open environment without feeling constrained by a predetermined path gives them a variety of options for how to reach their objectives or adjust when they are in difficult situations. Red Dead Redemption created 3D puzzles in a metaverse, for example, to promote involvement from many perspectives. The game demonstrates that self-presentation is possible in virtual spaces as well through action. By considering their decisions in a metaverse or virtual environment, people can grow and perhaps change for the better. In actuality, players are not just limited to what is accessible in a game's world. The metaverse's source code is occasionally available on the Internet, allowing users to alter it and generate fresh concepts by using third-party tools like programming languages and graphics programs. by fusing the metaverse with elements of gameplay that inspire players, such as obstacles, curiosity, or imagination. Players may express their ideas both within and beyond the virtual landscapes they explore.

In order to connect and have a good time, socializing entails communication with other people. Teamwork may be essential for effectiveness and productivity but having quality time with close friends may increase mutual trust and likeability. Numerous online games were created to meet social requirements by giving players a place to meet new people and engage in conversations that feel genuine and social. As a result of meeting others who enjoyed the series and had similar interests, those who participated under these circumstances reported an increase in social interaction. Character customization, which fulfills the requirement of self-presentation for avatar-interaction, was added to further improve the experiences. Socializing also takes place off the gaming platform in specialized online forums and social media platforms. Although it could seem irrelevant to the primary goal of the study, this could be significant for subsequent studies that are relevant. Video games that have a sizable fan base inevitably create communities outside their virtual settings. Players may exchange a wealth of information through these platforms, including comments, gaming advice, and personal narratives that are available for others to read. As a result, the metaverse would have the chance to impart knowledge via a distinctive social activity outside of its limits. As video games advanced, their complexity increased, giving rise to programs like Discord that enable users to interact, discuss, and contribute. By capitalizing on this trend, the metaverse and video games as a whole may not only improve user experiences but also draw in a wider audience, which would then interact socially within their individual communities and feed the cycle.

CONCLUSION

We have discussed the possibility for fusing the metaverse with video games and have provided numerous design strategies to foster soft skills. This approach is based on several research and numerous existing applications that have achieved success in the metaverse idea, gaming, or a mix of both. Metaverses offer a 3D virtual environment where users may explore and take part in various activities. In addition to being fun, video games have a special ability to instruct their users. Everyone may have access to greater invention and exploration if different aspects of both worlds were combined.

This report created a design approach based upon this metaverse and soft skills that would use game design to educate players communication and creativity. In order to accommodate people with diverse tastes and learning styles and to better prepare them for the actual world, it also addressed several aspects of each skill. If they are used effectively, gamers may be able to learn while enjoying their spare time without feeling forced to give up their leisure time. Instead of being one-size-fits-all solutions, these guidelines are meant to serve as a base for developers to build upon as they create new pieces of software that improve the metaverse and game design while also giving players the chance to learn soft skills.

REFERENCES

Ahad, A. D., Anshari, M., & Razzaq, A. (2017). Domestication of smartphones among adolescents in Brunei Darussalam. *International Journal of Cyber Behavior, Psychology and Learning*, *7*(4), 26–39. doi:10.4018/IJCBPL.2017100103

Almunawar, M. N., & Anshari, M. (2021). Digital enabler and value integration: Revealing the expansion engine of digital marketplace. *Technology Analysis and Strategic Management*, 1–11.

Almunawar, M. N., Anshari, M., & Lim, S. A. (2021). A framework for observing digital marketplace. *International Journal of Hyperconnectivity and the Internet of Things*, *5*(2), 57–73. doi:10.4018/IJHIoT.2021070104

Anshari, M. (2020, March). Workforce mapping of fourth industrial revolution: Optimization to identity. *Journal of Physics: Conference Series*, *1477*(7), 072023. doi:10.1088/1742-6596/1477/7/072023

Anshari, M., Almunawar, M. N., & Masri, M. (2022). Digital Twin: Financial Technology's Next Frontier of Robo-Advisor. *Journal of Risk and Financial Management, 15*(4), 163. doi:10.3390/jrfm15040163

Anshari, M., Almunawar, M. N., Masri, M., & Hamdan, M. (2019). Digital marketplace and FinTech to support agriculture sustainability. *Energy Procedia, 156*, 234–238. doi:10.1016/j.egypro.2018.11.134

Anshari, M., & Hamdan, M. (2022). Understanding knowledge management and upskilling in Fourth Industrial Revolution: Transformational shift and SECI model. *VINE Journal of Information and Knowledge Management Systems*. Advance online publication. doi:10.1108/VJIKMS-09-2021-0203

Anshari, M., Syafrudin, M., & Fitriyani, N. L. (2022). Fourth Industrial Revolution between Knowledge Management and Digital Humanities. *Information (Basel), 13*(6), 292. doi:10.3390/info13060292

Anshari, M., Syafrudin, M., Fitriyani, N. L., & Razzaq, A. (2022). Ethical Responsibility and Sustainability (ERS) Development in a Metaverse Business Model. *Sustainability, 14*(23), 15805. doi:10.3390u142315805

Folger, J. (2021). *What Does Metaverse Mean and How Does This Virtual World Work?* Retrieved from: https://www.investopedia.com/metaverse-definition-5206578

Gee, J. P. (2003). What video games have to teach us about learning and literacy. *Computers in Entertainment, 1*(1), 20. .950595 doi:10.1145/950566

Green, C. S., & Bavelier, D. (2003). Action video game modifies visual selective attention. *Nature, 423*(6939), 534–537. doi:10.1038/nature01647 PMID:12774121

Hamdan, M., Jaidin, J. H., Fithriyah, M., & Anshari, M. (2020, December). E-learning in time of COVID-19 pandemic: Challenges & experiences. In *2020 Sixth International Conference on e-Learning (econf)* (pp. 12-16). IEEE. 10.1109/econf51404.2020.9385507

Hasmawati, F., Samiha, Y. T., Razzaq, A., & Anshari, M. (2020). Understanding nomophobia among digital natives: Characteristics and challenges. *Journal of Critical Reviews, 7*(13), 122–131.

IndustryTrends. (2022). *Challenges in metaverse and how to overcome them.* Retrieved from: https://www.analyticsinsight.net/challenges-in-metaverse-and-how-to-overcome-them/

Jaman, S. F. I., & Anshari, M. (2021). Facebook as marketing tools for organizations: Knowledge management analysis. In *Research Anthology on Strategies for Using Social Media as a Service and Tool in Business* (pp. 117–131). IGI Global. doi:10.4018/978-1-7998-9020-1.ch007

Lee, L. H., Braud, T., & Zhou, P. (2021), *All One Needs to Know about Metaverse: A Complete Survey on Technological Singularity, Virtual Ecosystem, and Research Agenda.* Retrieved from: https://tuhat.helsinki.fi/ws/portalfiles/portal/169348619/METAVERSE.pdf

Patel, H. (2022), *The Metaverse Explained.* Retrieved from: https://www2.deloitte.com/content/dam/Deloitte/us/Documents/mergers-acqisitions/user-friendly-the-metaverse-explained.pdf

Rashmeet, K. (2022). *Challenges faced by the Metaverse in becoming a reality.* Retrieved from: https://medium.datadriveninvestor.com/challenges-faced-by-the-metaverse-in-becoming-a-reality-d02219d29370

Razzaq, A., Samiha, Y. T., & Anshari, M. (2018). Smartphone habits and behaviors in supporting students self-efficacy. *International Journal of Emerging Technologies in Learning*, *13*(2), 94. doi:10.3991/ijet.v13i02.7685

Sait, M. A., & Anshari, M. (2021). Industrial Revolution 4.0: A New Challenge to Brunei Darussalam's Unemployment Issue. *International Journal of Asian Business and Information Management*, *12*(4), 33–44. doi:10.4018/IJABIM.20211001.oa3

Samuel, B. P. (2022). *Potential Value For Your Company In The Metaverse.* Retrieved from: https://www.forbes.com/sites/peterbendorsamuel/2022/07/18/potential-value-for-your-company-in-the-metaverse/?sh=6dbccd2c514e

Sweet, J. (2022). *Meet Me in The Metaverse.* Retrieved from: https://www.accenture.com/_acnmedia/Thought-Leadership-Assets/PDF-5/Accenture-Meet-Me-in-the-Metaverse-Full-Report.pdf

Tharwani, K. (2022). *Problems & Disadvantages Of The Metaverse.* Retrieved from: https://www.opengrowth.com/resources/problems-disadvantages-of-the-metaverse

Chapter 9
Privacy and Security Concerns in the Metaverse

Muhd Hakeem Pg Haji Muhd Japar
Universiti Brunei Darussalam, Brunei

Muhammad Anshari
https://orcid.org/0000-0002-8160-6682
Universiti Brunei Darussalam, Brunei

Wardah Hakimah Haji Sumardi
Universiti Brunei Darussalam, Brunei

ABSTRACT

Every year, the metaverse grows to make the world more efficient and easy to use for all societies and industries. When connecting the virtual world to the real world and digital information, privacy and security are two of the most talked-about topics. This is because the metaverse has a lot of sensitive information. This chapter talks about some privacy and security problems in the metaverse and how they will affect the future. At the same time, even though the metaverse has become more advanced, its complexity produces a new situation where it raises the issues of privacy and security again. This chapter also explores and suggests countermeasures to combat privacy and security issues.

DOI: 10.4018/978-1-6684-6097-9.ch009

Copyright © 2023, IGI Global. Copying or distributing in print or electronic forms without written permission of IGI Global is prohibited.

INTRODUCTION

The journal article "Metaverse: Security and Privacy Issues" was published by Roberto Di Pietro and Stefano Crest in 2021. Both authors focus on today's essential issues regarding privacy and security related to almost all technology, known as metaverse, that people use or are involved in daily life, whether it relates to working life or daily activities. Myriads of journal articles and research papers regarding privacy and security on metaverse prove that privacy and security is not a new topic that has surfaced recently until today. This is because privacy and security have already been brought up and discussed a long time ago, almost more than two and a half centuries ago, which means that this topic area is not something that people can solve quickly or in a short amount of time since many authors nowadays still talk or do research regarding privacy and security on metaverse (Anshari et al., 2022). For example, some authors focused on improving what was achieved in the past few years: privacy and security that have already been strengthened to avoid any bad incident. This might happen without anyone's knowledge or in the future when people are already prepared for the possible bad outcome. However, some authors believe that privacy and security are not something that can be taken lightly even though everyday people make progress and improve.

Although there are many articles or books regarding this topic, Roberto and Stefano contributed to the analysis of the basis of a metaverse which led them to raise the issues of privacy and security in their research. As a result, it helps them to conclude their study by contributing a logical implication or suggestion of the metaverse in the future. Also, they have explored the potential research that privacy and security can do in the future that can lead other authors or researchers to find a new direction or topic that has not been discussed yet in the past. In this era of globalization, the increase of metaverse's privacy and security issues such as stolen personal information or security breach of the database becomes more familiar to people nowadays. Also, it is almost impossible to keep up with the new technology that keeps on increasing and improving, leading to more data or information needing to be protected and secure. Therefore, while new technology is introduced and keeps on updating every year, people also need to keep up to handle their privacy and security to avoid any incident that might occur in the future.

Background Studies on Privacy's Metaverse

Before the 1700s or prehistoric age, people could tell that privacy was not necessary at that time or care less because the technology was not advanced enough to focus genuinely on people or information's privacy. However, in 1789, the United State Constitution was introduced; where even though the right to privacy is not guaranteed or promised yet, the right to privacy is mentioned in the First, Third, Fourth, and Fifth amendments ("History of Privacy Timeline / safecomputing.umich.edu", 2022). This shows privacy started taking place in terms of an important topic that needed to be discussed and strengthened. After that, in 1980, Justice Louis Brandeis and Samuel Warren published a law review article about privacy, arguing about the right to privacy. They claimed that privacy became weak due to instant picture technology and newspaper companies; they then looked for a solution where the law at that time could help protect privacy ("History of Privacy Timeline / safecomputing.umich.edu", 2022). This demonstrates that problems regarding privacy already arose in the past when privacy was already difficult to control.

Furthermore, in 1973, people created the modern privacy legislation to make as the fundamentals from a report called Fair Information Practices, where The Department of Health, Education, and Welfare Secretary's Advisory Committee on Automated Personal Data Systems developed the landmark 1973 Records, Computers and the Rights of Citizens, Report of the Secretary's Advisory Committee on Automated Personal Data Systems ("History of Privacy Timeline / safecomputing.umich.edu", 2022). This shows that privacy becomes more important, like other legislation where people's right to confidentiality is broken. For instance, stolen information, a privacy law can be invoked to act, support, and protect further people or companies' privacy and make a contingency plan.

In 2003, data breach notification laws were introduced by California, and California was the first to implement them due to security breaches where the people of California's information was exposed to the public ("History of Privacy Timeline / safecomputing.umich.edu", 2022). The new law was immediately introduced after unexpected incidents happened, and California made an excellent and fast decision from happening again. In 2010, a Red Flag Rule was presented by the Federal Trade Commission (FTC) and the National Credit Union Administration (NUAC); where this rule would help from any identity theft that could happen to people or company to prevent stolen identity information ("History of Privacy Timeline / safecomputing.umich.edu", 2022).

Background Studies on Security's Metaverse

Before the evolution of cyber security became wildly prominent in the 21st century, security was also not advanced or careless due to unsophisticated technology like privacy, such as when the internet or network is invented yet or not wildly used by people. However, companies initially started to protect their computers in the 1960s (Murphey, 2019). According to Murphey (2019), security at that time was mainly based on physical measures but not internal or computer security, so people could not access the computer and learn how to use computer. For example, only basic security is added to protect computers, such as passwords and numerous layers of security protection (Murphey, 2019). Another example that security was not yet advanced at that time, such as no digital backup like iCloud, fire safety measures were applied to safeguard the room that fills with computers and other devices so any physical backup to other devices could be protected from any fire incident happening (Murphey, 2019). This would ensure that at that time, companies that utilize a room that fills with a myriad of computers and digital information would be heavily protected since there is no backup to the cloud.

In the 1970s, cyber security is taken to the next level, where security was taken seriously when some people tried to mess with poor security programs. This led to exposing loopholes that anyone with cyber security knowledge would be able to hack the program. A research project known as The Advanced Research Projects Agency Network (ARPANET) during the 1970s where a program created by Bob Thomas named 'CREEPER' was able to shift ARPANET's network to other networks and leaving a few signs as it moved to other places (Murphey, 2019). After that, the program was updated by another programmer known as Ray Tomlinson, who redesigned the program to make a copy of itself, then known as the first computer worm (Murphey, 2019).

Not long after that, he made a program called 'REAPER' to track the program 'CREEPER' and destroy it, which was then known as the beginning example of anti-virus software. Even though Bob Thomas and Ray Tomlinson created the program to mess around for fun, it concludes that the programs set off as a crucial purpose or objective to cyber security due the ARPANET's network is not secure enough since the program 'CREEPER' able to move ARPANET's network (Murphey, 2019). Due to this, according to Murphey (2019), it worries a lot of companies and the government because they created their network using telephone wires while linking to the computers that people were using to work. As a result of this, many people knew of this flaw, where people with hacking skills would be able to access the network without authorization to steal confidential data or information.

To the public from viruses, firewalls and antivirus programs were widely produced due to network security threats in the 1990s; a NASA researcher created the first firewall because of a virus attack at their base (Murphey, 2019). In the 2000s, as technology grew and became more advanced and more information was stored digitally, information security pursued as well to be more advanced because, at the same time, viruses also became more difficult and complex to handle without creating massive virus attacks on every device in every country (Murphey, 2019).

Related Trends

There are also many related articles about the metaverse in terms of privacy and security, such as Security and Privacy in the Metaverse: The Threat of the Digital Human by Lauren Buck and Rachel McDonnell, The Metaverse: Technology, Privacy and Security Risks, and the Road Ahead by Dr. Roberto Di Piero, and many more. These articles show that a myriad of authors interested in metaverse published related topics regarding the privacy and security of metaverse shows that the topic is vital and promising because it enables other readers or authors to keep up to date with nowadays problems and solutions that researchers provided.

Apart from that, it raises awareness for everyone who uses devices in their daily lives so people can take precautions when storing data or information digitally. Due to this, the metaverse plays a crucial role nowadays and in the future, primarily in privacy and security. Since metaverse affects people's privacy and security, the article chosen above is better and well-organized due to the authors explaining the issues of privacy and security, along with the countermeasures of the problem for developers and information security specialists to improve.

LITERATURE REVIEW

Privacy

Nowadays, organizations or companies can track people's activities even though they do not sign up for anything. This is because organizations or business companies can produce or market their products and services based on people's activities. Without knowing people's interests, business companies cannot make many sales, thus losing profits and wasting investment. One of the ways how people's privacy is known to organizations or business companies is by downloading their online application, and people need to accept the terms and conditions of using the product before they can use the application. Companies can use that information to know the user's interest by accepting the terms and conditions. It is common nowadays where an application needs a user to accept any terms and conditions before using the application to see the user's activities and analyze their behavior to make more products and services in the future that according to current user's behavior when using or downloading a specific application (Zulkarnain et al., 2021).

Even some of social media platform such as Facebook, Instagram, Twitter, TikTok, and many others keep track of users' activity and behavior (Anshari & Sumardi, 2020). Hence, when a user searches for a specific area in social media, such as sports, the social media algorithm will generate any related sports-related posts or news for the user. However, even though these may benefit companies to generate sales and profits, they may not be for the user who uses the products or services (Anshari et al., 2021a). This is because users might risk their personal information leaking to hackers. Some users may feel uncomfortable keeping track of their privacy, such as activities and behavior. Since these issues are happening nowadays and have been discussed in the past, what could happen to all privacy in the metaverse (Di Pietro & Cresci, 2021). For instance, users may not know when they use any smart devices, such as virtual reality devices, to track their movement and store them in the cloud (Dive, 2022). In the following section, both authors describe the capabilities of a metaverse in the data collection of users and applications.

1) User profiling in the metaverse

In today's era of the metaverse, it is almost impossible for the user not to have a profile on any digital media such as social media and many more, where sometimes users need to fill in their personal information such as email, location, date of birth and many more to access the Internet. Users may be able to avoid giving personal information if the user is only trying to search or browse, where users do not have to register or sign in to access information such as google. Although Google does not require its user to sign in, some default settings by the Internet or Google may be able to store the user's profile. According to Di Pietro and Cresci (2021), if the by-product of nowadays Internet is users connected with any social network, everyone and everything else is the product in the metaverse. This would mean that without users, the Internet or metaverse will act as nothing where it will not do or produce anything, such as e-commerce would not produce any sales because there is no user (Anshari et al., 2019; Anshari et al., 2021b). Thus, no target sales will make the e-commerce industry useless.

However, the metaverse is rapidly growing, and highly impossible not to get involved. It shows many benefits from the past few years, such as easing people. In addition to the previous point, users such as content creators, entrepreneurs, and businesses alike will be hugely involved where the metaverse act as a strong magnet that can gain users faster to expose in metaverse based on their passion and application whether it is a gaming industry, a business industry, healthcare industry and many more (Di Pietro & Cresci, 2021). This could indicate that metaverse will be involved in many industries where the more advanced system and technology will replace past technologies or automation (Anshari & Almunawar, 2018).

Despite that, it increases the risk of exposing user's information on the Internet or metaverse; where according to Di Pietro and Cresci (2021), due to vast industries already involved in the metaverse, it escalated considerable amounts of worries because storing many data in terms of volume and type. The authors show concern for users' profiles as storing many data will be exceedingly difficult or maintain its safety from unwanted incidents. Since the authors were concerned about user's profiles in the metaverse, they stated that Internet 2.0 authorized marketers like organizations or business companies to track and analyze user's activities when they used specific applications or a website, such as a mouse movement, what page what was open, the duration the users spend on the page, user's favorite site or pictures and many more (Di Pietro & Cresci, 2021; Hasmawati et al., 2020). In addition to the previous, every user needed to be identified in the metaverse for every device of their own, where the devices such as VR glass can be tracking the whereabouts of the user's location illegally (Wang et al., 2022). Other examples are sensors in the hospital. Since these sensors can collect patients' data, such as physical, behavioral, or mental problems, it can be dangerous if exposed to the public, or the information loses its integrity when the data is modified (Zhao et al., 2022).

This shows that the current Internet or metaverse keeps track of users' activity so that organizations or companies can use the data to make a profit based on every user's interest (Anshari & Almunawar, 2021). Some users with a background in information security or who are self-aware of nowadays privacy and security will stay alert when providing personal information that will be stored digitally. However, according to Di Pietro and Cresci (2021), some users that have no background in information security or are computer illiterate may not know that their online activity is recorded, and as a result of this, their personal information may be vulnerable or at risk that could expose to hackers or public if their right to privacy and security is not strong enough.

2) User privacy

User privacy is a very general and vast topic because it can cover many areas of privacy where there are specific areas that are only necessary that must be focused on; according to Di Pietro and Cresci (2021), personal information, behavior, and communications are the three types of areas primarily people focus on (Mulyani et al., 2019). Breaking down and narrowing the general topic into small topics allows people to focus and research more concisely and prevent them from going out of the topic where it could make a poor decision, irrelevant research, and waste of time. Although, by knowing the three areas for organizations or business companies, they would be able to acquire more data and information from users than they had before because they learned the areas they needed to focus on only (Di Pietro & Cresci, 2021; Anshari et al., 2021c).

In addition to communication, communication is the biggest platform where people and most organizations or companies exchange information, and some users may give their information voluntarily to untrusted people or fake agents since it is hard to tell if the person is legitimate or not (Zhao et al., 2022). It may be beneficial for them, but as a result, it could also lead to higher exposure, where a data breach would be catastrophic due to more data and information being stored (Di Pietro & Cresci, 2021). This would indicate that knowing the type of area to focus on will lead to storing more information and increase the risk to every user's privacy. One of the examples is social networking platforms such as Facebook and Twitter. These social networking platforms already collect user's personal information when they sign up or register where this is the standard practice for random organizations or hackers to search the user's personal information on their profile for malicious intent such as releasing it to the public (Di Pietro & Cresci, 2021).

This raises a question to the people and every information security specialist of how to prevent and reduce doxing at a minimum rate, even though some users' personal information may be helpful to other users (Di Pietro & Cresci, 2021). This is because Di Pietro and Cresci (2021) argue that it has something to do with the fact that the information about the user would know the user's habits and any characteristics in the real world if their information is leaked through the metaverse or the Internet.

In addition to the previous point, it would be almost impossible to know a user's habits and characteristics, such as physiological to obtain from the internet only, but with the help of nowadays metaverse where every technology has become more advanced, it would be easily possible due to how people and every industry became more closer between physical and virtual world (Di Pietro & Cresci, 2021). Consequently, the public will know the user's behavior if it leaks to the public, as the risk already increases due to the close relationship with the metaverse. According to Di Pietro and Cresci (2021), metaverse solves this by contributing an opportunity for utilizing online experience and relationships carried out offline or real-world problems that have never been done before or known, such as harmful incidents and frauds. In summary, while metaverse may increase in risking user's privacy, it also takes advantage of its technology to uncover flaws and solves real-world problems.

3) Countermeasures

Since privacy in the metaverse world is not entirely secure, it is not 100% vulnerable because as technology evolves and data collection gets massive, privacy is also improved to protect confidential or sensitive information as safely as possible. If privacy does not keep up with technological advancement, then all of it in the metaverse will be useless due to not being protected carefully. In addition to the previous point, educated people, such as scientists, professors, and many more, have already started to resolve problems to strengthen privacy in the metaverse world (Di Pietro & Cresci, 2021). This would indicate that every time privacy becomes a controversial topic, such as private data leaks in unexpected ways that people did not think of, there would be a researcher to help to overcome the problem, such as providing an idea to strengthen privacy more. Di Pietro and Cresci (2021) stated there are already a couple of answers that have been presented to update users' privacy to the next level, consisting of three central procedures.

The three procedures are: (i) creating a lot of fake accounts or an account that almost looks like the original user in order to cover the original user's movement or track; (ii) generating a personal copy of a public digital environment that is only for only specific user to use or not allowing other users to enter the public digital environment; (iii) authorize the user to be invincible, broadcast to other space, or other types of disguise where the user is unrecognizable by other user or network (Di Pietro & Cresci, 2021). For example, a user can generate an avatar that is almost like original information such as age and gender; thus, when the avatar is complete, the user can control information to display when other users see the information, like in the game called Second Life which is an open world social metaverse (Lee et al., 2021). Their proposed strategies will not just strengthen user privacy by keeping the user's activities in the network as minimal as possible but will also reduce the privacy data leaks to the outside world.

About the above three strategies, Di Pietro and Cresci (2021) suggested another solution or addition that could be added to the user's privacy, given that the three combinations are helpful under procedure number two, after the user exits from the public space, the authors recommended that the user administer a disguise where the user is unrecognizable and untraceable. This author's statement would mean that it ensures that the user's privacy is still protected, even though the user is no longer in the public digital space.

However, metaverse does not force its user to determine the level of protection of their privacy. Even though having the highest level of protection of user's privacy has it is beneficial rather than setting the level of privacy at low or medium, metaverse wanted its user freedom to choose how their control their privacy due to there are also benefiting from having low or medium levels of privacy than the highest. This is because, as stated by Di Pietro and Cresci (2021), although metaverse executed the three strategies above, users should have the ability or option to choose their privacy levels, such as providing a menu that is convenient for users where there is an option to choose the level of protection of privacy whether the users wanted low, medium, or high based on their preference and activities.

Users may no longer see their history or past activities when they enter the digital world again if the level of privacy protection is very high, which may be inconvenient for some users. Nevertheless, the solution provided just now by the metaverse is overly simplified and is still not strong enough to counter complex or almost impenetrable risks or attacks in nowadays metaverse; as a consequence, new or better solutions must be formulated where the authors also stated it might be an exciting challenge or journey to solve it (Di Pietro & Cresci, 2021).

Security

On top of privacy issues, as technology evolves and becomes more advanced, security threats will also become a controversial topic where metaverse must securely store everyone's information that stores digitally (Di Pietro & Cresci, 2021). This is because its value is priceless when technology or metaverse improves or becomes more advanced. Some organizations or hackers will try to exploit them for personal gains, such as selling sensitive information to the black market or exposing people's information to the public. Below is one of the few threats that have been going on in the metaverse world.

1) Humans in and out of the loop

According to Di Pietro and Cresci (2021), some of the security threats of the metaverse come from the existence of the complication of the metaverse itself. This is because it is simple enough to imagine for metaverse administration to go automation to handle many data in terms of connecting many users, services, applications, and goods than current Web platforms in order to implement many tasks by algorithms rather than with human handling it (Di Pietro & Cresci, 2021). It is unavoidable to go with past procedures where humans are the ones who are physically handling data as they could not keep up with nowadays metaverse.

Moreover, people will make more mistakes than artificial intelligence (AI) can make, such as human error, where artificial intelligence can work for longer without resting. Di Pietro and Cresci (2021) also agree that the implementation of algorithms by using AI capabilities can handle work more efficiently with high performance due to AI having significant scalability that can last a long time. Metaverse users can freely explore the physical and virtual worlds in socializing and economic business, such as using computer vision, intelligent voice, natural language processing, and many more using artificial intelligence technologies (Ning et al., 2021).

Despite of unmatched performance of AI technologies to do human tasks and solve complex algorithms, it has also been affected by several issues, especially security, such as prejudice that will lead to the unfair conclusion, absence of clarity, exposure to attacks and operations, and complex computational and energy of AI model which limit their competitiveness and needs (Di Pietro & Cresci, 2021).

Even though how complex AI is, there will be something affected, or an issue would raise, so people who make use of AI will have to take account of all these issues when advancing to more complex AI technologies in the metaverse where Di Pietro and Cresci (2021) also stated that daunting problems could happen due to complicated algorithms. Moreover, even nowadays, the security system is unsuccessful and works 100 percent in metaverse applications (Wang et al., 2022).

There are many examples of how security issues have become more common in the metaverse despite how advanced the technology has become over the past few years. One of the examples is related nowadays disease, where many people died from COVID-19 and vaccines due to misinformation (Di Pietro & Cresci, 2021). Even though COVID-19 and its vaccine are critical and severe incidents, some unresponsible people are still taking advantage of tempering the data or information.

2) Integrity and authentication in the metaverse

Two of the few security issues in the metaverse are integrity and authentication. Security integrity is protecting the originality of information from any unauthorized modification and ensuring that the information stays valid and legitimate. While security authentication is to determine whether a particular user is legitimate when accessing private data or information. This prevents any user from accessing any network or system without valid credentials.

According to Di Pietro and Cresci (2021), people are exposed to falsified information and fake users when interacting with the Internet on social networking platforms such as Facebook, Twitter, and many others. An example of falsified information is machine-generated text, where the information can create any information based on how complex the algorithm of the machine is. If the algorithm is complex, it could create very fake legitimate information without people noticing. Another example is bots, automated fake accounts, or users designed to interact with real users like usual. All these examples can lead to privacy attacks once the user is included in the trap that could attack the user's location data, smart devices, mobile, and many others (Nair et al., 2022).

Another example stated by the authors is that users can be digitally reproduced and created like the actual user on social networking platforms, detection software, or other users noticing (Di Pietro & Cresci, 2021). Another author also states that to protect the actual user's privacy, virtual clones that are almost like the real user could be generated to hide the real identities of the actual user (Nair et al., 2022). In summary, people expect these issues to be ongoing due to fake information, and users can hardly be detected by detection software.

3) Polarization and radicalization

Most security issues come from complex and insecure algorithms in the metaverse and automation and mechanization, but the characteristics of the metaverse itself can also raise a problem due to the metaverse acting as a singleton and its uniqueness (Di Pietro & Cresci, 2021). Even though the metaverse is one of the most prominent problem solvers, such as processing and handling data or information, its achievement depends on how many users or organizations are involved in the metaverse world (Di Pietro & Cresci, 2021). This is because without users using or interacting with metaverse, metaverse will not exist nor be functional.

One of the qualities of the metaverse is that it connects a myriad of platforms where users can go to any online platform or community of users based on their tastes and preferences and connect with other users with the same taste and preferences (Di Pietro & Cresci, 2021). The presence of an online platform would enable users to connect with other nations or communities in a new way, creating many users and increasing communities (Bermejo et al., 2022). This would allow able users to stay happy and not get bored with one platform only, thus, keeping the user stays connected with the metaverse.

Nevertheless, there are still consequences regardless of how beneficial connecting a myriad of different users to different online communities is. For example, in a multiplayer online game such as massively multiplayer online role-playing games (MMORPGs), all types of a nation of users can access different countries where which would be able for some users to bully or harass other users from different countries, such as harassing low-level players or opposite gender (Di Pietro & Cresci, 2021). This then raises a question for both authors what would happen if a different type of communities combined in one or shared metaverse (Di Pietro & Cresci, 2021).

ANALYSIS AND DISCUSSION

There are myriad ways to improve the report of the author's article so other readers or researchers can easily read the article.

1) Lack of case study or examples

One of the problems of the article is the preliminary case study or examples for some of the statements stated by the authors. This is because even though some points stated by the authors are valid, some readers or researchers need some examples that back up the statement stated. This is because if the statement is not backed by other means, some researchers may see it as an untrusted source to prevent misinformation (Razzaq et al., 2018). Therefore, improving the article provides case studies or examples from reliable sources so the article can be seen as legitimate. Another way is to make its reliable source by surveying metaverse privacy and security to people and any industry. With the survey, the authors can use the diagram to present the data or information, so it would be much more readable than explained by sentences. In addition, the survey questions can be pasted in an appendix so readers can look through the questions being asked in the survey.

2) Tabulate important points

Another problem is that since the authors stated many points, it may come quickly for readers to forget what was being stated. Moreover, since the article is written in essay format, reading the article for a while could make the reader lose focus and loss where he stops reading. One way to prevent readers from losing focus and remembering all the essential points is to tabulate all the critical points at the end of the article. So, if the readers wanted to refer to the article without reading the article over again to remember the points, the readers could go to the summary of all the points.

3) Collaborates with other researchers

Furthermore, another way to improve the article is to collaborate with other researchers. This is because, by collaborating with many researchers, there can share many ideas and information. At the same time, they can help each other by validating any information they find. For example, if a researcher does not know if the information that he or she finds is credible, he or she can ask help from other researchers. Therefore, the article may produce much legitimate information.

CONCLUSION

In conclusion, both authors discuss privacy and security issues in the metaverse. In contrast, as technology such as AI evolves, privacy and security also need to be strengthened and maintained so to avoid any possible incident that may happen in the future. The article Roberto Di Pietro and Stefano Cresci published is a very significant article that stated some points related to current issues. However, at the same time, the article can be improved further to be recognized as an excellent report. It is recommended that readers and researchers read this article to increase their knowledge and to further other research studies. This article may open doors to other discussions in other research papers.

REFERENCES

Anshari, M., Syafrudin, M., Fitriyani, N. L., & Razzaq, A. (2022). Ethical Responsibility and Sustainability (ERS) Development in a Metaverse Business Model. *Sustainability*, *14*(23), 15805. doi:10.3390u142315805

Anshari, M., Almunawar, M. N., Masri, M., & Hrdy, M. (2021a). Financial technology with ai-enabled and ethical challenges. *Society*, *58*(3), 189–195. doi:10.100712115-021-00592-w

Anshari, M., & Sumardi, W. H. (2020). Employing big data in business organisation and business ethics. *International Journal of Business Governance and Ethics*, *14*(2), 181–205. doi:10.1504/IJBGE.2020.106349

Anshari, M., Alas, Y., Razzaq, A., Shahrill, M., & Lim, S. A. (2021b). Millennials consumers' behaviors between trends and experiments. In Research Anthology on E-Commerce Adoption, Models, and Applications for Modern Business (pp. 1492-1508). IGI Global.

Anshari, M., Almunawar, M. N., Younis, M. Z., & Kisa, A. (2021c). Modeling Users' Empowerment in E-Health Systems. *Sustainability*, *13*(23), 12993. doi:10.3390u132312993

Anshari, M., Almunawar, M. N., Lim, S. A., & Al-Mudimigh, A. (2019). Customer relationship management and big data enabled: Personalization & customization of services. *Applied Computing and Informatics*, *15*(2), 94–101. doi:10.1016/j.aci.2018.05.004

Anshari, M., & Almunawar, M. N. (2021). Adopting open innovation for SMEs and industrial revolution 4.0. *Journal of Science and Technology Policy Management*.

Anshari, M., & Almunawar, M. N. (2018). Social customer relationship management, election and political campaign. *International Journal of Electronic Customer Relationship Management*, *11*(4), 332–346. doi:10.1504/IJECRM.2018.096239

Bermejo, C., & Hui, P. (2022). *Life, the Metaverse and Everything: An Overview of Privacy*. Ethics, and Governance in Metaverse., doi:10.13140/RG.2.2.35094.63042

Dive, D. (2022). *Metaverse Technology Opens Up a Wider World of Privacy Concerns*. Retrieved 10 September 2022, from https://news.bloomberglaw.com/privacy-and-data-security/metaverse-technology-opens-up-a-wider-world-of-privacy-concerns

Hasmawati, F., Samiha, Y. T., Razzaq, A., & Anshari, M. (2020). Understanding nomophobia among digital natives: Characteristics and challenges. *Journal of Critical Reviews*, *7*(13), 122–131.

Safecomputing.umich.edu. (2022). Retrieved 11 September 2022, from https://safecomputing.umich.edu/privacy/history-of-privacy-timeline

Holvast, J. (2009). History of Privacy. *The Future Of Identity In The Information Society*, 13-42. doi:10.1007/978-3-642-03315-5_2

Lee, L. H., Braud, T., Zhou, P., Wang, L., Xu, D., Lin, Z., . . . Hui, P. (2021). *All one needs to know about metaverse: A complete survey on technological singularity, virtual ecosystem, and research agenda*. arXiv preprint arXiv:2110.05352.

Mulyani, M. A., Razzaq, A., Sumardi, W. H., & Anshari, M. (2019, August). Smartphone adoption in mobile learning scenario. In *2019 International Conference on Information Management and Technology (ICIMTech)* (Vol. 1, pp. 208-211). IEEE. 10.1109/ICIMTech.2019.8843755

Murphey, D. (2019). *A history of information security - IFSEC Global | Security and Fire News and Resources*. Retrieved 16 September 2022, from https://www.ifsecglobal.com/cyber-security/a-history-of-information-security/

Nair, V., Garrido, G. M., & Song, D. (2022). *Exploring the Unprecedented Privacy Risks of the Metaverse*. arXiv preprint arXiv:2207.13176.

Ning, H., Wang, H., Lin, Y., Wang, W., Dhelim, S., Farha, F., . . . Daneshmand, M. (2021). *A Survey on Metaverse: The State-of-the-art, Technologies, Applications, and Challenges*. arXiv preprint arXiv:2111.09673.

Razzaq, A., Samiha, Y. T., & Anshari, M. (2018). Smartphone habits and behaviors in supporting students self-efficacy. *International Journal of Emerging Technologies in Learning*, *13*(2), 94. doi:10.3991/ijet.v13i02.7685

Wang, Y., Su, Z., Zhang, N., Xing, R., Liu, D., Luan, T., & Shen, X. (2022). A Survey on Metaverse: Fundamentals, Security, and Privacy. *IEEE Communications Surveys & Tutorials*. doi:10.1109/COMST.2022.3202047

Zhao, R., Zhang, Y., Zhu, Y., Lan, R., & Hua, Z. (2022). *Metaverse: Security and Privacy Concerns*. arXiv preprint arXiv:2203.03854.

Zulkarnain, N., Anshari, M., Hamdan, M., & Fithriyah, M. (2021, August). Big data in business and ethical challenges. In *2021 International Conference on Information Management and Technology (ICIMTech)* (Vol. 1, pp. 298-303). IEEE. 10.1109/ICIMTech53080.2021.9534963

Chapter 10
Sports in the Metaverse

Muhamad Danial Asyraf Mohamad
Universiti Brunei Darussalam, Brunei

ABSTRACT

The goal of this chapter is to present information on sports technology, specifically how the metaverse will affect the sports world and how well sports will adapt to life in the metaverse. The findings of the study conducted for the literature review have been described in the chapter, and the chapter has also investigated all the possible target outcomes. It has been proven that the sports industry is ready to enter the metaverse and has already taken action to do so as it guides the sporting world into the future.

INTRODUCTION

Sport is not a very unfamiliar word for most people. It has become part of life, society, culture, religion, or belief for a long time. Sport is described as an athletic activity demanding skill or physical prowess by Dictionary.com and included explicitly as sports are racing, golf, and fishing. An activity requiring physical exertion and skill in which a person or a team competes against another or others for enjoyment, according to the Oxford Dictionary, is what sport is (Steinberg, 2022). The following definition served as the basis for the editors' inclusion criteria while compiling all the world sports

DOI: 10.4018/978-1-6684-6097-9.ch010

Copyright © 2023, IGI Global. Copying or distributing in print or electronic forms without written permission of IGI Global is prohibited.

for the Encyclopedia of World Sport from Ancient Times to the Present; if an activity includes one or more of the following competitions involving two or more teams or people; play rules that make it possible to pick a winner; a key winning objective; The relative physical prowess of the participants will determine the winner. However, chance and strategy may also be involved (Topendsport, 2022). Wrestling and boxing are typically considered the earliest sports ever played; however, it is hard to tell. Running contests would have been among the first sports practiced, as it was the most basic form of human transportation (Thoughtco, 2022). Sports have a recorded history that dates back at least 3,000 years. This explains why so many early games featured the throwing of spears, stakes, and boulders, as well as one-on-one battling with opponents. Initially, sports typically required the preparation for battle or training as a hunter. The Ancient Greeks popularized organized sports by hosting the first Olympic Games in 776 BC, which featured contests including foot and chariot racing, discus, and javelin throwing. The history of some of the most popular athletic activities today is examined in the following list, which is not inclusive (Thoughtco, 2022). The fact that boys were raised playing sports may have contributed to the ancient Greeks' love of athletics. Today, we are living in a world of sports as a career. Sports careers include athletic and non-athletic occupations and encompass any employment connected to the sporting business. Jobs in the sports industry may be found both on the field with athletes and in support roles at sporting events such as athletes, Athletic directors, and trainers. During covid-19 pandemic restriction, greatly impacted the sports world. The worldwide COVID-19 epidemic has forced the closure of athletic facilities, swimming pools, and dancing and fitness studios. As a result, many people cannot actively engage in their regular outside solo or group athletic or physical activities (UN, 2022). The popularity of video games and esports is at an all-time high as more people are stuck at home.

According to Nielsen Games Video Game Tracking (VGT), 63% of gamers have increased their game-playing time since the COVID-19 outbreak. The four nations with the most significant percentage increases are the United States (46%), France (41%), the United Kingdom (28%), and Germany (23%) (Sourcing, 2022).

Sport existed before the internet and technologies. When technologies came, the sport evolved and changed. For global competitiveness, the sports sector is being progressively affected by technological innovation. In many situations, technology is present in sports, the participation, consumption, and viewing of sports (Ratten, 2020). At this time, wearable technology may avoid injuries, GPS pinpoints movements correctly, smartphones keep everyone up to date, and athletes wear sensors that transmit real-time information to a trainer's tablet (Onlinemasters, 2022; Anshari et al., 2019; Mulyani et al., 2019). Besides that, eSport is also a combination of sport and technology. While there are amateur leagues, multiplayer video game tournaments, known as Esports, are played amongst professionals. Not all video games can be categorized as eSports, despite this. Only those video games known as 'eSports,' which may be played either solo or in teams and allow for equal competition against other players, are eSports (Mapfre, 2022). eSport has recently gained a pouch of much; it may be included in the 2024 Olympic Games. Many competitive video games such as Counter-Strike: Global Offensive, FIFA, and Call of Duty are among the most popular forms (Thiel & John, 2018). As technologies keep moving forward, there is one fuse technology becoming one of the hot topics: Metaverses" and "universe" are combined to form the term metaverse. It is generally used to allude to Web 3.0, a much-celebrated future version of the internet. Online 3-D or virtually integrated settings that provided users access to virtual reality and augmented reality experiences are predicted to grow in popularity as the internet develops (Seekingalpha, 2022). A 3D representation of the internet is how many experts view the metaverse (Anshari et al., 2022). In essence, it's a location parallel to the real world, where people spend their time online (Anshari & Almunawar, 2021). A location where users and users may engage with one another using avatars. Others contend that the metaverse in its most comprehensive form is still hypothetical (Vice, 2022).

Around 6000 BC, the earliest mention of exercise equipment as we know it was made in ancient Chinese literature, describing the usage of stone lifting, archery, and weight throwing for personal fitness and military readiness. In the 2000s, fitness technology grew widely among severe athletes and regular exercisers. The fitness industry viewed this as the ideal chance to incorporate technology into the routine workout, leading to an explosion of technologically advanced exercise gear that enables users to track, broadcast, upload, and share practically every step made (Parrott, Ruyak & Liguori, 2020; Anshari et al., 2022). Technologies and sports have been fused as technologies significantly impact the development of the sports industry through many sectors, such as equipment, training, and recovery (Hasmawati et al., 2020. Wearable monitoring devices like Fitbits are becoming more popular, and the fitness industry uses social media to create and support sports communities, such as the Facebook group "UrbanRec" or the "RunKeeper" app (SportAus, 2022). The sports industry can dive into the future technology called Metaverse. The metaverse might give a new perspective to the sports industry on how people can watch and play sports. The metaverse has enormous promise for the sports sector. It may be used to build virtual stadiums where people can engage and watch sporting events. Additionally, it may be utilized to create a virtual practice area where participants can hone their abilities. Metaverse may also be used to construct virtual environments where fans can explore and discover more about their preferred teams and players (Ojeagbase, 2022). The reason for 'Sports in Metaverse' as the title of this report is because of the influence of sport on the planet and how, in the future, it will be altered through metaverse in which when the two worlds collide, it will drive the civilization of the humankind to a step forward.

The chapter aims to get as much detail on sports technologies, how the metaverse will up turn the sports world, and the status of sports adapting in the metaverse world. In the literature review, the report will present the research that has been done before and offers data regarding the updated technologies used in the sports industry, how metaverse can bring a new concept to sports, and the current progress of implementing metaverse in sport. This chapter will also discuss and analyze the findings by providing supporting data to conclude the chapter. In conclusion, it is expected to acknowledge and identify the current state of sport in the metaverse, the future of sports in the metaverse, and the latest technologies used in the sports industry.

LITERATURE REVIEW

Current Sports Technologies

Modern sports technology has wholly changed the sporting landscape. Fans can more easily engage with the game thanks to these technologies, and athletes can perform at their best. Sensors frequently drive technology in athletic and sporting goods. Athletes can have sensors embedded in their gear, clothes, and shoes. Depending on their capabilities, sensors may be used for various purposes, from tracking health and biometrics to providing real-time results to scoreboards. Sports utilize a variety of sensors, including heart rate monitors, to measure respiration and pulse rates. Inertial sensors analyze human motion and are helpful for injury and accident recovery. The accelerometers and gyroscopes monitor position, rotation, acceleration, and speed. GPS (Global Positioning System) devices monitor outside velocity measurements. LPS (Local Positioning System) devices can more accurately capture velocity measurements indoors than GPS. Utilizing sensors for velocity-based training (VBT), performance in the weight room is monitored. Utilize sleep trackers to monitor and improve sleeping habits. The frequency and precision of how strikes or footfalls land are determined by pressure sensors. One outstanding example is the Easton Power Sensor. This attachment, which records parameters including swing speed, power, and more, is placed on the end of a bat. Another exciting piece of sports technology is the Zepp 2 Golf Sensor, which offers 3D modeling of your golf swing.

Before the 2017–18 football season, an experiment using video aid referees will start, according to the International Football Association Board (IFAB). The technology will only affect crucial choices, including goals, red cards, penalties, and mistaken identification. After a lengthy testing phase, a final decision will be made on the technology's use. The Video Assistant Referee system, popularly known as VAR, was trialed for the first time in the Eredivisie in 2012. Subsequently, more thorough testing was permitted. A pitch-side monitor was used in the FIFA Club World Cup after the successful trial of VAR in a 2016 friendly between France and Italy. The A-league used VAR in its top-tier professional league for the first time in 2017, and the MLS, Bundesliga, and Serie A soon followed. In an FA Cup game, VAR was utilized for the first time in England, and La Liga adopted the system for the 2018–19 season. The World Cup saw the most extensive usage of it as the VAR rules were formally incorporated into football by the IFAB. From the 2019–20 season onward, VAR will be utilized in the Premier League and at every level of the Champions League for what FIFA refers to as 'game-changing decisions,' such as the legitimacy of goals, penalties, red cards, and offsides ("The Evolution of Tech in Sport | Hire Intelligence UK", 2022). The "video assistant referees" use new camera technology in sports to improve refereeing. With VAR, a group of referees in the control room review and rectify each missed or non-called play, goal, penalty call, and instance of mistaken identification (Reflexion, 2022).

The Hawk-Eye Officiating System is the only ball-tracking system to have passed the rigorous ITF testing procedures. It is precise, trustworthy, and valuable. One such device that is regarded as the best in many sports is Hawk-Eye. Hawk-Eye has transformed the athletic industry with its exceptional combination of innovation, expertise, and precision. The fundamental concept is to keep an eye on the ball's trajectory during the whole game. After processing this data, lifelike representations of the ball's travels are created. Andre Agassi, a tennis professional for over 20 years, is enthused about the technology since it will provide players, spectators, and television watchers with a completely new experience of the game (Bal & Dureja, 2012). The

Hawk-Eye technology, developed in the UK, would provide a clear answer on whether the ball has crossed the line. The Hawk Eye employs a camera on the goal line that records 600 frames per second. A computer analyzes the data, which is then relayed to the referee's headset or a gadget on his wrist. Football is another sport where the method is tested as part of the goal-line evaluation. After receiving approval from the football rules committee, the Premier League of the UK has decided to implement goal-line sensors. To enhance the television match official's (TMO) decision-making and promote player safety, rugby officials deployed Hawkeye technology at the 2015 Rugby World Cup. In this instance, improved video review is used in place of the ball-tracking equipment employed in other sports. The next-generation Hawk-Eye Live, which made line calls in real-time, was used for the 2020 US Open tennis tournament (Topendsports, 2022).

How Can the Metaverse Change Sports?

Sports lovers will soon benefit from a better watching experience thanks to the metaverse. By 2030, the metaverse business is predicted to be worth $824.53 billion, according to PR Newswire. Users can communicate virtually in the metaverse, a digital realm. Companies already use this technology to organize virtual conferences and events. The metaverse will, however, also significantly influence the sports sector (Ojeagbase, 2022). The metaverse would eliminate geographical and physical constraints to provide a better experience before, during, and after games. For instance, participants in the Metaverse Sports Arena might pose for photos with athletes, talk to their idols in real time, or go to a virtual bar to meet other fans. A panoramic picture of the whole game is available to spectators during games, and they can opt to zoom into any angle to see even more information. Additionally, supporters may enter the virtual field of play and run alongside players thanks to multi-view camera technology. They may cheer on their friends who might be located far away in the real world, observe from different vantage points, or sit alongside them ("What does the metaverse mean for sport? | SportBusiness", 2022). Thanks to the Metaverse, people may purchase digital goods like sports cards, autographs, and even play highlights. Digital goods purchased on secondary marketplaces are in great demand because of the hoopla surrounding the restricted releases of sports' best stars (Comcastsportstech, 2022). The sports business is seeking new methods to make money, considering the success of eSports. The sports business is now ready to enter the realm of eSports and use the power of the metaverse to establish new revenue streams. There are predicted to be 29.6

million monthly eSports viewers in the US alone in 2022. Businesses in the sports industry may now build their virtual worlds and provide customers with extraordinary experiences thanks to NFTs and blockchain. These experiences might range from VIP treatment to behind-the-scenes access. Users are prepared to pay for these experiences. Thus, firms in the sports industry may do well by offering them. Additionally, NFTs may be used to sell virtual assets (Ojeagbase, 2022). The appearance of their placements in the metaverse will need an adjustment on the part of brands and businesses, just as they had to learn how to adapt to new marketing channels like social media. Athletes may visit fields and stadiums in the virtual environment "Nikeland," which Nike and Roblox jointly created, to participate in sports like tag and dodgeball. According to Nike, the 2018 World Cup and Super Bowl will feature real-time highlights from athletic events. Players can use mobile device accelerometers to synchronize their motions in Nikeland with those in real life. To coincide with the Kentucky Derby, Stella Artois teamed up with Zed Run, an NFT platform where users can breed, train, and exchange virtual racing horses (Comcastsportstech, 2022). Brands may reach a bigger audience among sports viewers. A more significant number of options for integrated advertisements and branded partnerships across virtual worlds have surfaced as gaming and eSports have become more widely accepted. The most prominent native in-game ad example is FIFA's decision to introduce its programmatic bidding platform, which gives a variety of purchasers access to in-game ad space (Thompson, 2022).

Formula One drivers, for instance, may use immersive training for athletes to put on VR goggles and simulate the sensation of driving the route for an upcoming race so that they can learn the road and its turns in virtual reality (Marr, 2022). NBA commissioner Adam Silver presented "Coach Nat," a basketball coach from the metaverse, during the 2022 NBA All-Star Game in Cleveland. The upcoming crop of NBA talents is developed and trained by these artificially intelligent coaches. The coach will help young basketball players in the metaverse hone their skills (Tsui, 2022). The metaverse will alter how individuals maintain their health. Capable of doing actions like entering a boxing ring for brief sparring or possibly entering the ring versus AI (artificial intelligence) to practice techniques and playing team sports, such as football, from the comfort of one's home. Start an online football game with your friends versus an AI squad, or you might play a 5v5 football match with people worldwide ("What does the metaverse mean for the future of sports?", 2022). Even if they could be on the other side, the top sports trainers worldwide can be trained within one's living room via hologram.

The alternatives are nearly endless in this case. Sports training is already being used in the metaverse by businesses like cutting-edge bicycle maker Capti. Capti's gamified cycling platform relies on 3D environments created in the Unreal Engine, unlike popular manufacturers Peloton and Zwift. The platform may now be used with virtual worlds already in existence. In this way, it is feasible that individuals may ride their bikes to travel in Second Life or compete in Mario Cart races (ISPO, 2022).

Current Proof of Sports Existence in The Metaverse

The public land auction for high-end fan caves has begun in the Sports Metaverse. Landowners can purchase these structures in the first phase. There is a virtual environment dedicated to sports called the Sports Metaverse. These caverns make it possible to hang out with friends from around the globe, personalize their NFTs, play pool, watch sporting events, advertise, and lease their property to renters. It will also be possible to develop land with a specific use, such as a stadium or event space. The Sports Metaverse bills itself as the first virtual environment dedicated only to sports, bringing together well-known athletes, companies, and organizations. Users may exchange NFTs, purchase real estate, engage with famous athletes, and attend sporting events. Chris Worsey, CEO and Co-Founder of SportsIcon, stated, "we have together the greatest metaverse architects in the field, the most forward-thinking web3 companies, and some of the largest sports people of all time." According to Chris Worsey, the Sports Metaverse is the new frontier in sports, where billions of fans will be immediately linked and have access to their favorite sports brands and symbols (Economictimes, 2022). The NFTs feature a masterclass taught by notable sports figures. Football professionals like Romelu Lukaku, a striker for Chelsea in the English Premier League and Belgium's national team, provide fascinating insights into their experiences and training accomplishments. These contain videos of the celebrity on the practice field and interviews discussing the star's life story and how it shaped who they are now. The initiative also captured Lukaku, who will make a 3D appearance in the sports metaverse (Globenewswire, 2022).

The NBA and Google teamed together to bring fans to an immersive 3D metaverse called Google Pixel Arena on April 16, 2022, using the NBA app. Through the gyroscopes of their phones, it enables spectators to enter a 3D basketball arena and experience the daily life of NBA players. They may alter players' clothes and accessories, move them about the stadium or even the locker rooms, and a virtual player will represent each user. Users may participate in games on Google Pixel Arena and try to win as many points as possible. Users may interact with basketball lovers worldwide and enjoy the joy of the game by viewing 3D shot recaps of individuals' and teams' performances after games (Tsui, 2022). With its NBA Top Shots project, the NBA has also relied on digital fan merchandising since 2020. In this instance, the focus is on a particular category of trading cards—video trading cards. Each digital video trading card depicts an important event in the history of the NBA, and these NFTs may be collected and exchanged. LeBron James' dunk from the LA Lakers' game against the Houston Rockets on February 6, 2020, was the most expensive play, selling for $387,600 (ISPO, 2022). The National Basketball Association (NBA) has introduced a new virtual reality (VR) experience using Meta's Quest platform to engage fans in North America throughout the postseason. Anyone in the US or Canada who is at least 18 years old may visit 'NBA Lane,' advertised as an 'NBA- themed Wonderland' and can be accessed through the Horizon Worlds program. Games, content, and other interactive elements are provided throughout the experience, enhancing the league's reputation in the metaverse. In a free throw shootout game, for instance, participants strive to make the most baskets, while in a "low gravity dunk contest," competitors try to wow the judges by defying gravity (MCCASKILL, 2022).

With the assistance of Sony's virtual reality specialists, Manchester City has started construction on the first football stadium in the metaverse. The club's stadium will transform into the heart of Manchester City in a virtual reality environment thanks to image analysis and skeletal-tracking technology developed by Hawk-Eye, a tech and entertainment behemoth division. In the future, according to club executives working on the initiative, Manchester City will be able to pack the Eithad Stadium virtually several times over, enabling fans who may never travel to Manchester to watch live matches from the comfort of their homes anywhere in the globe (Cunningham, 2022). When Milan's league match versus Fiorentina was televised in this virtual environment on May 1, football fans in the Middle East and North Africa (Mena) area had the chance to see a world first that none of Europe's other top leagues had yet to try. With unique, cost-free digital tokens, Serie A offered 10,000 fans in the Mena area access to its metaverse virtual room, which included elements like a chat window for user interaction, a game to play, and a TV screen to watch the match (BBC, 2022). Manchester United has started producing and selling digital fan gear. Fans may buy these as NFTs to buy, accumulate, and possibly wear in the Metaverse in the future (ISPO, 2022).

ANALYSIS AND DISCUSSION

Current Sports Technologies

Technologies put the sports industry at the next level, which shows the standards and class. Technologies improve many factors in sports, from accuracy to performance. In sports, accuracy is critical to determine if it is a foul or not, the score, and many more. One of the technologies is a sensor. The sensor is a crucial device in tournaments or training that produces precision output. The 94Fifty is a rubberized indoor/outdoor ball that weighs less than 20 grams and is equipped with nine accelerometers (0.7 ounces). The sensors can measure speed, force (360-degree view), ball rotation, and ball arc. Additionally, the sensors can gauge the angle at which the ball, an inflated item, contacts a surface. The weight and rotation of the ball don't seem to be impacted by the sensors in the 94fifty. The sensors can also endure the force of dribbling, shooting on the backboard and rim, and passing to another player. The ball performs and feels exactly like a typical basketball. The sensors are compatible with Android and iOS, use Qi wireless charging, have a range of 90 feet from the smartphone used to collect the data, and have a battery life of up to eight hours. The Qi wireless charger operates on the magnetic induction theory, which enables power to be efficiently supplied to devices across short distances. Shot arc degree may be accurately measured using the 94Fifty instrumented ball. Coaches and players may find it helpful to get this information, especially if it is given in real-time. As a result, the 94Fifty offers trustworthy knowledge and prompt feedback for players and coaches on dribbling and shot angle. It will be interesting to observe if using the tool improves performance and engagement (Abdelrasoul, Mahmoud, Stergiou & Katz, 2015).

In football, VAR (Video Assistant Referee system) is one of the famous and latest technologies used in helping the referee and assistant referee analyze and execute the best and fair decision. As a fan of the English Premier League, the decision rule by VAR enhances the quality and standard of the referee and reduces human error. Motion capture technology has been utilized in recent research by the University of Bath to evaluate the efficacy of football's Video Assistant Referee (VAR) systems. According to the study, VAR helps avoid apparent errors but is not precise enough to render consistently accurate assessments. Following contentious rulings that might alter the game's outcome, several people have also questioned the accuracy and implementation of VAR, including well-known analysts like Gary Lineker and Alan Shearer. VAR critics also claim that it disrupts the game's rhythm. Nevertheless, some studies indicate that the frequency of fouls, offsides, and yellow cards has lessened. The Centre for Analysis of Motion, Entertainment Research, and Applications (CAMERA) at the University of Bath's Dr. Pooya Soltani stated: "VAR helps referees make accurate choices, but this study has proven it has distinct limitations. The frame rate and resolution of the VAR cameras occasionally cannot keep up with the quick movements, resulting in occasional blurring of the player or the ball (Bath, 2022).

The Hawk-Eye is one of the technologies currently used in tennis to detect the result or point in a match, whether in or out. Tennis is a fast-paced sport with rules regarding scoring points depending on the area where the ball hits the court. The International Tennis Federation evaluated Hawk-accuracy Eyes in approximately 800 trials before implementing the device at crucial competitions. According to Paul Hawkins, managing director of Hawk-Eye technology, the system is loved by everyone in tennis. According to Hawkins, Hawk-Eye had an average margin of error of 3.6 millimeters (0.14 inches) and was around 99.9 percent accurate. He continued, "Hawk-Eye isn't perfect, but it's pretty damn close." Hawk-Eye has placed ten cameras all around the tennis courts at Wimbledon. The system combines the ball's trajectory with images from the cameras to rebuild its most likely path. Hawk-Eye only shows what was statistically most likely to have happened, not what did (ESPN, 2022).

How Can the Metaverse Change Sports?

Metaverse is still new but not yet entirely there, but it will not stop from influencing—other factors such as sport. People love to watch sports and support their favorite ones. Metaverse can help fans and supporters gain a new set of experiences to watch their preferred sport in the future. With the element in the metaverse, sports fan can watch their team winning the match anywhere they want. Through multi-view camera technology, fans can even enter the field and stand beside the players, cheer alongside the football team, and observe the game from various angles. Finally, Metaverse enables people to interact with their friends in the same space even if they are physically apart. Fans will no longer attend sporting events but rather be in the thick of them while lounging on the couch or working at their computers (ISPO, 2022).

A new way of Marketing for the sports industry is through Metaverse. The teams cannot only promo or sell their services and merchandise but also provide a new form of virtual advertising for their sponsorship. The metaverse has no limitations or barriers, so the team can promote and sell NFT the way they want. This can help increase clubs' revenue and attract more sponsorship to the clubs. To represent digital trading sports cards, sporting events, digital memorabilia, and other sports-related objects, sports NFTs are verifiably unique digital assets developed on a blockchain. The issuing of sports NFTs gives fans a new method to interact with their favorite teams and athletes while giving athletes, clubs, and sports sponsors an opportunity to monetize in new ways. For instance, many fans are willing to spend money to acquire a piece of rare, valuable baseball memorabilia or a limited edition of virtual memorabilia of their favorite basketball team. Because of this, sports NFTs frequently trade for tens of thousands of dollars or more, and the value of some of the most valuable coins has significantly increased since they were issued. Autograph, a sports NFT platform founded by professional football player Tom Brady, offers autographed limited-edition sports collectibles from many top currents and former players, including Tony Hawk, Wayne Gretzky, and Naomi Osaka. Autograph supports NFTs that run on Polygon and Ethereum (Cryptonews, 2022).

In the metaverse as a new method for training in a unique and futuristic. Athletes and ordinary humans can also train in the metaverse for their health. To become a truly great athlete in any sport, repetitions are the key. But it can be challenging to get those reps in because of things like team availability and setup, restrictions, the physical toll on bodies, and even weather. Players may practice whenever they want, thanks to immersive learning, just as if they were on a field, court, slope, rink, or course. Athletes can speed up their training schedule while traveling by using a virtual reality (VR) sports environment. This enables them to complete total reps in the most realistic setting possible, ensuring they are fully prepared to give their all when it counts. The repetition of knowledge and skills necessary for peak athletic performance is made possible by Strivr's virtual reality sports training. Football players, particularly quarterbacks, spend weeks studying playbooks and videos to grasp the unique offenses that their coaches have created. Carson Palmer, a former quarterback for the Arizona Cardinals, had to memorize up to 250 plays each season. Palmer discovered that the training was more effective and enjoyable with Strivr's Immersive Learning system. He could don the headset home and be instantly transported back to field practice. He would be immersed in a realistic recreation of the play, with the action unfolding from his point of view almost precisely as he would experience it on the field (Strivr, 2022).

Current Proof of Sports Existence in The Metaverse

The sports industry has already shown its interest in the metaverse. As stated in the literature review, several sports clubs and organizations have engaged with technology companies to work together and achieve their objective of realizing the metaverse. The sports metaverse by SportsIcon is specifically combining the sports world and metaverse and provides many virtual services and activities related to sports. The sports metaverse shows the success of the implementation to the world. Another project called Sport Metaverse is a project being tested by blockchain sports fandom company Zetly. It uses the BSV blockchain's tokenized assets and the potential of VR/AR to forge deeper bonds between fans and their favorite sports teams. Based on fans' emotional connections with their favorite teams, Zetly is creating what it refers to as an 'All in One Sports Platform.' Beyond just purchasing tickets and supporting from the stands, interacting with the VR/AR features and tokenized digital environment will give them a greater sense of belonging and influence (Coingeek, 2022).

The National Basketball Association (NBA) is a sports organization that has already started developing a metaverse project. Many projects are already published in the metaverse world, such as google pixel arena and selling digital fan merchandise. To commemorate its 75th anniversary season, the league launched the NBA Lane campaign in October. The ad honors the best players in the game and the contemporary stars who have succeeded them. The NBA Lane experience can now be experienced first-hand, thanks to virtual reality. NBA Lane is accessible to adults in the United States and Canada through Horizon Worlds on Meta Quest 2 until June 30. Basketball enthusiasts may enter the NBA-themed metaverse through the immersive VR experience and celebrate their passion for the sport up close. A few entertaining pursuits in NBA Lane include Free Throw Shootout and Playing this minigame against friends. The person who makes the most baskets in motion wins. Fly high and overcome physics to win the Low-Gravity Dunk Contest. Sit back and watch the fantastic NBA entertainment on the big screen in front of the arena. Game highlights, player interviews, and other NBA content will all be included in the clips. Hold the newly released, virtual reality-recreated Larry O'Brien trophy for your selfie in the NBA Trophy Room. In virtual reality, take a selfie and show it to your pals in the real world (NBA, 2022).

Football is one of the largest sports in the world, with massive fans. Football also not missing the benefits that the metaverse brings. Like other sports, football has used many technologies to achieve standards and the best quality for the players, teams, and supporters. Currently, football is focusing on upgrading fans' virtual experience in watching the tournament and matches through the metaverse. FIFA, the body that oversees and develops football internationally, has submitted a trademark application for 'WORLD CUP 2026' to enter the metaverse and embrace the cryptocurrency world. FIFA plans to offer virtual stock trading, virtual clothes, virtual sports equipment, and services for processing digital and cryptocurrency transactions, according to the application submitted to the USPTO on July 14 (Cryptoflies, 2022). This move shows FIFA believes in the metaverse and is ready to invest more into it. A realistic metaverse simulation of the Etihad Stadium is being created by Manchester City and Sony so that fans from all over the world can visit it using their avatars. The possible migration into metaverse stadiums starts when many consumers are less concerned about the distinction between complex and possibly hazardous or inaccessible reality and ultra-realistic digital experiences. Somewhere along that route, a person's presence in a real drum loses much of its significance as a sign of their fandom. They may believe that the real thing is immensely more rewarding, but who are the 'true fans' then, and will they be able to make a convincing argument against change they do not like, and what will happen when reality can no longer be so readily defined (FT, 2022).

CONCLUSION

The sports world keeps up with globalization by using technologies to play a significant role in advancing and excelling in sports. The sports industry can now accept the metaverse as part of sports. These two worlds will be helping each other as the metaverse now is still developing and need more user participation, and sports can provide enormous user from the fan. Sports organizations such as NBA and FIFA are started working on building a metaverse project which shows the sports industry needs the metaverse. The metaverse will significantly impact the sports industry, especially in marketing and sponsorship. The Sports fan should view this transformation positively as it benefits the sports world and the fan itself as technologies constantly be updated and move forward to the future. The emergence of eSports can also help boost the partnership between the metaverse and the sports world as eSport have elements almost like the metaverse. Even though technology and sport are well paired, Metaverse is unique and different from the physical sport; now, it might be better for eSport occasionally.

REFERENCES

Abdelrasoul, E., Mahmoud, I., Stergiou, P., & Katz, L. (2015). The Accuracy of a Real Time Sensor in an Instrumented Basketball. *Procedia Engineering*, *112*, 202–206. doi:10.1016/j.proeng.2015.07.200

Anshari, M., Alas, Y., & Sulaiman, E. (2019). Smartphone addictions and nomophobia among youth. *Vulnerable Children and Youth Studies*, *14*(3), 242–247. doi:10.1080/17450128.2019.1614709

Anshari, M., & Almunawar, M. N. (2021). Adopting open innovation for SMEs and industrial revolution 4.0. *Journal of Science and Technology Policy Management*.

Anshari, M., Syafrudin, M., Fitriyani, N. L., & Razzaq, A. (2022). Ethical Responsibility and Sustainability (ERS) Development in a Metaverse Business Model. *Sustainability*, *14*(23), 15805. doi:10.3390u142315805

Bal, B., & Dureja, G. (2012). Hawk Eye: A Logical Innovative Technology Use in Sports for Effective Decision Making. *Sport Science Review*, *21*(1-2), 107–119. doi:10.2478/v10237-012-0006-6

Bath. (2022). *Motion capture reveals why VAR in football struggles with offside decisions*. Retrieved 23 September 2022, from https://www.bath.ac.uk/announcements/motion-capture-reveals-why-var-in-football-struggles-with-offside-decisions/#:~:text=The%20study%20suggests%20that%20VAR,red%20cards%2C%20penalties%20and%20offsides

BBC. (2022). *What does football look like in the metaverse?* Retrieved 22 September 2022, from https://www.bbc.com/sport/football/61473631

Coingeek. (2022). *Zetly's 'Sport Metaverse' gives fans an all-in-one bonding experience with their favorite teams.* Retrieved 23 September 2022, from https://coingeek.com/zetly-sport-metaverse-gives-fans-an-all-in-one-bonding-experience-with-their-favorite-teams/

Comcastsportstech. (2022). *Four Ways the Metaverse May Impact Sports Tech | Comcast SportsTech*. Retrieved 22 September 2022, from https://www.comcastsportstech.com/inside-track/four-ways-the-metaverse-may-impact-sports-tech/

Cryptoflies. (2022). *FIFA to Bring WORLD CUP 2026 to the Metaverse*. Retrieved 23 September 2022, from https://blog.cryptoflies.com/fifa-to-bring-world-cup-2026-to-the-metaverse/

Cryptonews. (2022). *Sports NFTs: What are They and Why are They So Popular?* Retrieved 23 September 2022, from https://cryptonews.com/exclusives/sports-nfts-what-are-they-why-are-they-so-popular.htm#:~:text=What%20are%20sports%20NFTs%3F,other%20types%20of%20sports%20items

Economictimes. (2022). *Sports Metaverse launches virtual land sale*. Retrieved 22 September 2022, from https://economictimes.indiatimes.com/markets/cryptocurrency/sports-metaverse-launches-virtual-land-sale/articleshow/92876154.cms?from=mdr

ESPN. (2022). *Study: Hawk-Eye not as accurate as people think*. Retrieved 23 September 2022, from https://www.espn.com/sports/tennis/wimbledon08/news/story?id=3452293

FT. (2022). *Football's future is in the metaverse*. Retrieved 23 September 2022, from https://www.ft.com/content/ee267372-15e6-459c-b786-da605f8d0258

Globenewswire. (2022). *SportsIcon Previews The Sports Metaverse with Legendary Athletes*. Retrieved 22 September 2022 from https://www.globenewswire.com/news-release/2022/03/23/2408882/0/en/SportsIcon-Previews-The-Sports-Metaverse-with-Legendary-Athletes.html

Hasmawati, F., Samiha, Y. T., Razzaq, A., & Anshari, M. (2020). Understanding nomophobia among digital natives: Characteristics and challenges. *Journal of Critical Reviews*, *7*(13), 122–131.

ISPO. (2022). *Metaverse: The Revolution of the Sports World*. Retrieved 22 September 2022, from https://www.ispo.com/en/trends/metaverse-revolution-sports-world

Mapfre. (2022). *The growing trend of Esports*. Retrieved 21 September 2022 from https://www.mapfre.com/en/insights/innovation/growing-trend-esports/

Marr, B. (2022). *How the Metaverse Is Changing Sports*. Retrieved 22 September 2022, from https://bernardmarr.com/how-the-metaverse-is-changing-sports/

McCaskill, S. (2022). *NBA launches Meta Quest VR environment to engage fans during playoffs*. Retrieved 22 September 2022, from https://www.sportspromedia.com/news/nba-lane-vr-meta-metaverse/

Mulyani, M. A., Razzaq, A., Sumardi, W. H., & Anshari, M. (2019, August). Smartphone adoption in mobile learning scenario. In *2019 International Conference on Information Management and Technology (ICIMTech)* (Vol. 1, pp. 208-211). IEEE. 10.1109/ICIMTech.2019.8843755

NBA. (2022). *NBA Lane comes to life through virtual reality*. Retrieved 23 September 2022, from https://www.nba.com/news/nba-lane-horizon-worlds-meta

Ojeagbase, S. (2022). *How Will Metaverse Transform Sports Industry?* Retrieved 21 September 2022, from https://www.completesports.com/how-will-metaverse-transform-sports-industry/

Onlinemasters. (2022). *How Technology is Revolutionizing Sports Training | Ohio University*. Retrieved 20 September 2022 from https://onlinemasters.ohio.edu/blog/how-technology-is-revolutionizing-sports-training/#:~:text=Compared%20to%20whiteboards%20and%20post,communication

Parrott, M., Ruyak, J., & Liguori, G. (2020). The History of Exercise Equipment. ACSM's Health &Amp. *Fitness Journal, 24*(6), 5–8. doi:10.1249/FIT.0000000000000612

Ratten, V. (2020). Sport technology: A commentary. *The Journal of High Technology Management Research, 31*(1), 100383. doi:10.1016/j.hitech.2020.100383

Reflexion. (2022). *New Examples of Sports Technology That's Changing The Game*. Retrieved 21 September 2022, from https://reflexion.co/blog/sports-technology/

Seekingalpha. (2022). *The Metaverse? What It Is & What You Should Know*. Retrieved 21 September 2022, from https://seekingalpha.com/article/4472812-what-is-metaverse

Sourcing. (2022). *COVID-19 Is Taking Gaming And eSports To The Next Level - HKTDC Newsbites*. Retrieved 20 September 2022, from https://sourcing.hktdc.com/newsbites/covid-19-is-taking-gaming-and-esports-to-the-next-level/

SportAus. (2022). Retrieved 21 September 2022, from https://www.sportaus.gov.au/participation/trends#holistic_health

Steinberg, L. (2022). *What Defines A "Sport"?* Retrieved 20 September 2022, from https://www.forbes.com/sites/leighsteinberg/2018/07/28/what-defines-a-sport/?sh=630d00aa2d66

Strivr. (2022). *Virtual Reality sports training systems*. Strivr. Retrieved 23 September 2022, from https://www.strivr.com/solutions/industries/sports/

The Evolution of Tech in Sport | Hire Intelligence UK. (2022). Retrieved 21 September 2022, from https://www.hire-intelligence.co.uk/evolution-of-technology-in-sport/

Thiel, A., & John, J. (2018). Is eSport a 'real' sport? Reflections on the spread of virtual competitions. *European Journal For Sport And Society*, *15*(4), 311–315. doi:10.1080/16138171.2018.1559019

Thompson, H. (2022). *As sports enter the metaverse, could brands win big?* Retrieved 22 September 2022, from https://www.thedrum.com/opinion/2022/07/20/sports-enter-

Thoughtco, (2022). *The History of Sports*. Retrieved 20 September 2022 from https://www.thoughtco.com/history-of-sports-1992447

Topendsport. (2022). *What Is A Sport?* Retrieved 20 September 2022 from https://www.topendsports.com/sport/what-is-a-sport.htm

Topendsports. (2022). *Technology in Sports*. Retrieved 21 September 2022, from https://www.topendsports.com/resources/technology.htm

Tsui, V. (2022). *What Happens When Metaverse Meets Sports Leagues?* Retrieved 22 September 2022, from https://www.jumpstartmag.com/what-happens-when-metaverse-meets-sports-leagues/

UN. (2022). *The impact of COVID-19 on sport, physical activity, and well-being and its effects on social development*. Retrieved 20 September 2022, from https://www.un.org/development/desa/dspd/2020/05/covid-19-sport/

Vice. (2022). *What Is the Metaverse? An Explanation.* Retrieved 21 September 2022, from https://www.vice.com/en/article/93bmyv/what-is-the-metaverse-internet-technology-vr

What does the metaverse mean for sport? | SportBusiness. (2022). Retrieved 22 September 2022, from https://www.sportbusiness.com/2021/11/what-does-the-metaverse-mean-for-sport/

What does the metaverse mean for the future of sports? (2022). Retrieved 22 September 2022, from https://www.javelinsportsinc.com/post/what-does-the-metaverse-mean-for-the-

Chapter 11
Applications of the Metaverse as Disruptive Innovation

Nur Nazihah Assyakirah Haji Isa
Universiti Brunei Darussalam, Brunei

ABSTRACT

The virtual world was made possible by big changes in computer hardware, graphics software, and computer software. Considering the function of a metaverse, which is a 3D virtual world with computing infrastructure that is available to everyone. By making products and services that are much better, more affordable, and easier to use, disruptive technologies can grow the industries they are already in or start whole new ones. Disruptive technology offers a big change in how things are done or processes are run. The metaverse uses a number of useful technologies to give users 3D experiences that are both immersive and unique. Marketing, education, travel, and healthcare are among the industries that the metaverse might have an impact on. This chapter discusses how these technologies could be used in digital medicine and the future of the medical metaverse. The authors also talk about the research that is being done to speed up the metaverse's adoption in global education and make it a better place to learn and teach.

DOI: 10.4018/978-1-6684-6097-9.ch011

Copyright © 2023, IGI Global. Copying or distributing in print or electronic forms without written permission of IGI Global is prohibited.

INTRODUCTION

Disruptive technologies either expand the industries they enter or create whole new ones when they bring products and services to market that are much more affordable, superior, and convenient. These disruptive technologies often have a negative impact on how individuals engage in the labour field by allowing those who lack technology literacy to do so and compete there (Kostoff et al., 2004). Disruptive technologies have the potential to either produce whole new technological products or result in substantial paradigm shifts in those already on the market when used to address new commercialization challenges (such as in systems or operations). They might potentially be fresh technological advancements or creative fusions of already existing ones (Walsh & Linton, 2000).

When physical and virtual space converge, the metaverse, an augmented virtual reality, is produced. Users engage in virtual interactions with one another and engage in virtual activities that may eventually result in real-world experiences while inhabiting this artificial environment. A virtual world that exists apart from reality is referred to as the "metaverse." Meta, which stands for transcendence and virtuality, and universe, which stands for the entire world, are its key phrases. According to Kim (2020), this phrase refers to the "digitized planet," a brand-new universe exemplified by digital media such as cellphones and the internet. Much effort and research went into making the metaverse a reality once the concept first emerged. The metaverse is a networked collection of 3-D virtual environments (Anshari et al., 2022). the first versions of Second Life: Mozilla Hubs, VRChat, Furcadia, and OpenSimulator (Siau et al., 2010). Virtual reality (VR) and augmented reality (AR), which enable multi-sensory interaction with digital people, things, and locations, are the foundations upon which the metaverse is created (Mystakidis, 2022). Even though the metaverse is still in its infancy, 3-D virtual worlds are already being utilised in many other industries, including healthcare, education, and others (Eschenbrenner et al., 2008; Thomason & Aydin, 2021). The following technologies are essential to the Metaverse architecture: blockchain, robotics, the internet of things, augmented reality (AR), virtual reality (VR), user interfaces, computer vision, artificial intelligence (AI), edge computing, computer networks, and hardware infrastructure (Anshari & Hamdan, 2022).

Metaverse makes use of several contemporary technologies. It develops an economic system based on blockchain technology, provides an immersive experience based on augmented reality, and uses digital twin technology to create a mirror image of the actual world. A variety of cutting-edge technologies must be included in the "Metaverse" tool to create a breakthrough Internet application and social structure that integrates, interacts, and links the real and virtual worlds (Ning et al., 2021). The potential effects transmitted by the Metaverse as one of the most recent expressions of technical growth have recently generated a lot of interest due to the rising chance that it will have a substantial impact on society in the near future (Razzaq et al., 2018). The Metaverse is a compelling and alluring socio-technical vision that claims shared, immersive, persistent, and transcendent cyberspace will be embedded with a variety of sensing devices, pervasive computing systems, and wireless communication networks that can perceive, think, feel, and react to human users and their virtual representations in the form of avatars with multiple identities and characters (Bibri, 2022). Due to the fusion of data-driven and immersive technologies, the Metaverse will be a platform on a 3D network of virtual worlds where people may socialise, engage, connect, learn, work, retail, play, and more.

HEALTHCARE AND METAVERSE

Healthcare is one of the most important components in guaranteeing the overall, physical, social, and mental health of all people globally. The basic objective of every healthcare system is to allocate its resources to projects that improve, maintain, repair, and advance healthcare services. Additionally, it significantly aids in a country's efficient industrialisation and economic expansion (Anshari, 2019). The connections between carers, patients, and other important stakeholder groups have improved as a result of this sector's considerable exposure to technological advancement and rapid expansion. The advent of telemedicine services has not significantly changed this tactic (Chengoden et al, 2022). Recent quick technological advances have unmatched chances to enhance healthcare (Anshari & Almunawar, 2019).

Systems for intelligent healthcare and smart health are proliferating in the healthcare industry (Anshari & Almunawar, 2018). Three cutting-edge technologies, including data science, metaverse, and artificial intelligence, are having an impact on and transforming the healthcare industry. The usage of metaverse in healthcare is one example of the disruptive developments that are anticipated in many areas of our life (Anshari et al., 2021). Physical contact between patients and doctors has been necessary for decades in order for doctors to diagnose patients' problems, prescribe medications, and conduct surgeries on patients (Marzaleh et al., 2022). The introduction of telehealth services has only marginally altered this strategy (Anshari et al., 2018). The recent fast breakthroughs in technology provide unparalleled opportunities to improve healthcare (Yang et al., 2022; Semivolos & Anshari, 2022). According to Chen and Zhang (2022), smart health, which integrates robotics with artificial intelligence, virtual reality, augmented reality, the Internet of medical devices, Web 3.0, intelligent cloud, edge, and quantum computing, offers a new approach in healthcare. There are two categories of digital health applications in the metaverse environment (Anshari et al., 2021).

The first is immersive environments, which are virtual or hybrid worlds that health care professionals and patients interact with for educational, therapeutic, or assistive purposes. The second is digital twins, which are representations of real-world entities that exist in virtual worlds and can be modified to gain insights (Damar, 2022). The application of augmented reality in the health industry has a substantial influence on the education and knowledge acquisition of prospective medical professionals.

Potential Application of The Metaverse to Healthcare

The Metaverse in medicine greatly assists in delivering complete healthcare as compared to the "handicraft workshop model" of healthcare, where diagnoses and treatments vary from doctor to doctor and hospital to hospital. Decisions would be made in line with the expert's recommendations and the results of the many Metaverse supporting technologies in a scenario with comprehensive healthcare (Anshari, Almunawar & Masri, 2022). There are several medical applications for the metaverse, such as research, physical examination, diagnosis, and insurance (Chengoden et al, 2022).

Surgeries

The metaverse is a crucial component of medical technology, especially in surgery. Currently, doctors use tools like VR headsets and haptic gloves to imitate actual surgical operations. This increases preparedness and efficiency in the operating room. By giving them quick access to data through augmented reality, surgeons can carry out procedures more quickly. Augmented reality can provide surgeons with rapid, easy, hands-free information on patients by superimposing 3D virtual representations onto the patient's body. Teachers and lecturers might do complicated operations in three dimensions in the metaverse.

According to a research by Morimoto et al. (2022), spine surgeons have had to adopt minimally invasive spine surgery (MISS), which has a high radiation exposure rate, over the past 20 years. Due to a lack of navigational signals and indirect vision, the digital revolution in spine surgery is accelerating. The 3D reconstruction images utilised during spine surgery can only be seen on a 2D flat monitor. Advanced spatial imagining 3D holographic viewing technologies help the digital transformation of spine surgery. Surface topography is used to examine posture. Because of its precise diagnosis and little radiation exposure, it is growing in popularity.

To gather patient data and facilitate patient monitoring, IoMT wearable sensors employed a concept for a device that uses augmented reality and aims to operate on the maxillofacial bones. The head-mounted wearable device used in the AR system captures a person's face traits and facilitates maxillofacial bone surgery. The product design assists practitioners in constructing a virtual plan by superimposing the patient details (Badiali et al., 2014).

Medical Diagnosis

The process of determining a patient's ailment from their symptoms is referred to as medical diagnosis. With the use of a number of cutting-edge technologies, including as extended digital twins, blockchain, 5G, and MIoT models that are AR and VR enabled, the usage of the Metaverse in healthcare substantially assists in the correct diagnosis of a patient's medical conditions. By overcoming its limitations in terms of connection, integration with and between real and virtual worlds, and human-computer interaction, the current medical IoT can be enhanced by the metaverse. Utilizing AR/VR glasses with the MIoT may help with holographic creation, emulation, real-world interaction, and integration, which makes complex problems in the healthcare sector easier to handle (Chengoden et al, 2022). Holography's applications in the medical sector have been thoroughly examined by Javaid et al. (2020). Experts from the real world and the metaverse may help medical professionals provide high-quality healthcare and diagnostics by talking with them and being present in any location digitally. This enables a treatment plan that complies with the standards set by the relevant regulatory organisations. The integration of blockchain technology with distributed ledger technology in the Metaverse will enable an efficient method of storing, exchanging, and programming health-based digital assets across multiple platforms, allowing the data to be used for making more informed and accurate diagnoses of a variety of medical conditions.

Ophthalmology

As we make tremendous progress towards making the Metaverse a reality, we are exploring the possible uses of the Metaverse in healthcare, particularly in the field of ophthalmology. Ophthalmology is a medical speciality that is particularly well-positioned for a range of Metaverse applications due to the visual nature of this new virtual technology that gives opportunities for unique applications. Potential applications include the creation of lifelike consulting avatars, individualised healthcare through data linking, and potential medicinal uses.

Users may interact and connect with virtual objects and other users in the Metaverse, where they also create their own avatars and personal assets. They may interact with one other and the virtual world by employing digital avatars as representations of themselves, as opposed to the fixed two-dimensional (2D) interface of video consultations (Park et al., 2021). Additionally, avatars are increasing the realism and "personal-touch" of remote consultations by making virtual diagnostic methods combining VR and AR more palpable (Iskander et al., 2021).

Clinical Applications That Could Be Made

a) *Education*

The general population may learn about eye health through VR and AR, according to studies by Gunasekeran et al. (2020). After using these immersive technologies in EyeCU, patients' awareness of glaucoma and the need of eye screening significantly increased, making remote health education more scaleable.

b) *Therapeutics*

Some of the therapeutic uses of AR and VR include surgical planning and execution, low vision therapy, amblyopia therapy, and even myopia management in children. Image-guided surgery, minimally invasive surgery, surgical planning, and simulation utilising VR simulators may all be done by surgeons using a surgery console. Due to the current introduction of 5G networks, network speeds have greatly risen, enabling the development of telesurgery, which in turn decreases healthcare costs, increases accessibility, and realises its promise for acute care (Abujassar et al., 2021).

c) *Diagnostics*

Using extended reality, it is possible to create immersive and interactive diagnostic content, display ocular imaging data, assess visual function, and test the visual field. Patients can understand how vision loss impacts function by using augmented reality (AR) and virtual reality (VR), including how glaucoma affects everyday activities, how vision-related impairments affect people, and how visual field loss affects functional vision (Jones et al., 2020; Goh et al., 2018; Lam et al., 2020; Gopalakrishnan et al., 2020).

Patient Monitoring

Due to the telepresence, digital twinning, and blockchain convergence, the healthcare sector will tremendously benefit from the Metaverse, especially in terms of patient monitoring. Telemedicine, sometimes referred to as telepresence in medicine, provides remote medical care (Gao & Gadekallu, 2022). A digital twin is a virtual, digital version of a product, system, or person created using real-world data that assists in comprehending its genuine counterpart. These patient test dummies can be used in emergency situations to predict how treatments or drugs will impact patients before they are even given. Medical data is among the most delicate and important types of data, thus employing blockchain technology may assist store and transfer them securely so that the data is not changed and is not jeopardised. The usage of AR/VR technologies for patient monitoring gives the user a sensation of "being there." Both patient-physician contacts and interactions between patients and members of their families are included by this. Patient monitoring via the Metaverse has the potential to significantly improve a patient's health state and consequently foster a comfortable environment for the patient by fostering meaningful connections between patients, healthcare providers, and family members.

EDUCATION AND METAVERSE

The virtual environment, which offers lifelike representations of people and may enhance the social elements of teaching and learning, is one of many causes contributing to the increased interest in the educational environment. Due to the fact that the term "Metaverse" is still relatively new, the study fills this gap by assessing the state-of-the-art of research in this area. As the metaverse has quickly assimilated into contemporary society, certain technologically based metaverse applications have already been implemented in schooling. Understanding the concept, the many types of technology, and examples of their application to education in the metaverse is crucial.

There are ways to use "Second Life," a virtual world, in combination with learning management systems, Metaverse, and Second Life. Focusing on the virtuality aspect, it was suggested that the Metaverse may be the next place where people might assemble and interact socially, mandating proactive use of it by higher education for teaching and learning purposes. In addition, it is said that the 3D virtual world enables interaction and communication through the use of avatars, which affects how people perceive your presence (Kemp & Livingstone, 2006). Through the dissemination of knowledge about the surroundings and how to influence them, the technology achieves its goal of emphasising the user's outside environment. The intimate world, in contrast, employs technology that focuses on the identity and behaviour of individuals or things and creates interior worlds of avatars or digital identities where users have agency in the digital environment (Tlili et al., 2022).

For instance, Lifelogging Metaverse logs standard information about people or things while using AR technology for Facebook or Instagram. The technique builds virtual maps and models in the Metaverse of Mirror Worlds using GPS technology on programmes like Google Earth or Google Maps. Avatars that interact digitally and represent a variety of identities are the foundation of the Metaverse technology used in virtual worlds (Davis et al., 2009).

The fields of education, learning, and development are always looking for new ways to combine platforms like the Metaverse with tried-and-true instructional techniques. Innovation is perhaps more important in the education and training industry than in any other. This is so that schools and universities, which do more than merely teach students, actively mould them for a future that goes beyond the workplace. The Metaverse is useful in many ways in the digital era, yet everyone wants to be a part of education's future. Everyone believes that education has to change as a result of the digital age's richness of ideas (Akçayr & Akçayr, 2017).

Augmented Reality, First

Augmented reality is one type of the external world's augmentation. It refers to a sort of technology that expands the actual physical world outside of an individual by using a location-aware system and interface with extra and layered networked information on the regions we encounter every day. The three types of interfaces that improve the world are GPS-based, marker-based, and see-through-based. By recognising a marker in a QR code or giving linked information suited for the user's location information, augmented reality may supplement already existing information with the use of a mobile device's built-in GPS and Wi-Fi (Jung & Kim, 2021). Additionally, real-time blending of the actual environment with virtual imagery is possible using glasses or lenses (Mulyani et al., 2021). Augmented reality has been proven to be beneficial for learning knowledge that is difficult to see directly or convey in words, professions that require continual practise and expertise, and fields with high costs and high risk (Kye et al., 2021).

Simulation content for augmented reality is an illustration of augmented reality in education. Simulation contributes to linking abstract pictures to actual objects by creating a link between the environment of the real world and virtual objects (Park, 2021). In the field of medicine, augmented reality technologies are being used in a wide variety of applications. A research team collaborating with university labs in a Seoul hospital has developed an augmented reality surgical platform for the spine. This platform projects a pedicle screw used for spinal fixation on a human body structure in real-time using an overlay picture based on augmented reality. To produce a productive teaching system that can be used to actual surgery, a spinal surgery education programme will also be developed based on this technology.

- While engaged in the learning setting, interactive experiences like reading, writing, and speaking are available.
- Comprehensive comprehension of subject matter that is hard to see or describe in text, and learners can build knowledge via experience
- Gain visual and three-dimensional understanding of unseen parts through virtual digital information, and use this knowledge to solve difficulties.

1. ***Lifelogging***

Lifelogging is a form of inner world enhancement. People use cellphones or the internet to record their daily lives in the realm of lifelogging. Instagram, Facebook, and Twitter are popular lifelogging sites. Recently, medical services that leverage biometric data saved on wearable technologies have been established. Some technology, such as Nike Plus, links sensors to monitor how much activity you get or where you are (Kye et al., 2021). The Classting artificial intelligence (AI) system in Korea offers as a prominent example of another sort of lifelogging. It is an educational social networking service and an online class community application (SNS). For instance, Classting AI evaluates students' academic achievement and provides level-appropriate training across all subject areas (Classiting. Artificial intelligence accomplishment change distribution by unit and screen for all disciplines, 2021)

The purpose of lifelogging is to effectively record everyday activities and thoughts. It may promote the use of the metaverse in education by placing an emphasis on personalised learning experiences. Therefore, the metaverse can be a crucial tool for expressing and putting feedback and learning into practise in one's daily life. Additionally, it makes it possible for systems to critically evaluate various forms of information. Lifelogging can aid in improving knowledge reconstruction and thinking about various learning situations.

Consequence for Education

Reviewing and reflecting on one's everyday activities helps one's capacity to represent and use information in the right way, and feedback from others on social media sites encourages reinforcement and incentives.

- Critically examine diverse data on the lifelogging platform and use collective intelligence to creatively recreate data.
- Examine your education and make improvements based on learning analytics data (e.g., dashboard).

Based on data from learning logs, teachers encourage learning in a personalised way, offer the right kind of help, and stop dropouts. (1.070 Words).

2. *Mirror Universe*

A virtual version or "reflection" of the actual world with improved information quality is referred to as a "mirror world." In the metaverse known as the mirror world, the look, content, and organisation of the actual world are transferred into virtual reality.

However, Kim (2020) asserted that the term "efficient expansion" is more appropriate than referring to these systems as exact replicas of the actual world. A mirror world metaverse is a location where living in the actual world is easy and efficient. In the real world, the internet or mobile applications may be used for all transactions. Examples of representational mirror worlds used in education include "virtual educational spaces" and "digital labs" that have been created in various mirror worlds.

The mirror world metaverse was further activated by the COVID-19 pandemic. In other words, the user is what enables the mirror world the most. Users can engage and play games with distant players while performing necessary tasks in the mirror world. The Fold it platform gives all users the opportunity to take part in scientific research through games (Kye et al., 2021).

Video conferencing programmes like Zoom, Webex, Google Meet, and Teams are examples of the mirror world. These video conferencing solutions are serving as the classroom in the real-time operation of non-face-to-face distant classrooms in the post-COVID-19 era. A virtual chat and business support platform for internet video conferencing called Gather Town. Its main capabilities include chatting, engaging with other networks, and creating spaces. Since it may be utilised to build the information and abilities required for learning while accurately simulating how the real world would appear in a mirror, the mirror world metaverse has immense educational potential.

Education-related implications: Learning occurs in the metaverse of the mirror world, which overcomes the geographical and physical constraints of teaching and learning.

- Use online video conferencing and collaboration technologies to conduct lessons in real time using representational mirror worlds like Zoom, WebEx, Google Meet, and Teams.
- Through the mirror world, students may achieve "learning by making" (for instance, in Minecraft, students construct and renovate iconic landmarks like the Eiffel Tower, Taj Mahal, Gyeongbokgung, and Bulguksa). By engaging with their digital legacy, users may better grasp history and culture.

3. ***Virtual reality***

Virtual reality is one type of the metaverse that replicates the inner world. Virtual reality technology includes capabilities for instant chat, avatars, and advanced 3D visuals. It seems to be fully virtual to users of this environment. Mixed reality and augmented reality are commonly contrasted with virtual reality. But according to Jung and Kim (2021), virtual reality manipulates the way our eyes function to cause us to view a flat image as three dimensional. Another description is that it is an online 3D world where many people may sign in simultaneously and interact by creating an avatar that represents themselves (Han, 2008).

In this virtual reality metaverse, people, places, and institutions are all built differently from how they are in the real world. The user's avatar completes the job by engaging with other players and travelling through an online environment filled with AI characters. The phrase "metaverse" is also used to describe virtual reality, but only in the narrow sense that it is a location where regular activities such as moving around and interacting with items happen as the actual body does.

- Practice can be done using virtual simulations in situations that are challenging to create because of their high costs and risks (e.g., fire scenes, flight control, dangerous surgery, etc.).
- Users can immerse themselves in moments and places that are not physically possible to experience, like the past or the future.

Users can develop strategic and comprehensive thinking skills, problem-solving abilities, and gain skills required for the actual world through 3D virtual world-based games (according to the features and types of planned games).

Potential Applications of The Metaverse in Education

Education today has a lot of pedagogical and technical assistance thanks to the technology and tools of the Metaverse, enabling students to engage in immersive learning that boosts motivation. Students' deep firsthand experience in the Metaverse fosters cooperation and skill development while also involving them in a variety of educational activities (Tarouco et al., 2013).

To create immersion, virtual technologies like Mixed Reality (MR), Virtual Reality (VR), Multi-User Virtual Environment (MUVE), and Augmented Reality must be combined (AR). The tools that serve as portals and enable immersion Metaverse settings also point to the need of multimodal immersion (Mystakidis et al., 2021). Because they enable psychological immersion, which promotes situational learning and transfer, these four types of technology are now the most common immersive interfaces in the Metaverse. They can enhance student learning in the classroom.

Gaming apps are another type of application that has been widely employed in the Metaverse to provide immersive educational experiences. The game that is played the most frequently is Pokémon Go. It permits the construction of fictitious interactive 3D characters with real-time VR and AR technology and the "luring" of Pokémon inside the game (Sourin, 2017).

The study of complex data for understanding, watching, controlling, and planning is the core concept of the Metaverse. Processing of this data can be based on the development of artificial intelligence (Duan et al., 2021). Due to the possibility of AI in the Metaverse, intelligent non-player characters (NPC) can now take on new roles as peers, teachers, and tutees. Future research may employ artificial intelligence to examine how students behave and interact in connection to their Metaverse performance levels and the establishment of new jobs (Hwang & Chien, 2022).

Mobile technologies, such mobile devices and geographic mobility, are also the most common in the Metaverse due to their ability to create a link between the medium and the learner and so boost authenticity in the virtual world. Learning can be enhanced when students utilise their Metaverse avatars on mobile devices. In a research by Estudante and Dietrich, a smartphone app (available for iOS and Android) was utilised to create a virtual world augmented reality for the Metaverse (2020). In addition to other virtual world instructions, teachers can use triggers to launch movies, text and picture calls, and Internet hyperlinks on students' displays in the actual world.

The Metaverse is linked with educational platforms when it is employed in education, allowing immersive surroundings to play a large role in instructional themes and making it easier to connect information (Wagner et al., 2013). Teachers can watch the dynamics of their students by analysing their behaviour thanks to technology in the field of sensors and wearables, such as the Microsoft HoloLens2 smart glasses and eye blinking (Barry et al., 2015). The most popular tool in the Metaverse for simulating models is OpenSim. It is a 3D application server that was initially created by Linden Labs Linden Research for Second Life. For academic institutions, the main benefit of OpenSim is how easily they can modify their development and design management systems and integrate them with LMS databases to create customised content (González Crespo et al., 2013).

ANALYSIS AND DISCUSSION

Hospital management is another field where applications of AI and data science are developing, being tried, and growing swiftly (Asha et al., 2022). Data published on the STATISTA website predicted that the global healthcare AI industry will grow at a pace of 55% between 2014 and 2021 (Figure 1). (Liu, 2021). Additionally, according to Sage Growth Partners, 90% of hospitals worldwide have an AI plan in place, and 75% of hospital administrators feel that AI is a key tool for the medical hospital environment in light of the COVID-19 epidemic (Yoganandhan et al., 2021). It is also expected that investment in AI for medical diagnostics would rise, from $505 million in 2020 to $387,87 billion in 2025. To reduce doctors' workloads, government initiatives will continue to increase demand for AI medical solutions (Sheel et al., 2022).

Figure 1. Growth rate for the AI healthcare market worldwide from 2014 to 2021 (published data from statista.com)

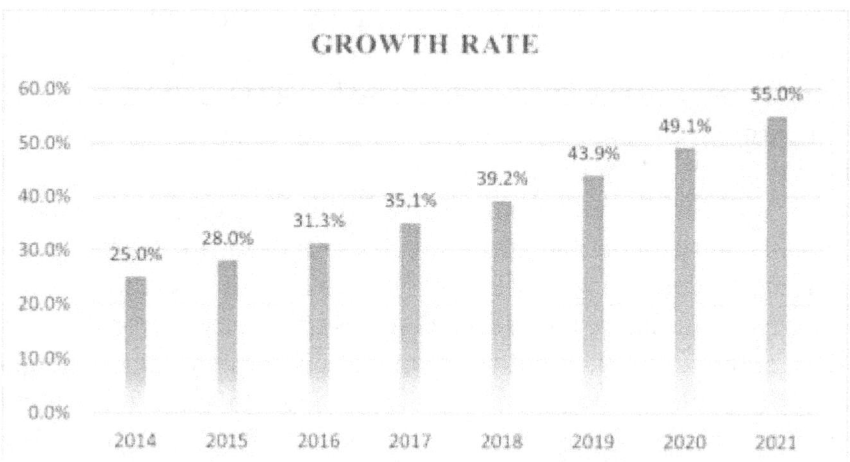

Clinical document management is a further use of AI and data science in hospital administration. Each year, more than 1.2 billion clinical papers are created. 20% of this data is structured, and structured data is ideal for computer storage and analysis. Around 80% of the data is also supplied in the form of clinical paperwork, pictures taken during medical procedures, and comments made by physicians. Data science may thus be used to study and analyse a huge number of clinical papers and data in order to reduce the workload of the healthcare professional. The seven categories for the AI applications utilised in hospital management are shown in Table 1. For each category, a list of articles that serve as examples is provided.

METAVERSE IN EDUCATION EVOLUTION

According to Tarouco et al. (2013), students may experience an immersive learning environment using the Metaverse, which also offers the potential for collaborative learning and a high level of involvement. It may both assist professors in designing their teaching methods in the Metaverse and assist students in learning more effectively by examining how the Metaverse is used in various settings.

The neighbourhood ages as a whole along with us. Events that impact a person's education individually may have a range of repercussions on education in society as a whole. Despite the fact that it might be challenging to categorise or distinguish between the various age groups, several studies provide a variety of labels, dates, and analyses for each generation type (Moore et al., 2017).

It is critical to designate generational groups because of the technology's quick development and incorporation with schooling, especially for future generations like Gen Alpha. As a result, it was also revealed how the education-related Metaverse came to be and how it changed through time. Table 1 displays the several generations that the literature emphasises. Based on the participants' educational backgrounds and the year that each Metaverse research was conducted, generation types were categorised. For example, because the participants in a research with high school students in 2020 would be between the ages of 16 and 24 in 2022, the study would normally be labelled as Gen Z (Tootell et al., 2014).

Huang et al (2022) claim that The Metaverse is positively affecting education. In comparison to traditional classrooms, students are more interested in learning through games in the Metaverse, and they have a great motivation to practise science on mobile devices (Estudante, & Dietrich, 2020). Furthermore advantageous, metaverse instruction in virtual classrooms like Second Life can promote multilingual student communication and raise academic standards (Kanematsu et al., 2010).

Table 1. Generation (Gen) differences

Table 1 Generation (Gen) differences

Generation Type	Baby Boomer	Gen X	Gen Y/ Millennials	Gen Z/ iGeneration	Gen Alpha
Years range	1946–1964	1965–1980	1981–1994	1995–2010*	2010–2025*
Age range as in 2022	58–76	43–57	28–42	12–27	1–12
New Technology	Television	Computers	Internet	Smart phones	Virtual Reality/ Augmented Reality
Learning style	Rote, hands-on**	Self-directed, mix traditional with technology**	Groups, lots of tests**	Groups, lots of tests, online, 'gamification'**	Online, blended, 'gamification'

*As referenced in (Jha, 2020; Nagy & Kolcsey, 2017)

**As referenced in (Moore & Frazier, 2017)

The Metaverse, with its more flexibility, higher creativity, and lower risk, may potentially broaden traditional learning by providing experiences that would otherwise be unattainable. Additionally, it boosts pupils' involvement and motivation (Erturk & Reynolds, 2020; Tarouco et al., 2013).

Students who cannot physically be present in the classroom can nonetheless participate in class and submit resources. Students can engage with peers and lecturers in the Metaverse using their avatars. Students could therefore have an immersive educational experience that improves their desire to study. Siyaev and Jo (2021), for example, investigated the use of mixed reality in maintenance to provide an engaging learning environment for aircraft maintenance. The usage of OpenSim in educational virtual environments and the dissemination of information through open courses in the Metaverse were both investigated by González Crespo et al. (2013). In order to teach mathematics via augmented reality and mobile learning, Reyes (2020) developed the Metaverse (Anshari et al., 2021b). In the metaverse, for instance, Roblox and Zepeto have created a new social space for individuals who couldn't go outdoors due to COVID-19 to congregate and unwind. This area has become a place for new forms of social contact. Additionally, there is more flexibility to produce and share. The user can do anything they want if there is no set goal. Depending on their preferred amount of freedom, users can partake in a range of activities in the real world, such as travelling and shopping. Additionally, they could discuss activities like flight and space travel, which are challenging in the real world due to physical constraints. By actively utilising the features of the metaverse, it will be possible to design educational activities that may indefinitely improve students' flexibility and experience. Lastly, using virtualization to deliver fresh experiences with a high level of immersion. As a potential remedy for the shortcomings of conventional 2D-based online and remote courses, the metaverse is growing in favour. In the metaverse, it is also possible to create a singular experience that transcends space and time. Through the use of metaverse-based education, which has the advantage of enabling interactivity on par with face-to-face learning, the use of limitless space and data is made feasible (Kye et. al, 2021).

David Baker's team, for example, used a protein folding simulation to discover the crystal structure of a monomeric retroviral protease, in contrast to Metaverse in healthcare. A possible AID therapy's protein structure was found by 60,000 participants using a digital lab in just 10 days, allowing people to fold protein amino acid chains. Thanks to advancements in the tactile sensing environment, robots can already simulate human-level touch. You'll need hardware, simulators, libraries, benchmarks, and data sets to build a touch-sensitive AI system. DIGIT is a compact, robotic, high-resolution tactile fingertip sensor for in-hand handling. Using simulators like TACTO, robotics advances are prototyped, fixed, and benchmarked. Robotics has an influence on senior care, prosthetics, rehabilitation, and assistive surgery. Acceptability, usefulness, cost, and practical applications are crucial components (Ganapathy, 2022).

FUTURE DIRECTIONS

The growth of digital or precision medicine will be aided by the metaverse's rise, which will open up endless possibilities in the field of healthcare. However, the ongoing advancement of digital technology unavoidably also comes with it certain unnoticed risks. The medical industry is distinct from other industries and has its own set of ethics and regulations. According to Yilmaz et al., extensive usage of metaverse applications can have a variety of adverse impacts, such as virtual addiction, social isolation, behavioural problems, and an increase in worry and stress (2022). In his study, Kuş (2021) asserts that while metaverse technology presents a range of opportunities and solutions in the fields of collaboration, education, cultural production, and the economy, it also carries a number of worries and potential risks, much like those posed by earlier developed technologies.

It is said that due to its commercial nature, metaverse technology is thought to always include these weaknesses. This is true even if it offers security for the virtual economy, security for the technology it incorporates (such edge computing and blockchain), and trust in the secure storage and display of data. Mamun (2022) asserts that for healthcare organisations, private/proprietary blockchains—which need authorisation to join the network—are preferable than public blockchains.

Another issue is that, despite the fact that AI is better at making accurate diagnoses than human doctors, most machine learning and deep learning systems are unable to explain how they came to a certain result. Patients' knowledge of and trust in AI and data science systems are constrained as a result of human doctors' failure to adequately explain the diagnosis they are given. In all kinds of relationships, acceptance is necessary for trust to exist (Siau & Shen, 2003; Siau & Wang, 2018). However, given the potential of AI, machine learning and deep learning must cooperate to create an AI that can be explained and made transparent to everyone.

Another inherent challenge in a medical hospital environment is the complex interaction that exists between patients and hospitals. Despite the fact that AI and data science technologies may result in lower costs and shorter wait times for patients, patients may still not be happy for a variety of reasons, such as poor health outcomes, unfulfilled expectations, and unclear communication. Stefanini and others (2012).

Patients' impressions of health robots and AI systems are less trustworthy because they lack human emotions like empathy and compassion (Siau & Wang, 2018). Because of this, patients typically place more trust in their doctors than in the more accurate AI systems (Bedué & Fritzsche, 2021).

The recognised issues with Metaverse in education may be divided into pedagogical, technical, and other categories (Huang et al., 2022). Network congestion, smartphone interface issues, bad design, issues with blink capture technologies, and the creation of guidelines for digital cohabitation are some examples of technical challenges.

According to reports, a smartphone's UI may limit how many pupils may use it at once, which would reduce their ability to work in teams and their degree of communication (Estudante & Dietrich, 2020). The mechanism of the eye-blink is typically connected to emotional responses when students discuss a variety of topics. This complicates the use of blink capture technology since problems with the student's eyes may interfere with the recording of blinking activity (Barry et al., 2015).

However, from a pedagogical standpoint, the growth of the Metaverse is constrained by the design of digital resources. Teachers must develop, improve, and provide the Metaverse server administrators with the digital resources integrated into the metaverse (Daz et al., 2020). However, as evidenced by numerous applications' lack of educational framework and instructor competencies, digital resources were not appropriately built (Erturk & Reynolds, 2020). Additionally, it should be highlighted that students have trouble managing their time. Students find it more challenging to use the Metaverse's virtual environment due to time management issues and technological challenges (Belei et al., 2011). The final one is the rigidity of Metaverse applications in education, which will likewise require a lot of work, design, and practise. High design and practise expenses as well as a lack of quantity analysis are further difficulties.

Furthermore, it is clear that a lot of cutting-edge technology, like Blockchain, have not yet been put into use. This will improve user security and perhaps even thwart cheating. Another potential issue is whether the ICT-based competencies described in the research are sufficient to prepare instructors and students for this novel educational setting (the Metaverse in Education), or whether additional abilities are needed for improved teaching and learning.

CONCLUSION

The metaverse holds out the possibility of innovation and development. Despite some of the current difficulties, Metaverse will continue to be developed and used. The properties of the Metaverse technology in the healthcare and educational sectors, as well as possible Metaverse applications in both, were covered in this paper. The metaverse is anticipated to have an influence on our daily lives and the economy in addition to gaming, entertainment, health, and lifestyle. The social, cultural, and commercial activities across the whole metaverse are also moving to the new platform. The potential of the metaverse as a cutting-edge platform for social interaction is virtually endless. It provides a unique, immersive experience together with a high degree of creative and sharing flexibility.

REFERENCES

Abujassar, R. S., Yaseen, H., & Al-Adwan, A. S. (2021). A highly effective route for real-time traffic using an IOT smart algorithm for Tele-surgery using 5G networks. *Journal of Sensor and Actuator Networks*, *10*(2), 30. doi:10.3390/jsan10020030

Ahmadi Marzaleh, M., Peyravi, M., & Shaygani, F. (2022). A revolution in health: Opportunities and challenges of the Metaverse. *EXCLI Journal*, *21*, 791–792. doi:10.17179/excli2022-5017 PMID:35949490

Akçayır, M., & Akçayır, G. (2017). Advantages and challenges associated with augmented reality for education: A systematic review of the literature. *Educational Research Review*, *20*, 1–11. doi:10.1016/j.edurev.2016.11.002

Anshari, M. (2019). Redefining electronic health records (EHR) and electronic medical records (EMR) to promote patient empowerment. *IJID*, *8*(1), 35–39. doi:10.14421/ijid.2019.08106

Anshari, M., & Almunawar, M. N. (2018). Pervasive Mobile Health. In *Encyclopedia of Information Science and Technology* (4th ed., pp. 5908–5917). IGI Global.

Anshari, M., & Almunawar, M. N. (2019, August). Big Data in Healthcare for Personalization & Customization of Healthcare Services. In *2019 International Conference on Information Management and Technology (ICIMTech)* (Vol. 1, pp. 73-77). IEEE.

Anshari, M., Almunawar, M. N., & Lim, S. A. (2018, February). Big data and open government data in public services. In *Proceedings of the 2018 10th International Conference on Machine Learning and Computing* (pp. 140-144). 10.1145/3195106.3195172

Anshari, M., Almunawar, M. N., & Masri, M. (2022). Digital Twin: Financial Technology's Next Frontier of Robo-Advisor. *Journal of Risk and Financial Management*, *15*(4), 163. doi:10.3390/jrfm15040163

Anshari, M., Almunawar, M. N., Masri, M., & Hrdy, M. (2021b). Financial technology with ai-enabled and ethical challenges. *Society*, *58*(3), 189–195. doi:10.100712115-021-00592-w

Anshari, M., Almunawar, M. N., & Razzaq, A. (2021). Developing talents vis-à-vis fourth industrial revolution. *International Journal of Asian Business and Information Management, 12*(4), 20–32. doi:10.4018/IJABIM.20211001.oa2

Anshari, M., Almunawar, M. N., Younis, M. Z., & Kisa, A. (2021a). Modeling Users' Empowerment in E-Health Systems. *Sustainability, 13*(23), 12993. doi:10.3390u132312993

Anshari, M., & Hamdan, M. (2022). Enhancing e-government with a digital twin for innovation management. *Journal of Science and Technology Policy Management.*

Anshari, M., Syafrudin, M., Fitriyani, N. L., & Razzaq, A. (2022). Ethical Responsibility and Sustainability (ERS) Development in a Metaverse Business Model. *Sustainability, 14*(23), 15805. doi:10.3390u142315805

Asha, S., Kanchana Devi, V., & Sahaja Vaishnavi, G. (2022). Artificial Intelligence in Healthcare Data Science with Knowledge Engineering. Handbook of Intelligent Healthcare Analytics, 255–283. doi:10.1002/9781119792550.ch12

Badiali, G., Ferrari, V., Cutolo, F., Freschi, C., Caramella, D., Bianchi, A., & Marchetti, C. (2014). Augmented reality as an aid in maxillofacial surgery: Validation of a wearable system allowing maxillary repositioning. *Journal of Cranio-Maxillo-Facial Surgery, 42*(8), 1970–1976. doi:10.1016/j.jcms.2014.09.001 PMID:25441867

Barry, D. M., Ogawa, N., Dharmawansa, A., Kanematsu, H., Fukumura, Y., Shirai, T., Yajima, K., & Kobayashi, T. (2015). Evaluation for students' learning manner using eye blinking system in Metaverse. *Procedia Computer Science, 60*, 1195–1204. doi:10.1016/j.procs.2015.08.181

Bedué, P., & Fritzsche, A. (2021). Can we trust AI? An empirical investigation of trust requirements and guide to successful AI adoption. *Journal of Enterprise Information Management.*

Belei, N., Noteborn, G., & De Ruyter, K. (2011). It's a brand-new world: Teaching brand management in virtual environments. *Journal of Brand Management, 18*(8), 611–623. doi:10.1057/bm.2011.6

Bibri, S. E. (2022). The social shaping of the metaverse as an alternative to the imaginaries of data-driven Smart Cities: A Study in Science, technology, and Society. *Smart Cities, 5*(3), 832–874. doi:10.3390martcities5030043

Chen, D., & Zhang, R. (2022). Exploring research trends of emerging technologies in Healt Metaverse: A Bibliometric analysis. SSRN *Electronic Journal*. doi:10.2139/ssrn.3998068

Chengoden, R., Victor, N., Huynh-The, T., Yenduri, G., Jhaveri, R. H., Alazab, M., . . . Gadekallu, T. R. (2022). *Metaverse for Healthcare: A Survey on Potential Applications, Challenges and Future Directions*. arXiv preprint arXiv:2209.04160.

Classting AI. (n.d.). *Classiting. Artificial intelligence analysis screen for all subjects and distribution table of achievement change by unit*. Retrieved September 24, 2022, from https://www.classting.ai/

Damar, M. (2022). What the Literature on Medicine, Nursing, Public Health, Midwifery, and Dentistry Reveals: An Overview of the Rapidly Approaching Metaverse. *Journal of Metaverse*, *2*(2), 62–70. doi:10.57019/jmv.1132962

Davis, A., Murphy, J., Owens, D., Khazanchi, D., & Zigurs, I. (2009). Avatars, people, and virtual worlds: Foundations for research in metaverses. *Journal of the Association for Information Systems*, *10*(2), 90–117. doi:10.17705/1jais.00183

Díaz, J., Saldana, C., & Avila, C. (2020). Virtual world as a resource for hybrid education. *Int. J. Emerg. Technol. Learn.*, *15*(15), 94–109.

Duan, H., Li, J., Fan, S., Lin, Z., Wu, X., & Cai, W. (2021). Metaverse for social good. *Proceedings of the 29th ACM International Conference on Multimedia*. 10.1145/3474085.3479238

Erturk, E., & Reynolds, G. B. (2020). The expanding role of immersive media in education. In *International Conference on E-Learning* (pp. 191–194). Academic Press.

Eschenbrenner, B., Nah, F. F.-H., & Siau, K. (2008). 3-D virtual worlds in education. *Journal of Database Management*, *19*(4), 91–110. doi:10.4018/jdm.2008100106

Estudante, A., & Dietrich, N. (2020). Using augmented reality to stimulate students and difuse escape game activities to larger audiences. *Journal of Chemical Education*, *97*(5), 1368–1374. doi:10.1021/acs.jchemed.9b00933

Gao, Q., & Gadekallu, T. R. (2022). Design of telemedicine information query system based on Wireless Sensor Network. *EAI Endorsed Transactions on Pervasive Health and Technology*, *8*(4), e1. Advance online publication. doi:10.4108/eetpht.v8i4.674

Goh, R. L., Kong, Y. X., McAlinden, C., Liu, J., Crowston, J. G., & Skalicky, S. E. (2018). Objective assessment of activity limitation in glaucoma with smartphone virtual reality goggles: A pilot study. *Translational Vision Science & Technology*, *7*(1), 10. doi:10.1167/tvst.7.1.10 PMID:29372112

González Crespo, R., Escobar, R. F., Joyanes Aguilar, L., Velazco, S., & Castillo Sanz, A. G. (2013). Use of ARIMA mathematical analysis to model the implementation of expert system courses by means of free software OpenSim and Sloodle platforms in virtual university campuses. *Expert Systems with Applications*, *40*(18), 7381–7390. doi:10.1016/j.eswa.2013.06.054

Gopalakrishnan, S., Jacob, C. E., Kumar, M., Karunakaran, V., & Raman, R. (2020). Comparison of visual parameters between normal individuals and people with low vision in a virtual environment. *Cyberpsychology, Behavior, and Social Networking*, *23*(3), 171–178. doi:10.1089/cyber.2019.0235 PMID:32150699

Gunasekeran, D. V., Low, R., Gunasekeran, R., Chan, B., Ong, H. Y., Raje, D., Mi, H., Pavesio, C., Nguyen, Q. D., & Agrawal, R. (2020). Population Eye Health Education using augmented reality and virtual reality: Scalable tools during and beyond COVID-19. *BMJ Innovations*, *7*(2), 278–283. doi:10.1136/bmjinnov-2020-000522

Gutierrez, G. (2020). Artificial intelligence in the intensive care unit. *Annual Update in Intensive Care and Emergency Medicine*, *2020*, 667–681. doi:10.1007/978-3-030-37323-8_51 PMID:32204716

Hamdan, M., Jaidin, J. H., Fithriyah, M., & Anshari, M. (2020, December). E-learning in time of COVID-19 pandemic: Challenges & experiences. In *2020 Sixth International Conference on e-Learning (econf)* (pp. 12-16). IEEE. 10.1109/econf51404.2020.9385507

Han, H. W. (2008). A study on typology of virtual world and its development in metaverse. *Journal of Digital Contents Society*, *9*(2), 317–323.

Hawks, C., & Krasniansky, A. (2022). *Digital health enters the metaverse.* https://rockhealth.com/insights/digital-health-enters-the-metaverse/

Hwang, G.-J., & Chien, S.-Y. (2022). Definition, roles, and potential research issues of the metaverse in education: An artificial intelligence perspective. *Computers and Education: Artificial Intelligence*, *3*, 100082. doi:10.1016/j.caeai.2022.100082

Iskander, M., Ogunsola, T., Ramachandran, R., McGowan, R., & Al-Aswad, L. A. (2021). Virtual reality and augmented reality in ophthalmology: A contemporary prospective. *Asia-Pacific Journal of Ophthalmology*, *10*(3), 244–252. doi:10.1097/APO.0000000000000409 PMID:34383716

Javaid, M., Haleem, A., & Khan, I. H. (2020). Holography applications toward medical field: An overview. *The Indian Journal of Radiology & Imaging*, *30*(3), 354–361. doi:10.4103/ijri.IJRI_39_20 PMID:33273770

Jones, P. R., Somoskeöy, T., Chow-Wing-Bom, H., & Crabb, D. P. (2020). Seeing other perspectives: Evaluating the use of virtual and augmented reality to simulate visual impairments (openvissim). *NPJ Digital Medicine*, *3*(1), 32. Advance online publication. doi:10.103841746-020-0242-6 PMID:32195367

Jung, E. J., & Kim, N. H. (2021). Virtual and augmented reality for Vocational Education:A review of major issues. *Korean Association for Educational Information and Media*, *27*(1), 79–109. doi:10.15833/KAFEIAM.27.1.079

Kemp, J., & Livingstone, D. (2006). Putting a Second Life "Metaverse" skin on learning management systems. *Proceedings of the Second Life Education Workshop at the Second Life Community Convention*, 20.

Kim, S. (2020). *Metaverse: Digital world, world of emerging items*. PlanB Design.

Kostoff, R. N., Boylan, R., & Simons, G. R. (2004). Disruptive Technology Roadmaps. *Technological Forecasting and Social Change*, *71*(1-2), 141–159. doi:10.1016/S0040-1625(03)00048-9

Kuş, O. (2021). Metaverse: 'Dijital büyük patlamada'fırsatlar ve endişelere yönelik algılar. *Intermedia International E-journal*, *8*(15), 245–266. doi:10.21645/intermedia.2021.109

Kye, B., Han, N., Kim, E., Park, Y., & Jo, S. (2021). Educational applications of metaverse: Possibilities and limitations. *Journal of Educational Evaluation for Health Professions*, *18*, 32. doi:10.3352/jeehp.2021.18.32 PMID:34897242

Lam, A. K., To, E., Weinreb, R. N., Yu, M., Mak, H., Lai, G., Chiu, V., Wu, K., Zhang, X., Cheng, T. P., Guo, P. Y., & Leung, C. K. (2020). Use of virtual reality simulation to identify vision-related disability in patients with glaucoma. *JAMA Ophthalmology*, *138*(5), 490. doi:10.1001/jamaophthalmol.2020.0392 PMID:32191274

Liu, S. H. (2021). *Global healthcare artificial intelligence market growth rate 2014-2021*. https://www.statista.com/statistics/938794/global-healthcare-artificial-intelligence-market-growth-rate/

Mamun, Q. (2022). Blockchain technology in the future of healthcare. *Smart Health (Amsterdam, Netherlands)*, *23*, 100223. doi:10.1016/j.smhl.2021.100223

Moore, K., Jones, C., & Frazier, R. S. (2017). Engineering education for generation Z. *American Journal of Engineering Education*, *8*(2), 111–126. doi:10.19030/ajee.v8i2.10067

Morimoto, T., Kobayashi, T., Hirata, H., Otani, K., Sugimoto, M., Tsukamoto, M., Yoshihara, T., Ueno, M., & Mawatari, M. (2022). XR (extended reality: Virtual reality, augmented reality, mixed reality) technology in Spine Medicine: Status Quo and quo vadis. *Journal of Clinical Medicine*, *11*(2), 470. doi:10.3390/jcm11020470 PMID:35054164

Mulyani, M. A., Yusuf, S., Siregar, P., Nurihsan, J., Razzaq, A., & Anshari, M. (2021, August). Fourth Industrial Revolution and Educational Challenges. In *2021 International Conference on Information Management and Technology (ICIMTech)* (Vol. 1, pp. 245-249). IEEE. 10.1109/ICIMTech53080.2021.9535057

Mystakidis, S. (2022). Metaverse. *Encyclopedia*, *2*(1), 486–497. doi:10.3390/encyclopedia2010031

Mystakidis, S., Fragkaki, M., & Filippousis, G. (2021). Ready teacher One: Virtual and Augmented Reality Online Professional Development for K-12 school teachers. *Computers*, *10*(10), 134. doi:10.3390/computers10100134

Ning, H., Wang, H., Lin, Y., Wang, W., Dhelim, S., Farha, F., Ding, J., & Daneshmand, M. (2021, November 18). *A survey on Metaverse: The state-of-the-art, technologies, applications, and challenges.* https://arxiv.org/abs/2111.09673

Park, M. S. (2021, January 11)., *Development of AR technology-based spine surgery platform.* 이투데이. Retrieved September 24, 2022, from https://www.etoday.co.kr/news/view/1982781

Park, S., Kim, S. P., & Whang, M. (2021). Individual's social perception of virtual avatars embodied with their habitual facial expressions and facial appearance. *Sensors (Basel), 21*(17), 5986. doi:10.339021175986 PMID:34502877

Razzaq, A., Samiha, Y. T., & Anshari, M. (2018). Smartphone habits and behaviors in supporting students self-efficacy. *International Journal of Emerging Technologies in Learning, 13*(2), 94. doi:10.3991/ijet.v13i02.7685

Reyes, C. E. G. (2020). Perception of high school students about using Metaverse in augmented reality learning experi- ences in mathematics. Pixel-Bit. *Media and Education Magazine, 58*, 143–159.

Semivolos, A., & Anshari, M. (2023). The Application of Artificial Intelligence to the Process of Logistic During COVID-19. In *Handbook of Research on Artificial Intelligence and Knowledge Management in Asia's Digital Economy* (pp. 1–11). IGI Global.

Sheel, N., Verma, L. P., Kumar, S., & Singh, T. P. (2022). Artificial Intelligence and analytics for better decision-making and strategy management. *Decision Intelligence Analytics and the Implementation of Strategic Business Management*, 31–43. doi:10.1007/978-3-030-82763-2_3

Siau, K., Nah, F. F.-H., Mennecke, B. E., & Schiller, S. Z. (2010). Co-creation and collaboration in a virtual world. *Journal of Database Management, 21*(4), 1–13. doi:10.4018/jdm.2010100101

Siau, K., & Wang, W. (2018). Building Trust in Artificial Intelligence, Machine Learning, and Robotics. *Cutter Business Technology Journal, 31*(2), 47–53.

Siyaev, A., & Jo, G. S. (2021b). Towards aircraft maintenance Metaverse using speech interactions with virtual objects in mixed reality. *Sensors (Basel), 21*(6), 2066. doi:10.339021062066 PMID:33804253

Sourin, A. (2017). Case study: Shared virtual and augmented environments for creative applications. *Research and Development in the Academy, Creative Industries and Applications*, 49–64. doi:10.1007/978-3-319-54081-8_5

Stefanini, A., Aloini, D., Gloor, P., & Pochiero, F. (2021). Patient satisfaction in emergency department: Unveiling complex interactions by wearable sensors. *Journal of Business Research, 129*, 600–611. doi:.jbusres.2019.12.038 doi:10.1016/j

Tarouco, L., Gorziza, B., Correa, Y., Amaral, E. M., & Muller, T. (2013). Virtual Laboratory for Teaching Calculus: An immersive experience. *2013 IEEE Global Engineering Education Conference (EDUCON)*. 10.1109/EduCon.2013.6530195

Thomason, J., & Aydın, Ö. (2021). MetaHealth-How will the Metaverse Change Health Care? *Journal of Metaverse*, *1*, 13–16.

Tlili, A., Huang, R., Shehata, B., Liu, D., Zhao, J., Metwally, A. H., Wang, H., Denden, M., Bozkurt, A., Lee, L.-H., Beyoglu, D., Altinay, F., Sharma, R. C., Altinay, Z., Li, Z., Liu, J., Ahmad, F., Hu, Y., Salha, S., ... Burgos, D. (2022). Is metaverse in education a blessing or a curse: A combined content and bibliometric analysis. *Smart Learning Environments*, *9*(1), 24. Advance online publication. doi:10.118640561-022-00205-x

Tootell, H., Freeman, M., & Freeman, A. (2014). Generation alpha at the intersection of technology, play and motivation. *2014 47th Hawaii International Conference on System Sciences*. 10.1109/HICSS.2014.19

Wagner, R., Piovesan, S. D., Passerino, P. D., & de Lima, J. V. (2013). Using 3D virtual learning environments in new perspective of education. *2013 12th International Conference on Information Technology Based Higher Education and Training*. 10.1109/ITHET.2013.6671019

Walsh, S. T., & Linton, J. D. (2000). Infrastructure for emergent industries based on discontinuous innovations. *Engineering Management Journal*, *12*(2), 23–32. doi:10.1080/10429247.2000.11415071

Yang, Y., Siau, K., Xie, W., & Sun, Y. (2022). Smart health. *Journal of Organizational and End User Computing*, *34*(1), 1–14. doi:10.4018/JOEUC.308814

Yılmaz, F., Mete, A. H., Türkön, B. F., & İnce, Ö. (2022). Sağlık Hizmetlerinin Geleceğinde Metaverse Ekosistemi ve Teknolojileri: Uygulamalar, Fırsatlar ve Zorluklar. *Eurasian Journal of Health Technology Assessment*, *6*(1), 1–22. doi:10.52148/ehta.1082705

Yoganandhan, A., Rajesh Kanna, G., Subhash, S. D., & Hebinson Jothi, J. (2021). Retrospective and prospective application of robots and Artificial Intelligence in global pandemic and epidemic diseases. *Vacunas*, *22*(2), 98–105. doi:10.1016/j.vacun.2020.12.004 PMID:33841058

Chapter 12
Business Future With the Metaverse

Tazkia Tahira
University of Muhammadiyah Malang, Indonesia

Fien Zulfikarijah
University of Muhammadiyah Malang, Indonesia

ABSTRACT

This research is about the metaverse as the next evolutionary step in doing business. In addition, the purpose of this research is to get to know more about the metaverse, ranging from positive and negative impacts to business opportunities and business strategies in the metaverse. This metaverse is a proof of the technological development that occurs and does not only refer to one type of technology. However, it leads to ways to utilise the technology. The metaverse is important because it has stylistic ideas that might help us organise society to be more productive, shared standards, and protocols that bring different virtual worlds (the metaverse) and augmented reality into one open metaverse that can help people work together. The study revealed that the metaverse is very important to expand business reachability so that users can explore this virtual world in real life. The metaverse will be co-created and responsibly built so that any type of business can be realised in the future.

DOI: 10.4018/978-1-6684-6097-9.ch012

Copyright © 2023, IGI Global. Copying or distributing in print or electronic forms without written permission of IGI Global is prohibited.

INTRODUCTION

The metaverse is a virtual world or space that replicates or clones human activities and real-world activities for use in the virtual world. The term "metaverse" came to life in 1992 in a novel called "Snow Crash," written by Neal Stephenson. At that time, the concept of "metaverse" referred to the virtual world that combined physical and digital aspects. In the metaverse era, there are several business opportunities that can be obtained by the community, one of which is NFTs. NFT, or non-fungible token, is a token (based on the programme code on the blockchain) that represents digital files, including photos, images, songs, sound recordings, videos, and games. Thus, NFTs are digital-based assets, so they are relatively easy to trade because they do not require more expensive real space. Meanwhile, the research method used was qualitative and descriptive, using secondary data based on phenomena and analysis from relevant references. This is supported by the results (Sari, 2022), which state that NFT is one of the easiest business opportunities to do in the metaverse era (Anshari et al., 2022).

There are still many people who doubt whether the Metaverse is a business worth running. The answer is that the metaverse is the path for your business's development towards the next step. The chapter discusses what makes the metaverse important for future business applications. The Metaverse must grow in order for users to explore this virtual world in real life.Many large companies, such as Facebook (Meta), have prepared all the supporting components needed to design the Metaverse; maybe Facebook will develop new technology or be ready to create a Metaverse in the future. There are several other large companies that will also make their own metaverses, such as Microsoft, Google, MicroDox, and many more. These companies will invest billions of dollars over the next few years to make the metaverse a reality. This is also one of the reasons why the Metaverse is important, but there is still another reason: the Metaverse has a style idea that might help us organise society to be more productive (in addition to reality or the real world) into one open Metaverse. A metaverse that allows people to collaborate and reduces duplication of effort.

BACKGROUND

Before discussing the business model that exists in the metaverse world, we will explain what the metaverse is, how to join the metaverse, the advantages and disadvantages of the metaverse, and much more. The chapter will also provide tips on what types of businesses people in the metaverse can have. Metaverse is a combination of two words, namely “meta” and “universe,” where the meaning of “meta” is digital and “universe” is the universe. When these two words are combined, they mean “the digital universe.” This may sound very simple, but the metaverse is different from the digital world we know. The digital world we know may only be limited to using the internet to help with our daily activities such as doing schoolwork, playing games, etc. The metaverse is an open door through which we can truly be present and do what we can.

As an example of the metaverse, consider the game “The Sims,” in which we can only select clothes from the system for the character or avatar to wear in the game. The difference is that in the metaverse, the characters or avatars we play can use more than that. It’s as if we become them in the virtual world, choosing clothes, choosing hair colors, and doing other activities. Cindrum has a different perspective on the metaverse.

The metaverse is a real world created by the convergence of virtuality and reality. a virtual world that interacts with the real world on an entirely new level. The metaverse is the next evolutionary step (level of evolution) after the internet and social media. The metaverse alters not only how we connect to the internet but also what we connect to it with. The metaverse is a virtual world or space that replicates or clones human and real-world activities for use in the virtual world. It’s as if we have two different “bodies” in two worlds, and later, what happens in the real world could happen in the virtual world. It is no wonder that in the future, the marketing world will head into the metaverse. The gamevertising trend is one example, which uses terminology to present brand ads in game exposure that is similar to real-world exposure.

There are still many who doubt whether the Metaverse is a business worth running. The answer is that the metaverse is the path for your business’s development towards the next step. The Metaverse must grow in order for users to explore this virtual world in real life. Many large companies, such as Facebook (Meta), have prepared all the supporting components needed to design the Metaverse; maybe Facebook will develop new technology or be ready to create a Metaverse in the future. There are several other large companies that will also make their own metaverses, such as Microsoft,

Google, MicroDox, and many more. These companies will invest billions of dollars over the next few years to make the metaverse a reality. This is also one of the reasons why the Metaverse is important, but there is still another reason: the Metaverse has a style idea that might help us organise society to be more productive (in addition to reality or the real world) into one open Metaverse. A metaverse that allows people to collaborate and reduces duplication of effort.

Concept of Metaverse

The concept of "metaverse" referred to the virtual world, which combines physical and digital aspects. Metaverse invites a lot of attention from well-known companies such as Apple, Facebook, Microsoft, and many more. Why is that so? Metaverse can change the way we do business. For example, if we run a bread shop, we can use artificial intelligence robots from the Metaverse in sales, and this will also train apprentices or their employees by using the Metaverse. If we want to be at the forefront of business competition, we must begin planning our entry into the metaverse. We may not have enough experience with this virtual reality (metaverse) world.

In order to understand whether our product fits our target audience or not. Before we make any decisions, it's important to understand if the Metaverse is suitable for our target audience. For example, if most of our customers are young, the world of digital or the metaverse might be a great place for them to invest. First, learn his competence. To be at the forefront of business competition, it's important that we know what they're doing in the metaverse. This means we learn what kind of experience other brands or companies offer or how they interact with customers, and whether it will work for your brand. Second, find opportunities for our brand to participate. Once we understand what the metaverse is, it's time to find opportunities that your brand can participate in. by sponsoring events, creating virtual offices or platforms, and much more. There are still different ways for our brand to get involved in the digital world, or metaverse. Therefore, it is very important for us to start strategizing on how to enter this exciting virtual world. The metaverse has the potential to transform everything from entertainment, gaming, and retail to how we work and socialise (Juna et al., 2022).

What are the negative and positive impacts of the metaverse? The first are some of the shortcomings or negative impacts of the metaverse. The metaverse may be very tempting for us to enter, but at that moment, it is one of the biggest dangers. "The more perfect the experience in the virtual world, the greater the danger of addiction.

Social media has changed society and politics in ways we couldn't initially imagine. So be wise when using something; in order to avoid becoming addicted, we must be able to limit our use. In addition to addiction, there is a risk of cybercrime. Crimes committed in the metaverse are simple to commit, such as violence, persecution, etc. Worse crimes can also be experienced, especially by women, namely harassment. Because of the ease of doing things in the virtual world, it is not impossible that this inappropriate action will happen a lot in the future, especially to women. In addition, privacy is compromised. The metaverse has the potential to erode our privacy even further. It is likely that the high wall separating private life from the public could collapse. This can cause privacy data to be easily known.

In addition to the negative impact generated by the metaverse, there are several positive impacts. Based on my research about the metaverse, namely:

- *Experience*

The metaverse can make us anyone, and we can be anywhere. In addition, we can also realise the fantasies we have. This experience can be a new leap in technological development.

- *Increase Productivity*

With this metaverse, developers hope that in addition to playing and interacting, users can also increase their productivity. Remembering that this virtual world is like a fantasy world will certainly make us feel more excited.

- *Making Money*

As explained above, this metaverse can change the way we do business. Because the Metaverse is a vast virtual world, it can help your business grow and become more well-known.

Metaverse Applications

Many people will ask how much money can be made from the metaverse. It all depends on what kind of business you run, what products or brands you have, how quickly you adopt trends, and how creative you are in the metaverse. Metaverse is an all-round internet world that is presented on a virtual platform (Almunawar & Anshari, 2021). Users can do many activities in it, ranging from investing to doing work remotely, such as in the real world. Even so, in order to be able to plunge into the virtual world of the Metaverse, there are some things that must be prepared first. Metaverse requires support from modern devices that collect data, such as mobile phones and VR or AR glasses. In addition, Metaverse will require the internet as its main access, supported by technological developments that are now increasingly sophisticated (Anshari & Almunawar, 2021; Anshari, 2020). Later, users will require a variety of devices to make metaverse activities more real and simple to carry out (Anshari et al., 2020; Razzaq et al., 2018).

The metaverse has changed how we do business in today's digital world, but not only that, the metaverse has also changed our lifestyle. Without our knowing it, we enter the world of the metaverse, as evidenced by shopping. We are now beginning to believe that online shopping is more practical, with the Metaverse making it easier for us to shop because we can directly try the goods we buy. In addition, many companies are changing their marketing strategies to be all-digital, including their online advertising purchases. It will be predicted that NFTs or other cryptoassets will become the currency that prevails in the metaverse. This has the potential to convert all future transactions to all-digital transactions.

Why was the metaverse created? One reason for creating the metaverse is to create an experience so that a person has a feeling of presence as if they were in a different place. This will give you a completely different feeling than a 2D app or web page can offer. For example, you will be able to create your own virtual office space instead of just making phone calls. You will be able to sit like a hologram on the sofa with the person you want to talk to. It will really feel as if you are in one place, even if we are in a different state or hundreds of miles apart. Facebook already has a professional version of the ongoing metaverse. Horizon Workrooms is a mobile app that allows Oculus Sports employees to enter virtual offices and hold meetings. How can the metaverse have implications for the future? The transformative potential of the metaverse can be realised with a strong foundation. This foundation consists of four technological pillars that will later become the backbone of the new environment, namely:

- *Holographic Construction*

This construction is used to build geometric models in the virtual world that can later be seen from the device to create an immersive environment for users. This holographic construction also allows users to, for example, view virtual reality versions of buildings and apartments.

- *Holographic Simulation*

By having a person's virtual partner or object react similarly to a person or object in the real world, for example, these simulations aim to balance or align the virtual and real worlds.

- *Integration of virtuality into Reality*

This integration is used to develop 3D maps of the world to achieve more accurate positioning.

- *The Interconnectedness of Virtuality in Reality*

This connection requires transformation between the real and virtual worlds through changes that exist in the virtual world. So later, these two worlds will be related to each other to see what transformation will happen. That metaverse will never materialise if it is self-made. The metaverse will be co-created and responsibly built so that it can all be realised in the future. There will be no company that will build the Metaverse alone; there will definitely be cooperation globally and internationally with artists, content creators, entrepreneurs, policymakers, and many more. The metaverse will also be built with a strong framework and foundation to create a space or place where people can feel safe, comfortable, secure, and private.

Metaverse Business Model

Metaverse combines two points of view based on blockchain technology, and in accordance with general trends, these are some of the business models that Metaverse will have in the future, as discussed below.

1. **NFT Sales (Non-Fungible Token)**

NFTs are a type of digital asset that is expanding in popularity. From visual artwork to food and unusual tweets, this one object is causing the effects of tulip mania among young investors. NFTs are bought and sold online, and are often paid for with cryptocurrency, and are generally encoded using basic software similar to other crypto assets. NFTs are also generally rated as one of the very limited transaction processes and have a unique identifier code. why do people really want non fungible tokens? This happens because NFTs allow buyers to own the original item. Not only that, NFTs also contain built-in authentication, which serves as proof of ownership.

How NFTs work. NFTs are part of the blockchain. Therefore, the NFT buyer can later verify that he is the sole owner of the asset he has purchased. Once paid, no one can cancel the ownership rights to the NFT held by the buyer. NFTs are also digital assets that cannot be reproduced repeatedly. Nft owned by the buyer is unique and can be proven through proof of purchase in blockchain with cryptocurrency / crypto. **How to buy and sell NFTs?** NFTs must go through the NFT minting process which is the process of converting digital files into a collection of cryptocurrencies or assets in the blockchain. The process requires marketplaces as third parties or minting agents, such as OpenSea, MakersPlace, Mintable, or Theta Drop. **How is NFT implemented in a business station?** NFTs are often used as a link between physical assets, such as proof of ownership of land or other property. Deed/proof of physical ownership that can be stored is considered more secure in the blockchain with a short verification process. Buyers also do not have to worry about the danger of valuable certificates being lost or stolen by others. Because, their ownership data is already recorded in the blockchain. After all the above explanations about NFTs you may be thinking what are the true benefits of NFTs. A brief explanation based on Blockchains is rare and cannot be faked, its high value makes it easy to resell, eternal and irrevocable ownership rights, Copyright can only be held and managed by the buyer, andsecurity against high assets.

2. **Vox Sales**

The blockchain-based CryptoVoxels game built in the virtual world (Metaverse) is built on the Ethereum blockhain network. In this game you can build, develop, and sell your property on the streets of CryptoVoxels. Your land is held by you, your ownership is documented forever on the blockchain. The virtual world of CryptoVoxels is a world where participants control most of the assets. The Ethereum blockchain network serves as the basis for this application. The users buy rare earth NFTs to own a piece of the world. This is because NFTs symbolize land in the game and their holdings can be tracked because each field is unique. Even if you only own a piece of land in CryptoVoxels, you can still build it and make money from it on the same land as in the real world. CryptoVoxels gives users the freedom to design their own WEARABLES NFTs. In accordance with the overall look and feel of the platform, these voxel-filled items are displayed in the game.

3. Construction

Landowners who own multiple plots of land in the Metaverse have limited time and energy to carry out construction. Other landowners usually hire a team of professionals to build their plots and to expand the branding or brand they own. The demand to hire such a team of professionals has led to the emergence of third-party construction services within the Metaverse such as MetaEstate and Voxel Architects. Origin City the main island of CryptoVoxels within the Metaverse has four of the most popular buildings with the largest number of visitors such as, SpaceAge, StoneAge, GlassAge, and Welcome all built by Voxel Architects.

4. Digital Parcel Rental

Digital cars can be bought and rented just like real estate in the real world. According to the results of data analysis by CV Analytics, many landowners have multiple plots and most of the landowners do not plan to build their own plots, they prefer to make investments in the long run. Therefore, the market for renting natural land has arisen spontaneously. Here landowners can rent out their unused land to others who need it for construction.

5. Immersive Experience

Metaverse is a natural place based on professional architectural design with deep experience in using 3D equipment. Therefore, when entering the metaverse world usually refers or we can look at the experience of people who are too focused in designing virtual environments and forget reality. This immersive learning experience can also serve as a business opportunity within the Metaverse. For example, the synthesis training environment in the Metaverse is based on ugmented reality which can offer a realistic and engaging training experience. The virtual world of the Metaverse can be remade physically as well as mentally with a real-life picture. Metaverse offers a continuous network of virtual worlds and real worlds that can create better prospects for virtual training.

6. Game

Virtual games have properties that can make them easy to integrate into the Metaverse. One blockchain-based game is sandbox community-based blockchain gaming platform where creators can turn voxel assets and wars that exist in the game into NFTs on the blockchain. In addition, the game can certainly be part of other Metaverse platforms. Through on-chain gaming players can enjoy in-game fun while investing in NFTs.

7. Selling Clothes

In the Metaverse there are some things that will never replace the real world. For example, clothing, food, boards, and transportation, that's our basic needs in the real world. In particular selling clothing online has gone from the introduction of 2D graphics in the past to developing to 3D in the future. If we see others trying on clothes must be different sensations by trying on the clothes themselves. By using a 3D scanner, you can now put a 3D virtual version of the outfit to yourself in the 3D virtual version.

8. KTV (Karaoke Television) Online

For people who like TV Karaoke this is their way of socializing. But in the real world it's hard for people who are at a great distance to meet on Karaoke TV. However, in the Metaverse all those wishes can be realized. You can KTV with people who are far away or people who don't even know you for you to duet together.

9. Data Services

Data is many, various, and can be anywhere of course no exception Metaverse. The Metaverse requires visitor data for each admission ticket, the prospective buyer needs historical data on the package sold, and the prospective seller also needs market data to establish the requested on the package he sold. Data support is needed for the above, and professional data analytics service providers can be a very important business in the Metaverse.

10. **Pop up Ads in the Game World**

Ads in the Metaverse are usually holograms or popups. As an illustration in mmorpg-themed games, there is usually an advertisement like a hologram in front of the avatar that is being played. Many things have been taken into account from this advertisement, both in terms of appearance, convenience for users so as not to be disturbed by their activities while in the Metaverse. The curls can appear in certain places or at certain events, and you as a manufacturer just do your research and strategy, where the popup ads will appear to users.

Here are some companies that have launched their own version of Metaverse, namely:

1. **Roblox**

Roblox Corporation (RBLX) video game platform. N) that went public this year. Envisioning the metaverse as a place for "people to come together in millions of 3D experiences to learn, work, play, create, and socialize." Roblox aims to give users and developers a way to create a digital world. The CEO of Roblox also said about shopping in the future and running a business within the platform, which has its own virtual economy with support by its Robux currency.

2. **Microsoft**

CEO of Microsoft Corp. (MSFT. O) Satya Nadella in a mid-year meeting said the company was working to build a "corporate metaverse". That is when the digital and physical worlds meet in offer. Microsoft, which owns xbox and world-building game Minecraft, is also a key player in the gaming world.

3. **Facebook**

Facebook, which will start trading as a Meta Platform on Dec. 1, said it wanted to be seen as a metaverse company rather than social media. The tech giant, which has about 3 billion users, has invested heavily in Augmented

Reality and Virtual Reality and has built its VR environment Horizon, accessed through its Quest headset.

4. Tencent

Chinese tech giant Tencent Holdings Ltd (0700.HK) is the world's largest video game company by revenue. Tencent also has stakes in major gaming studios such as Epic Games and Activision Blizzard. The South China Morning Post reported this year that Tencent has registered many metaverse-related trademarks for its social site QQ.

5. Amazon

E-commerce giant Amazon.com Inc (AMZN. O), which is the world's largest cloud services vendor and has many media offerings, also has potential as a big player in the metaverse. Amazon, which has developed many of its own devices and applications, has the potential to leverage the Metaverse as the business of the future. By creating a virtual reading room for example.

Since Mark Zuckerberg, CEO of Facebook (Meta), introduced his idea to the world, the "Metaverse" has attracted a lot of attention, as well as the pros and cons of the public, investors, and even technology observers. "The Metaverse is a bad idea if we all sit back and watch through it (VR/AR) and feel like something normal," said Robert McNamee, one of Facebook's early investors.According to him, the possibility of the spread of the phenomenon should be a concern for many people from now on. The most obvious danger from this technology is the tendency to make people lazier to move and socialise in the real world. Physical health is also a major problem, such as with vision disorders and obesity, which lurk among metaverse users. Because of the pleasure of surfing the metaverse using avatars that may be self-images that are not conveyed in the real world, it can be difficult for users to accept the situation in the real world. This happens because of the Metaverse's ability to allow its users to display a different self-image from reality. Data theft and manipulation of a person can be more freely done in the metaverse.

In the midst of controversy or problems that occur, the metaverse has a variety of potential benefits. For people with disabilities or elderly Metaverses, this is an opportunity for them to explore this virtual world without involving physical movement like people in general do in the real world (Mulyani et al., 2019; Hamdan et al., 2020). Other companies will also be encouraged to think about marketing and customer outreach concepts through the Metaverse.

Judging from the pattern of technological development that occurs, it is very likely that the Metaverse will become a common technology in the future. There could be a virtual school that teaches sciences that can only be utilised in the metaverse. If managed properly, the Metaverse will certainly be a benefit to many people in the world. Therefore, the problem that occurs is not whether or not this technology is developed. However, how is the direction of its development and the application of ethics to its users? Do not let technology enslave humans; that way, the Metaverse can provide many benefits.

CONCLUSION

The metaverse is the real world created by the convergence of virtuality and reality, which is a virtual world that interacts with the real world on a whole new level. Metaverse is the next evolutionary step after the advent of the internet and social media. Metaverse is altering not only how we connect to the internet but also what we connect to it with. So do not be surprised if, in the future, the world of marketing will go into the metaverse. One example is the gamevertising trend, where the terminology that presents brand advertisements in game exposure is similar to the real world. There are still many people who doubt whether the Metaverse is a decent place to run a business. The explanation is that the metaverse is a path for developing your business to the next step. Then the term "metaverse" itself appeared in 1992 in a novel called Snow Crash, written by Neal Stephenson. At that time, the concept of "metaverse" referred to a virtual world that combined physical and digital aspects. Metaverse is the sundries of the internet world brought together on a virtual platform. Users can perform many activities in it, from doing work remotely to investing like in the real world. One business opportunity that has been widely recognised by many people is the easiest NFT to do in Metaverse. Metaverse has several dangers in its use, such as cybercrime, data theft, addiction, and physical health disorders. Aside from that, the metaverse has numerous potentials or benefits, particularly for people with disabilities and the elderly. The metaverse will also be built with a strong framework and foundation to create a space or place where people can feel safe, comfortable, secure, and private. If we are wise in using the metaverse, there will be no loss in its use.

REFERENCES

Almunawar, M. N., & Anshari, M. (2021). Digital enabler and value integration: Revealing the expansion engine of digital marketplace. *Technology Analysis and Strategic Management*, 1–11.

Anshari, M. (2020, March). Workforce mapping of fourth industrial revolution: Optimization to identity. *Journal of Physics: Conference Series*, *1477*(7), 072023. doi:10.1088/1742-6596/1477/7/072023

Anshari, M., & Almunawar, M. N. (2021). Adopting open innovation for SMEs and industrial revolution 4.0. *Journal of Science and Technology Policy Management*.

Anshari, M., Almunawar, M. N., Lim, S. A., & Al-Mudimigh, A. (2019). Customer relationship management and big data enabled: Personalization & customization of services. *Applied Computing and Informatics*, *15*(2), 94–101. doi:10.1016/j.aci.2018.05.004

Anshari, M., Almunawar, M. N., & Masri, M. (2020). An overview of financial technology in Indonesia. *Financial technology and disruptive innovation in ASEAN*, 216-224.

Anshari, M., Syafrudin, M., Fitriyani, N. L., & Razzaq, A. (2022). Ethical Responsibility and Sustainability (ERS) Development in a Metaverse Business Model. *Sustainability*, *14*(23), 15805. doi:10.3390u142315805

Hamdan, M., Jaidin, J. H., Fithriyah, M., & Anshari, M. (2020, December). E-learning in time of COVID-19 pandemic: Challenges & experiences. In *2020 Sixth International Conference on e-Learning (econf)* (pp. 12-16). IEEE. 10.1109/econf51404.2020.9385507

Juna, M. A., Anshari, M., Ahmad, N., & Hamdan, M. (2022). Working from home, COVID-19 and multi-dimensional model of well-being theory. *International Journal of Work Organisation and Emotion*, *13*(3), 230–259. doi:10.1504/IJWOE.2022.126957

Mulyani, M. A., Razzaq, A., Sumardi, W. H., & Anshari, M. (2019, August). Smartphone adoption in mobile learning scenario. In *2019 International Conference on Information Management and Technology (ICIMTech)* (Vol. 1, pp. 208-211). IEEE. 10.1109/ICIMTech.2019.8843755

Mystakidis. (2022). *Metaverse*. Multidisciplinary Digital Publishing Institute.

Razzaq, A., Samiha, Y. T., & Anshari, M. (2018). Smartphone habits and behaviors in supporting students self-efficacy. *International Journal of Emerging Technologies in Learning, 13*(2), 94. doi:10.3991/ijet.v13i02.7685

Sari. (2022). *Pemanfaatan NFT sebagai peluang bisnis pada era Metaverse*. Jurnal Akrab Juara.

Sari, D. P. (2022). Pemanfaatan NFT Sebagai Peluang Bisnis Pada Era Metaverse. *Jurnal Akrab Juara, 7*(1), 237–245. https://dspace.uii.ac.id/handle/123456789/29069

Compilation of References

Abdelrasoul, E., Mahmoud, I., Stergiou, P., & Katz, L. (2015). The Accuracy of a Real Time Sensor in an Instrumented Basketball. *Procedia Engineering*, *112*, 202–206. doi:10.1016/j.proeng.2015.07.200

Abdlkarim, D., & Holland, P. (n.d.). *A Methodological Framework to Assess the Accuracy of Virtual Reality Hand-Tracking Systems: A case study with the Oculus Quest 2*. doi:10.1101/2022.02.18.481001

Abu-Bakar, M. M. (2017). *Shariah Analysis of Bitcoin, Cryptocurrency and Blockchain*. Blossom.

Abujassar, R. S., Yaseen, H., & Al-Adwan, A. S. (2021). A highly effective route for real-time traffic using an IOT smart algorithm for Tele-surgery using 5G networks. *Journal of Sensor and Actuator Networks*, *10*(2), 30. doi:10.3390/jsan10020030

Adams, G. L., & Lamont, B. (2003). Knowledge management systems and developing sustainable competitive advantage. *Journal of Knowledge Management*, *7*(2), 142–154. doi:10.1108/13673270310477342

Ahad, A. D., Anshari, M., & Razzaq, A. (2017). Domestication of smartphones among adolescents in Brunei Darussalam. *International Journal of Cyber Behavior, Psychology and Learning*, *7*(4), 26–39. doi:10.4018/IJCBPL.2017100103

Ahmadi Marzaleh, M., Peyravi, M., & Shaygani, F. (2022). A revolution in health: Opportunities and challenges of the Metaverse. *EXCLI Journal*, *21*, 791–792. doi:10.17179/excli2022-5017 PMID:35949490

Akçayır, M., & Akçayır, G. (2017). Advantages and challenges associated with augmented reality for education: A systematic review of the literature. *Educational Research Review*, *20*, 1–11. doi:10.1016/j.edurev.2016.11.002

Alam, N., Gupta, L., & Zameni, A. (2019). *Fintech and Islamic Finance: Digitalization, Development and Disruption*. Palgrave MacMillan. doi:10.1007/978-3-030-24666-2

Alexander, M. W., Truel, A. D., & Zhao, J. J. (2012). Expected advantages and disadvantages of online learning: Perceptions from college students who have not taken online courses. *Issues in Information Systems*, *13*(2), 193–200. doi:10.48009/2_iis_2012_193-200

Almunawar, M. N., & Anshari, M. (2022). Customer acceptance of online delivery platform during the COVID-19 pandemic: the case of Brunei Darussalam. *Journal of Science and Technology Policy Management.*

Almunawar, M. N., Anshari, M., & Lim, S. A. (2020). Customer acceptance of ride-hailing in Indonesia. *Journal of Science and Technology Policy Management.*

Almunawar, M. N., & Anshari, M. (2021). Digital enabler and value integration: Revealing the expansion engine of digital marketplace. *Technology Analysis and Strategic Management*, 1–11.

Almunawar, M. N., Anshari, M., & Lim, S. A. (2021). A framework for observing digital marketplace. *International Journal of Hyperconnectivity and the Internet of Things*, *5*(2), 57–73. doi:10.4018/IJHIoT.2021070104

Anshari, M., & Almunawar, M. N. (2021). Adopting open innovation for SMEs and industrial revolution 4.0. *Journal of Science and Technology Policy Management.*

Anshari, M., & Hamdan, M. (2022). Enhancing e-government with a digital twin for innovation management. *Journal of Science and Technology Policy Management.*

Anshari, M., Alas, Y., Razzaq, A., Shahrill, M., & Lim, S. A. (2021b). Millennials consumers' behaviors between trends and experiments. In Research Anthology on E-Commerce Adoption, Models, and Applications for Modern Business (pp. 1492-1508). IGI Global.

Anshari, M., Almunawar, M. N., & Masri, M. (2020). An overview of financial technology in Indonesia. *Financial technology and disruptive innovation in ASEAN*, 216-224.

Anshari, M. (2019). Redefining electronic health records (EHR) and electronic medical records (EMR) to promote patient empowerment. *IJID*, *8*(1), 35–39. doi:10.14421/ijid.2019.08106

Anshari, M. (2020, March). Workforce mapping of fourth industrial revolution: Optimization to identity. *Journal of Physics: Conference Series*, *1477*(7), 072023. doi:10.1088/1742-6596/1477/7/072023

Anshari, M., Alas, Y., & Sulaiman, E. (2019). Smartphone addictions and nomophobia among youth. *Vulnerable Children and Youth Studies*, *14*(3), 242–247. doi:10.1080/17450128.2019.1614709

Anshari, M., & Almunawar, M. N. (2018). Pervasive Mobile Health. In *Encyclopedia of Information Science and Technology* (4th ed., pp. 5908–5917). IGI Global.

Anshari, M., & Almunawar, M. N. (2018). Social customer relationship management, election and political campaign. *International Journal of Electronic Customer Relationship Management*, *11*(4), 332–346. doi:10.1504/IJECRM.2018.096239

Anshari, M., & Almunawar, M. N. (2019, August). Big Data in Healthcare for Personalization & Customization of Healthcare Services. In *2019 International Conference on Information Management and Technology (ICIMTech)* (Vol. 1, pp. 73-77). IEEE.

Anshari, M., Almunawar, M. N., & Lim, S. A. (2018, February). Big data and open government data in public services. In *Proceedings of the 2018 10th International Conference on Machine Learning and Computing* (pp. 140-144). 10.1145/3195106.3195172

Anshari, M., Almunawar, M. N., Lim, S. A., & Al-Mudimigh, A. (2019). Customer relationship management and big data enabled: Personalization & customization of services. *Applied Computing and Informatics, 15*(2), 94–101. doi:10.1016/j.aci.2018.05.004

Anshari, M., Almunawar, M. N., & Masri, M. (2022). Digital Twin: Financial Technology's Next Frontier of Robo-Advisor. *Journal of Risk and Financial Management, 15*(4), 163. doi:10.3390/jrfm15040163

Anshari, M., Almunawar, M. N., Masri, M., & Hamdan, M. (2019b). Digital marketplace and FinTech to support agriculture sustainability. *Energy Procedia, 156*, 234–238. doi:10.1016/j.egypro.2018.11.134

Anshari, M., Almunawar, M. N., Masri, M., & Hrdy, M. (2021a). Financial technology with ai-enabled and ethical challenges. *Society, 58*(3), 189–195. doi:10.100712115-021-00592-w

Anshari, M., Almunawar, M. N., & Razzaq, A. (2021). Developing talents vis-à-vis fourth industrial revolution. *International Journal of Asian Business and Information Management, 12*(4), 20–32. doi:10.4018/IJABIM.20211001.oa2

Anshari, M., Almunawar, M. N., Younis, M. Z., & Kisa, A. (2021c). Modeling Users' Empowerment in E-Health Systems. *Sustainability, 13*(23), 12993. doi:10.3390u132312993

Anshari, M., & Hamdan, M. (2022). Understanding knowledge management and upskilling in Fourth Industrial Revolution: Transformational shift and SECI model. *VINE Journal of Information and Knowledge Management Systems*. Advance online publication. doi:10.1108/VJIKMS-09-2021-0203

Anshari, M., Hamdan, M., Ahmad, N., Ali, E., & Haidi, H. (2022a). COVID-19, artificial intelligence, ethical challenges and policy implications. *AI & Society*, 1–14. doi:10.100700146-022-01471-6 PMID:35607368

Anshari, M., Sakalayen, Q., Fithriyah, M., & Lim, S. A. (2022c). Decision Aid in Logistics during COVID-19 Induced Disruption and Significance of a Digital Ecosystem. In *2022 International Conference on Decision Aid Sciences and Applications (DASA)* (pp. 1371-1377). IEEE. 10.1109/DASA54658.2022.9765144

Anshari, M., & Sumardi, W. H. (2020). Employing big data in business organisation and business ethics. *International Journal of Business Governance and Ethics, 14*(2), 181–205. doi:10.1504/IJBGE.2020.106349

Anshari, M., Syafrudin, M., & Fitriyani, N. L. (2022). Fourth Industrial Revolution between Knowledge Management and Digital Humanities. *Information (Basel), 13*(6), 292. doi:10.3390/info13060292

Anshari, M., Syafrudin, M., Fitriyani, N. L., & Razzaq, A. (2022). Ethical Responsibility and Sustainability (ERS) Development in a Metaverse Business Model. *Sustainability, 14*(23), 15805. doi:10.3390u142315805

Asha, S., Kanchana Devi, V., & Sahaja Vaishnavi, G. (2022). Artificial Intelligence in Healthcare Data Science with Knowledge Engineering. Handbook of Intelligent Healthcare Analytics, 255–283. doi:10.1002/9781119792550.ch12

Asif, S. (2018). The halal and haram aspect of cryptocurrencies in Islam. *Journal of Islamic Banking and Finance*, 91-101.

Awosika, E. (2022, March 14). *Why Should Businesses Care About The Metaverse?* Retrieved from Business Tech Guides: https://businesstechguides.co/importance-of-metaverse-for-businesses

Badiali, G., Ferrari, V., Cutolo, F., Freschi, C., Caramella, D., Bianchi, A., & Marchetti, C. (2014). Augmented reality as an aid in maxillofacial surgery: Validation of a wearable system allowing maxillary repositioning. *Journal of Cranio-Maxillo-Facial Surgery, 42*(8), 1970–1976. doi:10.1016/j.jcms.2014.09.001 PMID:25441867

Bal, B., & Dureja, G. (2012). Hawk Eye: A Logical Innovative Technology Use in Sports for Effective Decision Making. *Sport Science Review, 21*(1-2), 107–119. doi:10.2478/v10237-012-0006-6

Barney, J. (1991). Firm resources and sustained competitive advantage. *Journal of Management, 17*(1), 99–120. doi:10.1177/014920639101700108

Barry, D. M., Ogawa, N., Dharmawansa, A., Kanematsu, H., Fukumura, Y., Shirai, T., Yajima, K., & Kobayashi, T. (2015). Evaluation for students' learning manner using eye blinking system in Metaverse. *Procedia Computer Science, 60*, 1195–1204. doi:10.1016/j.procs.2015.08.181

Bath. (2022). *Motion capture reveals why VAR in football struggles with offside decisions*. Retrieved 23 September 2022, from https://www.bath.ac.uk/announcements/motion-capture-reveals-why-var-in-football-struggles-with-offside-decisions/#:~:text=The%20study%20suggests%20that%20VAR,red%20cards%2C%20penalties%20and%20offsides

BBC. (2022). *What does football look like in the metaverse?* Retrieved 22 September 2022, from https://www.bbc.com/sport/football/61473631

Bedué, P., & Fritzsche, A. (2021). Can we trust AI? An empirical investigation of trust requirements and guide to successful AI adoption. *Journal of Enterprise Information Management.*

Belei, N., Noteborn, G., & De Ruyter, K. (2011). It's a brand-new world: Teaching brand management in virtual environments. *Journal of Brand Management, 18*(8), 611–623. doi:10.1057/bm.2011.6

Berawi, M. A. (2018). Utilizing Big Data In Industry 4.0: Managing Competitive Advantages And Business Ethics. *International Journal of Technology, 3*(3), 430–433. doi:10.14716/ijtech.v9i3.1948

Bermejo, C., & Hui, P. (2022). *Life, the Metaverse and Everything: An Overview of Privacy.* Ethics, and Governance in Metaverse., doi:10.13140/RG.2.2.35094.63042

Bibri, S. E. (2022). The social shaping of the metaverse as an alternative to the imaginaries of data-driven Smart Cities: A Study in Science, technology, and Society. *Smart Cities*, *5*(3), 832–874. doi:10.3390martcities5030043

Bibri, S. E., & Allam, Z. (2022). The Metaverse as a Virtual Form of Data-Driven Smart Urbanism: On Post-Pandemic Governance through the Prism of the Logic of Surveillance Capitalism. *Smart Cities*, *5*(2), 715–727. doi:10.3390martcities5020037

Birch, K. (2022, February 17). *JP Morgan is first leading bank to launch in the metaverse.* Retrieved from FinTech Magazine: https://fintechmagazine.com/banking/jp-morgan-becomes-the-first-bank-to-launch-in-the-metaverse

Bloomberg - Are you a robot ? (2021). Retrieved 30 September 2022, from https://www.bloomberg.com/professional/blog/metaverse-may-be-800-billion-market-next-tech-platform/

Bonk, C. J., & Graham, C. R. (Eds.). (in press). *Handbook of blended learning: Global Perspectives, local designs*. Pfeiffer Publishing.

Bouheraoua, S., Mohamad, S., Kasri, N. S., & Abdullah, S. (2015). Shariah Issues in Intangible Assets. *Jurnal Syariah*, 287-324.

Brown, J. (2017). *Hadith: Muhammad's legacy in the medieval and modern world.* Simon and Schuster.

Cardinal, L. B., Alessandri, T. M., & Turner, S. F. (2001). Knowledge codifiability, resources, and science-based innovation. *Journal of Knowledge Management*, *5*(2), 195–204. doi:10.1108/13673270110393266

Carrillo, A. (2022, June 24). *Gucci unveils an NFT gallery with 'The Next 100 Years of Gucci'.* Retrieved from Input Magazine: https://www.inputmag.com/style/gucci-100-years-nft-gallery

Cascales, A., Pérez-López, D., & Contero, M. (2013). Study on parent's acceptance of the augmented reality use for preschool education. *Procedia Computer Science*, *25*, 420–427. doi:10.1016/j.procs.2013.11.053

Chauhan, P., & Sood, M. (2021). Big Data: Present and Future. *IEEE Computer Society*, *54*(4), 59–65. doi:10.1109/MC.2021.3057442

Chen, D., & Zhang, R. (2022). Exploring research trends of emerging technologies in Healt Metaverse: A Bibliometric analysis. SSRN *Electronic Journal*. doi:10.2139/ssrn.3998068

Chengoden, R., Victor, N., Huynh-The, T., Yenduri, G., Jhaveri, R. H., Alazab, M., . . . Gadekallu, T. R. (2022). *Metaverse for Healthcare: A Survey on Potential Applications, Challenges and Future Directions.* arXiv preprint arXiv:2209.04160.

City, A. M. (2022). *How the metaverse will change the world.* Retrieved 30 September 2022, from https://www.cityam.com/how-the-metaverse-will-change-the-world/#:~:text=The%20metaverse%2C%20by%20offering%20a,so%20as%20to%20solve%20problems

Classting AI. (n.d.). *Classiting. Artificial intelligence analysis screen for all subjects and distribution table of achievement change by unit.* Retrieved September 24, 2022, from https://www.classting.ai/

Coingeek. (2022). *Zetly's 'Sport Metaverse' gives fans an all-in-one bonding experience with their favorite teams.* Retrieved 23 September 2022, from https://coingeek.com/zetly-sport-metaverse-gives-fans-an-all-in-one-bonding-experience-with-their-favorite-teams/

Collins, C. (2008). Looking to the future: Higher education in the Metaverse. *EDUCAUSE Review, 43*(5), 51–63.

Comcastsportstech. (2022). *Four Ways the Metaverse May Impact Sports Tech | Comcast SportsTech.* Retrieved 22 September 2022, from https://www.comcastsportstech.com/inside-track/four-ways-the-metaverse-may-impact-sports-tech/

Conway, M., & O'Connor, D. (2016). Social media, big data, and mental health: Current advances and ethical implications. *Current Opinion in Psychology, 9*, 77–82. doi:10.1016/j.copsyc.2016.01.004 PMID:27042689

Cryptoflies. (2022). *FIFA to Bring WORLD CUP 2026 to the Metaverse.* Retrieved 23 September 2022, from https://blog.cryptoflies.com/fifa-to-bring-world-cup-2026-to-the-metaverse/

Cryptonews. (2022). *Sports NFTs: What are They and Why are They So Popular?* Retrieved 23 September 2022, from https://cryptonews.com/exclusives/sports-nfts-what-are-they-why-are-they-so-popular.htm#:~:text=What%20are%20sports%20NFTs%3F,other%20types%20of%20sports%20items

Dadayan, L., & Ferro, E. (n.d.). *When Technology Meets the Mind: A Comparative Study of the Technology Acceptance Model.* Academic Press.

Damar, M. (2022). What the Literature on Medicine, Nursing, Public Health, Midwifery, and Dentistry Reveals: An Overview of the Rapidly Approaching Metaverse. *Journal of Metaverse, 2*(2), 62–70. doi:10.57019/jmv.1132962

Darroch, J., & McNaughton, R. (2002). Examining the link between knowledge management practices and types of innovation. *Journal of Intellectual Capital, 3*(3), 210–222. doi:10.1108/14691930210435570

Davis, A., Murphy, J., Owens, D., Khazanchi, D., & Zigurs, I. (2009). Avatars, people, and virtual worlds: Foundations for research in metaverses. *Journal of the Association for Information Systems, 10*(2), 90–117. doi:10.17705/1jais.00183

Davis, F. (1989). Perceived Usefulness, Perceived Ease of Use, and User Acceptance of Information Technology. *Management Information Systems Quarterly, 13*(3), 319. doi:10.2307/249008

Denholm, J. A., Protopsaltis, A., & de Freitas, S. (2013). The value of Team-Based Mixed-Reality (TBMR) games in higher education. *International Journal of Game-Based Learning, 3*(1), 18–33. doi:10.4018/ijgbl.2013010102

Dhamdere, S. N. (2015). Importance of knowledge management in the higher educational institutes. *Turkish Online Journal of Distance Education*, *16*(1), 162–183. doi:10.17718/tojde.34392

Díaz, J., Saldana, C., & Avila, C. (2020). Virtual world as a resource for hybrid education. *Int. J. Emerg. Technol. Learn.*, *15*(15), 94–109.

Dionisio, J., Burns, W. III, & Gilbert, R. (2013). 3D Virtual Worlds and the Metaverse. *ACM Computing Surveys*, *45*(3), 1–38. doi:10.1145/2480741.2480751

Dive, D. (2022). *Metaverse Technology Opens Up a Wider World of Privacy Concerns*. Retrieved 10 September 2022, from https://news.bloomberglaw.com/privacy-and-data-security/metaverse-technology-opens-up-a-wider-world-of-privacy-concerns

Dixon, R. (2022). *What You Need to Know About How the Metaverse Will Affect Business*. Retrieved from https://www.entrepreneur.com/article/415480

Duan, H., Li, J., Fan, S., Lin, Z., Wu, X., & Cai, W. (2021). Metaverse for social good. *Proceedings of the 29th ACM International Conference on Multimedia*. 10.1145/3474085.3479238

Economictimes. (2022). *Sports Metaverse launches virtual land sale*. Retrieved 22 September 2022, from https://economictimes.indiatimes.com/markets/cryptocurrency/sports-metaverse-launches-virtual-land-sale/articleshow/92876154.cms?from=mdr

Erturk, E., & Reynolds, G. B. (2020). The expanding role of immersive media in education. In *International Conference on E-Learning* (pp. 191–194). Academic Press.

Eschenbrenner, B., Nah, F. F.-H., & Siau, K. (2008). 3-D virtual worlds in education. *Journal of Database Management*, *19*(4), 91–110. doi:10.4018/jdm.2008100106

ESPN. (2022). *Study: Hawk-Eye not as accurate as people think*. Retrieved 23 September 2022, from https://www.espn.com/sports/tennis/wimbledon08/news/story?id=3452293

Estudante, A., & Dietrich, N. (2020). Using augmented reality to stimulate students and difuse escape game activities to larger audiences. *Journal of Chemical Education*, *97*(5), 1368–1374. doi:10.1021/acs.jchemed.9b00933

Farjami, S., Taguchi, R., Nakahira, K. T., Nunez Rattia, R., Fukumura, Y., & Kanematsu, H. (2011). Multilingual problem based learning in metaverse. *Knowledge-Based and Intelligent Information and Engineering Systems*, 499–509. doi:10.1007/978-3-642-23854-3_53

Firmansyah, R., Putri, D. M., Wicaksono, M. G. S., Putri, S. F., & Widianto, A. A. (2021). The university students' perspectives on the advantages and disadvantages of online learning due to COVID-19. *Proceedings of 2nd Annual Management, Business and Economic Conference (AMBEC 2020)*, 183. 10.2991/aebmr.k.210717.025

Fithriyah, M., Masri, M., Almunawar, M. N., & Anshari, M. (2022). Financial Inclusion and Mobile Payment to Empower Small and Medium-Sized Enterprises: Post-COVID-19 Business Strategy. In FinTech Development for Financial Inclusiveness (pp. 50-59). IGI Global.

Folger, J. (2021). *What Does Metaverse Mean and How Does This Virtual World Work?* Retrieved from: https://www.investopedia.com/metaverse-definition-5206578

FT. (2022). *Football's future is in the metaverse.* Retrieved 23 September 2022, from https://www.ft.com/content/ee267372-15e6-459c-b786-da605f8d0258

Gao, Q., & Gadekallu, T. R. (2022). Design of telemedicine information query system based on Wireless Sensor Network. *EAI Endorsed Transactions on Pervasive Health and Technology*, *8*(4), e1. Advance online publication. doi:10.4108/eetpht.v8i4.674

Garrison, D., & Kanuka, H. (2004). Blended learning: Uncovering its transformative potential in higher education. *The Internet and Higher Education*, *7*(2), 95–105. doi:10.1016/j.iheduc.2004.02.001

Gee, J. P. (2003). What video games have to teach us about learning and literacy. *Computers in Entertainment, 1*(1), 20. .950595 doi:10.1145/950566

Germain, J. (2022, March 17). *A Step Into Meta's VR Meeting World, Horizon Workrooms.* Retrieved from Tech News World: https://www.technewsworld.com/story/a-step-into-metas-vr-meeting-world-horizon-workrooms-87448.html

Gestalt, A. (2022). *10 Ways the Metaverse Will Change the World - Listverse.* Retrieved 30 September 2022, from https://listverse.com/2022/04/30/10-ways-the-metaverse-will-change-the-world/

Globenewswire. (2022). *SportsIcon Previews The Sports Metaverse with Legendary Athletes.* Retrieved 22 September 2022 from https://www.globenewswire.com/news-release/2022/03/23/2408882/0/en/SportsIcon-Previews-The-Sports-Metaverse-with-Legendary-Athletes.html

Goh, R. L., Kong, Y. X., McAlinden, C., Liu, J., Crowston, J. G., & Skalicky, S. E. (2018). Objective assessment of activity limitation in glaucoma with smartphone virtual reality goggles: A pilot study. *Translational Vision Science & Technology*, *7*(1), 10. doi:10.1167/tvst.7.1.10 PMID:29372112

González Crespo, R., Escobar, R. F., Joyanes Aguilar, L., Velazco, S., & Castillo Sanz, A. G. (2013). Use of ARIMA mathematical analysis to model the implementation of expert system courses by means of free software OpenSim and Sloodle platforms in virtual university campuses. *Expert Systems with Applications*, *40*(18), 7381–7390. doi:10.1016/j.eswa.2013.06.054

Gopalakrishnan, S., Jacob, C. E., Kumar, M., Karunakaran, V., & Raman, R. (2020). Comparison of visual parameters between normal individuals and people with low vision in a virtual environment. *Cyberpsychology, Behavior, and Social Networking*, *23*(3), 171–178. doi:10.1089/cyber.2019.0235 PMID:32150699

Gourlay, S. (n.d.). *The SECI model of knowledge creation: some empirical shortcomings.* Academic Press.

Green, C. S., & Bavelier, D. (2003). Action video game modifies visual selective attention. *Nature*, *423*(6939), 534–537. doi:10.1038/nature01647 PMID:12774121

Gunasekeran, D. V., Low, R., Gunasekeran, R., Chan, B., Ong, H. Y., Raje, D., Mi, H., Pavesio, C., Nguyen, Q. D., & Agrawal, R. (2020). Population Eye Health Education using augmented reality and virtual reality: Scalable tools during and beyond COVID-19. *BMJ Innovations*, *7*(2), 278–283. doi:10.1136/bmjinnov-2020-000522

Gutierrez, G. (2020). Artificial intelligence in the intensive care unit. *Annual Update in Intensive Care and Emergency Medicine*, *2020*, 667–681. doi:10.1007/978-3-030-37323-8_51 PMID:32204716

Hamdan, M., Ahmad, N., Jaidin, J. H., & Anshari, M. (2020b). Internationalisation in Brunei's higher education and its policy implications: Case study of Universiti Brunei Darussalam. *TEST Engineering and Management*, *83*, 764–779.

Hamdan, M., Jaidin, J. H., Fithriyah, M., & Anshari, M. (2020, December). E-learning in time of COVID-19 pandemic: Challenges & experiences. In *2020 Sixth International Conference on e-Learning (econf)* (pp. 12-16). IEEE. 10.1109/econf51404.2020.9385507

Han, J., Heo, J., & You, E. (2021, October). Analysis of metaverse platform as a new play culture: Focusing on roblox and zepeto. In *Proceedings of the 2nd International Conference on Human-centered Artificial Intelligence (Computing4Human 2021). CEUR Workshop Proceedings*. https://ceur-ws.org/Vol-3026/paper3.pdf

Han, H. W. (2008). A study on typology of virtual world and its development in metaverse. *Journal of Digital Contents Society*, *9*(2), 317–323.

Harris, P., Connolly, J., & Feeney, L. (2009). Blended learning: Overview and recommendations for successful implementation. *Industrial and Commercial Training*, *41*(3), 155–163. doi:10.1108/00197850910950961

Hasmawati, F., Samiha, Y. T., Razzaq, A., & Anshari, M. (2020). Understanding nomophobia among digital natives: Characteristics and challenges. *Journal of Critical Reviews*, *7*(13), 122–131.

Hawks, C., & Krasniansky, A. (2022). *Digital health enters the metaverse*. https://rockhealth.com/insights/digital-health-enters-the-metaverse/

Hazari, S. (2021, February 19). *The Benefits Of Online Learning During The Pandemic*. London College of Contemporary Arts. https://www.lcca.org.uk/blog/student-life/the-benefits-of-online-learning-during-the-pandemic/

Hofacker, C. F., Malthouse, E. C., & Sultan, F. (2016). Big Data and consumer behavior: Imminent opportunities. *Journal of Consumer Marketing*, *33*(2), 89–97. doi:10.1108/JCM-04-2015-1399

Holvast, J. (2009). History of Privacy. *The Future Of Identity In The Information Society*, 13-42. doi:10.1007/978-3-642-03315-5_2

Howson, P., & de Vries, A. (2022). Preying on the poor? Opportunities and challenges for tackling the social and environmental threats of cryptocurrencies for vulnerable and low-income communities. *Energy Research & Social Science*, *84*, 102394. doi:10.1016/j.erss.2021.102394

Hwang, G. J., & Chien, S. Y. (2022). Definition, roles, and potential research issues of the metaverse in education: An artificial intelligence perspective. *Computers and Education: Artificial Intelligence*, *3*, 100082. doi:10.1016/j.caeai.2022.100082

IndustryTrends. (2022). *Challenges in metaverse and how to overcome them.* Retrieved from: https://www.analyticsinsight.net/challenges-in-metaverse-and-how-to-overcome-them/

Isaac, M. (2021). *To Build the Metaverse, Meta First Wants to Build Stores*. Retrieved 30 September 2022, from https://www.nytimes.com/2021/11/05/technology/facebook-stores-meta-metaverse.html

Iskander, M., Ogunsola, T., Ramachandran, R., McGowan, R., & Al-Aswad, L. A. (2021). Virtual reality and augmented reality in ophthalmology: A contemporary prospective. *Asia-Pacific Journal of Ophthalmology*, *10*(3), 244–252. doi:10.1097/APO.0000000000000409 PMID:34383716

ISPO. (2022). *Metaverse: The Revolution of the Sports World.* Retrieved 22 September 2022, from https://www.ispo.com/en/trends/metaverse-revolution-sports-world

Jagannathan, S. (n.d.). *Education Meets The Metaverse: Reimagining The Future Of Learning*. World Bank Group. Retrieved September 20, 2022, from https://olc.worldbank.org/about-olc/education-meets-the-metaverse-reimagining-the-future-of-learning

Jaman, S. F. I., & Anshari, M. (2021). Facebook as marketing tools for organizations: Knowledge management analysis. In *Research Anthology on Strategies for Using Social Media as a Service and Tool in Business* (pp. 117–131). IGI Global. doi:10.4018/978-1-7998-9020-1.ch007

Javaid, M., Haleem, A., & Khan, I. H. (2020). Holography applications toward medical field: An overview. *The Indian Journal of Radiology & Imaging*, *30*(3), 354–361. doi:10.4103/ijri.IJRI_39_20 PMID:33273770

Jensen, L., & Konradsen, F. (2017). A review of the use of virtual reality head-mounted displays in education and training. *Education and Information Technologies*, *23*(4), 1515–1529. doi:10.100710639-017-9676-0

Jones, P. R., Somoskeöy, T., Chow-Wing-Bom, H., & Crabb, D. P. (2020). Seeing other perspectives: Evaluating the use of virtual and augmented reality to simulate visual impairments (openvissim). *NPJ Digital Medicine*, *3*(1), 32. Advance online publication. doi:10.103841746-020-0242-6 PMID:32195367

Juna, M. A., Anshari, M., Ahmad, N., & Hamdan, M. (2022). Working from home, COVID-19 and multi-dimensional model of well-being theory. *International Journal of Work Organisation and Emotion*, *13*(3), 230–259. doi:10.1504/IJWOE.2022.126957

Jung, E. J., & Kim, N. H. (2021). Virtual and augmented reality for Vocational Education:A review of major issues. *Korean Association for Educational Information and Media, 27*(1), 79–109. doi:10.15833/KAFEIAM.27.1.079

Kamenov, K. (2017). *The 4th Wave in Technology | Part 1 | Accenture*. Retrieved 30 September 2022, from https://www.accenture.com/gb-en/blogs/blogs-immersive-experience-wave-learning-ropes

Kasraie, N., & Alahmad, A. (2014). Investigating the Reasons Institutions of Higher Education in the USA and Canada Utilize Blended Learning. *Mevlana International Journal of Education, 4*(1), 67–81. doi:10.13054/mije.13.68.4.1

Kemp, J., & Livingstone, D. (2006). Putting a Second Life "Metaverse" skin on learning management systems. *Proceedings of the Second Life Education Workshop at the Second Life Community Convention*, 20.

Kensinger, R. (2021). *Metaverse*. doi:10.13140/RG.2.2.19971.22564

Kim, S. (2020). *Metaverse: Digital world, world of emerging items*. PlanB Design.

Kostoff, R. N., Boylan, R., & Simons, G. R. (2004). Disruptive Technology Roadmaps. *Technological Forecasting and Social Change, 71*(1-2), 141–159. doi:10.1016/S0040-1625(03)00048-9

Kumar, A. (2022, July 10). *The Metaverse In eLearning*. eLearning Industry. https://elearningindustry.com/the-metaverse-in-elearning

Kuş, O. (2021). Metaverse: 'Dijital büyük patlamada'fırsatlar ve endişelere yönelik algılar. *Intermedia International E-journal, 8*(15), 245–266. doi:10.21645/intermedia.2021.109

Kye, B., Han, N., Kim, E., Park, Y., & Jo, S. (2021). Educational applications of metaverse: Possibilities and limitations. *Journal of Educational Evaluation for Health Professions, 18*, 32. doi:10.3352/jeehp.2021.18.32 PMID:34897242

Lam, A. K., To, E., Weinreb, R. N., Yu, M., Mak, H., Lai, G., Chiu, V., Wu, K., Zhang, X., Cheng, T. P., Guo, P. Y., & Leung, C. K. (2020). Use of virtual reality simulation to identify vision-related disability in patients with glaucoma. *JAMA Ophthalmology, 138*(5), 490. doi:10.1001/jamaophthalmol.2020.0392 PMID:32191274

Lang, B. (2020). *Social VR App 'VRChat' is Seeing Record Usage Amidst the Pandemic*. Retrieved 30 September 2022, from https://www.roadtovr.com/vrchat-record-users-coronavirus/

Lee, L. H., Braud, T., & Zhou, P. (2021), *All One Needs to Know about Metaverse: A Complete Survey on Technological Singularity, Virtual Ecosystem, and Research Agenda.* Retrieved from: https://tuhat.helsinki.fi/ws/portalfiles/portal/169348619/METAVERSE.pdf

Lee, L. H., Braud, T., Zhou, P., Wang, L., Xu, D., Lin, Z., . . . Hui, P. (2021). *All one needs to know about metaverse: A complete survey on technological singularity, virtual ecosystem, and research agenda.* arXiv preprint arXiv:2110.05352.

Lee, L. H., Lin, Z., Hu, R., Gong, Z., Kumar, A., Li, T., ... Hui, P. (2021). *When Creators Meet the Metaverse: A Survey on Computational Arts*. Academic Press.

Liang, R., & Chen, D.-T. V. (2012). Online learning: Trends, potential and challenges. *Creative Education, 03*(08), 1332–1335. doi:10.4236/ce.2012.38195

Liu, S. H. (2021). *Global healthcare artificial intelligence market growth rate 2014-2021*. https://www.statista.com/statistics/938794/global-healthcare-artificial-intelligence-market-growth-rate/

Mamun, Q. (2022). Blockchain technology in the future of healthcare. *Smart Health (Amsterdam, Netherlands), 23*, 100223. doi:10.1016/j.smhl.2021.100223

Mapfre. (2022). *The growing trend of Esports*. Retrieved 21 September 2022 from https://www.mapfre.com/en/insights/innovation/growing-trend-esports/

Marr, B. (2022). *How the Metaverse Is Changing Sports*. Retrieved 22 September 2022, from https://bernardmarr.com/how-the-metaverse-is-changing-sports/

McCaskill, S. (2022). *NBA launches Meta Quest VR environment to engage fans during playoffs*. Retrieved 22 September 2022, from https://www.sportspromedia.com/news/nba-lane-vr-meta-metaverse/

McDevitt, C. (2021, October 27). *The Future of Crypto Assets Regulation in the UAE*. Retrieved from Hadef & Partners: https://www.lexology.com/library/detail.aspx?g=88c0f35c-7ea5-439b-90d7-df3fe4f70586

McDowell, M. (2021, November 24). *Virtual stores: Fashion's new mode of shopping*. Retrieved from Vogue Business: https://www.voguebusiness.com/technology/virtual-stores-fashions-new-mode-of-shopping

Meta. (2021). *The Facebook Company Is Now Meta | Meta*. Retrieved 30 September 2022, from https://about.fb.com/news/2021/10/facebook-company-is-now-meta/

Milmo, D. (2021). Enter the metaverse: the digital future Mark Zuckerberg is steering us toward. *The Guardian*. Retrieved from https://www.theguardian.com/technology/2021/oct/28/facebook-mark-zuckerberg-meta-metaverse

Moore, K., Jones, C., & Frazier, R. S. (2017). Engineering education for generation Z. *American Journal of Engineering Education, 8*(2), 111–126. doi:10.19030/ajee.v8i2.10067

Morimoto, T., Kobayashi, T., Hirata, H., Otani, K., Sugimoto, M., Tsukamoto, M., Yoshihara, T., Ueno, M., & Mawatari, M. (2022). XR (extended reality: Virtual reality, augmented reality, mixed reality) technology in Spine Medicine: Status Quo and quo vadis. *Journal of Clinical Medicine, 11*(2), 470. doi:10.3390/jcm11020470 PMID:35054164

Mulyani, M. A., Razzaq, A., Sumardi, W. H., & Anshari, M. (2019, August). Smartphone adoption in mobile learning scenario. In *2019 International Conference on Information Management and Technology (ICIMTech)* (Vol. 1, pp. 208-211). IEEE. 10.1109/ICIMTech.2019.8843755

Mulyani, M. A., Yusuf, S., Siregar, P., Nurihsan, J., Razzaq, A., & Anshari, M. (2021, August). Fourth Industrial Revolution and Educational Challenges. In *2021 International Conference on Information Management and Technology (ICIMTech)* (Vol. 1, pp. 245-249). IEEE. 10.1109/ICIMTech53080.2021.9535057

Murphey, D. (2019). *A history of information security - IFSEC Global | Security and Fire News and Resources*. Retrieved 16 September 2022, from https://www.ifsecglobal.com/cyber-security/a-history-of-information-security/

Mystakidis. (2022). *Metaverse*. Multidisciplinary Digital Publishing Institute.

Mystakidis, S. (2022). Metaverse. *Encyclopedia*, *2*(1), 486–497. doi:10.3390/encyclopedia2010031

Mystakidis, S., Fragkaki, M., & Filippousis, G. (2021). Ready teacher One: Virtual and Augmented Reality Online Professional Development for K-12 school teachers. *Computers*, *10*(10), 134. doi:10.3390/computers10100134

Nair, V., Garrido, G. M., & Song, D. (2022). *Exploring the Unprecedented Privacy Risks of the Metaverse*. arXiv preprint arXiv:2207.13176.

Narin, N. G. (2021). A Content Analysis of the Metaverse Articles. *Journal of Metaverse*, 17-24.

NBA. (2022). *NBA Lane comes to life through virtual reality*. Retrieved 23 September 2022, from https://www.nba.com/news/nba-lane-horizon-worlds-meta

Nichols, S., & Patel, H. (2002). Health and safety implications of virtual reality: A review of empirical evidence. *Applied Ergonomics*, *33*(3), 251–271. doi:10.1016/S0003-6870(02)00020-0 PMID:12164509

Ning, H., Wang, H., Lin, Y., Wang, W., Dhelim, S., Farha, F., . . . Daneshmand, M. (2021). *A Survey on Metaverse: The State-of-the-art, Technologies, Applications, and Challenges*. arXiv preprint arXiv:2111.09673.

Ning, H., Wang, H., Lin, Y., Wang, W., Dhelim, S., Farha, F., Ding, J., & Daneshmand, M. (2021, November 18). *A survey on Metaverse: The state-of-the-art, technologies, applications, and challenges*. https://arxiv.org/abs/2111.09673

Nonaka, I. (1994). *A Dynamic Theory of Organizational Knowledge Creation*. Academic Press.

Nonaka, I., & Takeuchi, H. (n.d.). *The Knowledge-Creating Company*. Academic Press.

Nonaka, I., Toyama, R., & Konno, N. (n.d.). *SECI, Ba and Leadership: A Unified Model of Dynamic Knowledge Creation*. www.elsevier.com/locate/lrp

Nonaka, I., & Toyama, R. (2003). The knowledge-creating theory revisited: Knowledge creation as a synthesizing process. *Knowledge Management Research and Practice*, *1*(1), 2–10. https://doi.org/10.1057/palgrave.kmrp.8500001

Ohkubo, S. (2015, August 24). *People, Process, Platform, Partnership, and Problem Solving: The 5P Approach to Strengthening Knowledge Management Capacity and Culture*. Learning Lab. https://usaidlearninglab.org/community/blog/people-process-platform-partnership-and-problem-solving-5p-approach-strengthening

Ojeagbase, S. (2022). *How Will Metaverse Transform Sports Industry?* Retrieved 21 September 2022, from https://www.completesports.com/how-will-metaverse-transform-sports-industry/

Onlinemasters. (2022). *How Technology is Revolutionizing Sports Training | Ohio University*. Retrieved 20 September 2022 from https://onlinemasters.ohio.edu/blog/how-technology-is-revolutionizing-sports-training/#:~:text=Compared%20to%20whiteboards%20and%20post,communication

Park, M. S. (2021, January 11)., *Development of AR technology-based spine surgery platform*. 이투데이. Retrieved September 24, 2022, from https://www.etoday.co.kr/news/view/1982781

Park, S., Kim, S. P., & Whang, M. (2021). Individual's social perception of virtual avatars embodied with their habitual facial expressions and facial appearance. *Sensors (Basel)*, *21*(17), 5986. doi:10.339021175986 PMID:34502877

Park, S.-M., & Kim, Y.-G. (2022). A Metaverse: Taxonomy, components, applications, and open challenges. *IEEE Access: Practical Innovations, Open Solutions*, *10*, 4209–4251. doi:10.1109/ACCESS.2021.3140175

Parrott, M., Ruyak, J., & Liguori, G. (2020). The History of Exercise Equipment. ACSM's Health &Amp. *Fitness Journal*, *24*(6), 5–8. doi:10.1249/FIT.0000000000000612

Patel, H. (2022), *The Metaverse Explained*. Retrieved from: https://www2.deloitte.com/content/dam/Deloitte/us/Documents/mergers-acqisitions/user-friendly-the-metaverse-explained.pdf

Peppard, J., & Ward, J. (2004). Beyond strategic information systems: Towards an IS capability. *The Journal of Strategic Information Systems*, *13*(2), 167–194. doi:10.1016/j.jsis.2004.02.002

Pyka, A. (2002). Innovation networks in economics: From the incentive-based to the knowledge-based approaches. *European Journal of Innovation Management*, *5*(3), 152–163. doi:10.1108/14601060210436727

Rahman, M. T. (2016, July 2). Customers' Attitude towards Online Shopping: The Case of Bangladesh. *World Journal of Social Sciences*, *6*(2), 82–91.

Ramesh, U. V., Harini, A., Gowri, C. S. D., Durga, K. V., Druvitha, P., & Kumar, K. S. (2022). Metaverse: Future of the Internet. *International Journal of Research Publication and Reviews*, *3*(2), 93–97.

Rashmeet, K. (2022). *Challenges faced by the Metaverse in becoming a reality*. Retrieved from: https://medium.datadriveninvestor.com/challenges-faced-by-the-metaverse-in-becoming-a-reality-d02219d29370

Ratten, V. (2020). Sport technology: A commentary. *The Journal of High Technology Management Research*, *31*(1), 100383. doi:10.1016/j.hitech.2020.100383

Ravi, P. (2022, April 24). *Metaverse — A Stepping-Stone To New-Gen Education*. Mindtree. https://www.mindtree.com/insights/blog/metaverse-stepping-stone-new-gen-education

Razzaq, A., Samiha, Y. T., & Anshari, M. (2018). Smartphone habits and behaviors in supporting students self-efficacy. *International Journal of Emerging Technologies in Learning*, *13*(2), 94. doi:10.3991/ijet.v13i02.7685

Reflexion. (2022). *New Examples of Sports Technology That's Changing The Game*. Retrieved 21 September 2022, from https://reflexion.co/blog/sports-technology/

Reyes, C. E. G. (2020). Perception of high school students about using Metaverse in augmented reality learning experi- ences in mathematics. Pixel-Bit. *Media and Education Magazine*, *58*, 143–159.

Safecomputing.umich.edu. (2022). Retrieved 11 September 2022, from https://safecomputing.umich.edu/privacy/history-of-privacy-timeline

Sait, M. A., & Anshari, M. (2021). Industrial Revolution 4.0: A New Challenge to Brunei Darussalam's Unemployment Issue. *International Journal of Asian Business and Information Management*, *12*(4), 33–44. doi:10.4018/IJABIM.20211001.oa3

Sait, S., & Lim, H. (2006). *Land, Law and Islam*. Zed Books. doi:10.5040/9781350221017

Samuel, B. P. (2022). *Potential Value For Your Company In The Metaverse.* Retrieved from: https://www.forbes.com/sites/peterbendorsamuel/2022/07/18/potential-value-for-your-company-in-the-metaverse/?sh=6dbccd2c514e

Sanders, N. (2016). How to Use Big Data to Drive Your Supply Chain. *California Management Review*, *58*(3), 26–48. doi:10.1525/cmr.2016.58.3.26

Sandkuhl, K. (2015). Knowledge Reuse: Survey of Existing Techniques and Classification Approach. *Lecture Notes in Business Information Processing*, *205*, 126–148. doi:10.1007/978-3-319-17551-5_5

Sari, D. P. (2022). Pemanfaatan NFT Sebagai Peluang Bisnis Pada Era Metaverse. *Jurnal Akrab Juara, 7*(1), 237–245. https://dspace.uii.ac.id/handle/123456789/29069

Sari. (2022). *Pemanfaatan NFT sebagai peluang bisnis pada era Metaverse*. Jurnal Akrab Juara.

Seekingalpha. (2022). *The Metaverse? What It Is & What You Should Know*. Retrieved 21 September 2022, from https://seekingalpha.com/article/4472812-what-is-metaverse

Semivolos, A., & Anshari, M. (2023). The Application of Artificial Intelligence to the Process of Logistic During COVID-19. In *Handbook of Research on Artificial Intelligence and Knowledge Management in Asia's Digital Economy* (pp. 1–11). IGI Global.

Shanbhag, R. (2020). Maintaining Strategic Information Systems. *International Journal of IT & Knowledge Management*, *13*(2), 19–21.

Shani, A. B. R., Sena, J. A., & Olin, T. (2003). Knowledge management and new product development: A study of two companies. *European Journal of Innovation Management*, *6*(3), 137–149. doi:10.1108/14601060310486217

Sheel, N., Verma, L. P., Kumar, S., & Singh, T. P. (2022). Artificial Intelligence and analytics for better decision-making and strategy management. *Decision Intelligence Analytics and the Implementation of Strategic Business Management*, 31–43. doi:10.1007/978-3-030-82763-2_3

Siau, K., Nah, F. F.-H., Mennecke, B. E., & Schiller, S. Z. (2010). Co-creation and collaboration in a virtual world. *Journal of Database Management, 21*(4), 1–13. doi:10.4018/jdm.2010100101

Siau, K., & Wang, W. (2018). Building Trust in Artificial Intelligence, Machine Learning, and Robotics. *Cutter Business Technology Journal, 31*(2), 47–53.

Singh, H. (2003). Building effective blended learning programs. *Educational Technology, 43*, 51–54.

Sirakaya, M., & Cakmak, E. K. (2018). The effect of augmented reality use on achievement, misconception and course engagement. *Contemporary Educational Technology, 9*(3), 297–314. doi:10.30935/cet.444119

Siyaev, A., & Jo, G. S. (2021b). Towards aircraft maintenance Metaverse using speech interactions with virtual objects in mixed reality. *Sensors (Basel), 21*(6), 2066. doi:10.339021062066 PMID:33804253

Smith, S. (2022). *Meta Quest 2 review: The affordable VR headset we've been waiting for.* Retrieved 30 September 2022, from https://www.laptopmag.com/reviews/oculus-quest-2

Sourcing. (2022). *COVID-19 Is Taking Gaming And eSports To The Next Level - HKTDC Newsbites*. Retrieved 20 September 2022, from https://sourcing.hktdc.com/newsbites/covid-19-is-taking-gaming-and-esports-to-the-next-level/

Sourin, A. (2017). Case study: Shared virtual and augmented environments for creative applications. *Research and Development in the Academy, Creative Industries and Applications*, 49–64. doi:10.1007/978-3-319-54081-8_5

Sousa, K., & Oz, E. (2015). *Management Information Systems*. Cengage Learning.

SportAus. (2022). Retrieved 21 September 2022, from https://www.sportaus.gov.au/participation/trends#holistic_health

Srivastava, K., Chaudhury, S., & Das, R. (2014). Virtual reality applications in mental health: Challenges and perspectives. *Industrial Psychiatry Journal, 23*(2), 83. doi:10.4103/0972-6748.151666 PMID:25788795

Stefanini, A., Aloini, D., Gloor, P., & Pochiero, F. (2021). Patient satisfaction in emergency department: Unveiling complex interactions by wearable sensors. *Journal of Business Research, 129*, 600–611. doi:.jbusres.2019.12.038 doi:10.1016/j

Steinberg, L. (2022). *What Defines A "Sport"?* Retrieved 20 September 2022, from https://www.forbes.com/sites/leighsteinberg/2018/07/28/what-defines-a-sport/?sh=630d00aa2d66

Stewart, J. M. (2002). A blended e-learning approach to intercultural training. *Industrial and Commercial Training, 34*(7), 269–271. doi:10.1108/00197850210447264

Strivr. (2022). *Virtual Reality sports training systems*. Strivr. Retrieved 23 September 2022, from https://www.strivr.com/solutions/industries/sports/

Swant, M. (2021, August 25). *Ralph Lauren Is Now Selling Digital Apparel For Avatars Inside Of Zepeto*. Retrieved from Forbes: https://www.forbes.com/sites/martyswant/2021/08/25/ralph-lauren-is-now-selling-digital-apparel-for-avatars-inside-of-zepeto

Sweet, J. (2022). *Meet Me in The Metaverse*. Retrieved from: https://www.accenture.com/_acnmedia/Thought-Leadership-Assets/PDF-5/Accenture-Meet-Me-in-the-Metaverse-Full-Report.pdf

Tamer Cavusgil, S., Calantone, R. J., & Zhao, Y. (2003). Tacit knowledge transfer and firm innovation capability. *Journal of Business and Industrial Marketing*, *18*(1), 6–21. doi:10.1108/08858620310458615

Tarouco, L., Gorziza, B., Correa, Y., Amaral, E. M., & Muller, T. (2013). Virtual Laboratory for Teaching Calculus: An immersive experience. *2013 IEEE Global Engineering Education Conference (EDUCON)*. 10.1109/EduCon.2013.6530195

Taylor, S., & Soneji, S. (2022). Bioinformatics and the Metaverse: Are We Ready? *Frontiers in Bioinformatics, 2*. doi:10.3389/fbinf.2022.863676

Tharwani, K. (2022). *Problems & Disadvantages Of The Metaverse*. Retrieved from: https://www.opengrowth.com/resources/problems-disadvantages-of-the-metaverse

The Evolution of Tech in Sport | Hire Intelligence UK. (2022). Retrieved 21 September 2022, from https://www.hire-intelligence.co.uk/evolution-of-technology-in-sport/

Thiel, A., & John, J. (2018). Is eSport a 'real' sport? Reflections on the spread of virtual competitions. *European Journal For Sport And Society*, *15*(4), 311–315. doi:10.1080/16138171.2018.1559019

Thomas, D. (2021, August 27). *Dolce & Gabbana Is Bringing NFTs To The Traditional World Of Couture*. Retrieved from Vogue: https://www.vogue.co.uk/fashion/article/dolce-and-gabbana-nfts-couture

Thomason, J., & Aydın, Ö. (2021). MetaHealth-How will the Metaverse Change Health Care? *Journal of Metaverse*, *1*, 13–16.

Thompson, H. (2022). *As sports enter the metaverse, could brands win big?* Retrieved 22 September 2022, from https://www.thedrum.com/opinion/2022/07/20/sports-enter-

Thoughtco, (2022). *The History of Sports*. Retrieved 20 September 2022 from https://www.thoughtco.com/history-of-sports-1992447

Tlili, A., Huang, R., Shehata, B., Liu, D., Zhao, J., Metwally, A. H., Wang, H., Denden, M., Bozkurt, A., Lee, L.-H., Beyoglu, D., Altinay, F., Sharma, R. C., Altinay, Z., Li, Z., Liu, J., Ahmad, F., Hu, Y., Salha, S., ... Burgos, D. (2022). Is metaverse in education a blessing or a curse: A combined content and bibliometric analysis. *Smart Learning Environments*, *9*(1), 24. Advance online publication. doi:10.118640561-022-00205-x

Tootell, H., Freeman, M., & Freeman, A. (2014). Generation alpha at the intersection of technology, play and motivation. *2014 47th Hawaii International Conference on System Sciences*. 10.1109/HICSS.2014.19

Topendsport. (2022). *What Is A Sport?* Retrieved 20 September 2022 from https://www.topendsports.com/sport/what-is-a-sport.htm

Topendsports. (2022). *Technology in Sports*. Retrieved 21 September 2022, from https://www.topendsports.com/resources/technology.htm

Tsui, V. (2022). *What Happens When Metaverse Meets Sports Leagues?* Retrieved 22 September 2022, from https://www.jumpstartmag.com/what-happens-when-metaverse-meets-sports-leagues/

UN. (2022). *The impact of COVID-19 on sport, physical activity, and well-being and its effects on social development*. Retrieved 20 September 2022, from https://www.un.org/development/desa/dspd/2020/05/covid-19-sport/

Vice. (2022). *What Is the Metaverse? An Explanation*. Retrieved 21 September 2022, from https://www.vice.com/en/article/93bmyv/what-is-the-metaverse-internet-technology-vr

Wagner, R., Piovesan, S. D., Passerino, P. D., & de Lima, J. V. (2013). Using 3D virtual learning environments in new perspective of education. *2013 12th International Conference on Information Technology Based Higher Education and Training*. 10.1109/ITHET.2013.6671019

Walsh, S. T., & Linton, J. D. (2000). Infrastructure for emergent industries based on discontinuous innovations. *Engineering Management Journal*, *12*(2), 23–32. doi:10.1080/10429247.2000.11415071

Wang, Y., Su, Z., Zhang, N., Xing, R., Liu, D., Luan, T., & Shen, X. (2022). A Survey on Metaverse: Fundamentals, Security, and Privacy. *IEEE Communications Surveys & Tutorials*. doi:10.1109/COMST.2022.3202047

What does the metaverse mean for sport? | SportBusiness. (2022). Retrieved 22 September 2022, from https://www.sportbusiness.com/2021/11/what-does-the-metaverse-mean-for-sport/

What does the metaverse mean for the future of sports ? (2022). Retrieved 22 September 2022, from https://www.javelinsportsinc.com/post/what-does-the-metaverse-mean-for-the-

Wilson, C. (2019). Cryptocurrencies: The Future of Finance? *Contemporary Issues in International Political Economy*, 359-394.

Wilson, K. B., Karg, A., & Ghaderi, H. (2021). Prospecting non-fungible tokens in the digital economy: Stakeholders and ecosystem, risk and opportunity. *Business Horizons*.

Wohlgenannt, I., Simons, A., & Stieglitz, S. (2020). Virtual reality. *Business & Information Systems Engineering*, *62*(5), 455–461. doi:10.100712599-020-00658-9

Wong, J. (2022). *How Will the Metaverse Impact Businesses in The Consumer Goods Sector?* from https://www.forbes.com/sites/forbestechcouncil/2022/01/19/how-will-the-metaverse-impact-businesses-in-the-consumer-goods-sector

Xiong, J., Hsiang, E.-L., He, Z., Zhan, T., & Wu, S.-T. (2021). Augmented reality and virtual reality displays: Emerging technologies and future perspectives. *Light, Science & Applications*, *10*(1), 216. https://doi.org/10.1038/s41377-021-00658-8

Yan, Y., Chen, K., Xie, Y., Song, Y., & Liu, Y. (2019). The Effects of Weight on Comfort of Virtual Reality Devices. https://doi.org/10.1007/978-3-319-94706-8_27.

Yang, Y., Siau, K., Xie, W., & Sun, Y. (2022). Smart health. *Journal of Organizational and End User Computing*, *34*(1), 1–14. doi:10.4018/JOEUC.308814

Yao, Q. (2018). A systematic framework to understand central bank digital currency. *Science China. Information Sciences*, *61*(3), 1–8. doi:10.100711432-017-9294-5

Yılmaz, F., Mete, A. H., Türkön, B. F., & İnce, Ö. (2022). Sağlık Hizmetlerinin Geleceğinde Metaverse Ekosistemi ve Teknolojileri: Uygulamalar, Fırsatlar ve Zorluklar. *Eurasian Journal of Health Technology Assessment*, *6*(1), 1–22. doi:10.52148/ehta.1082705

Yoganandhan, A., Rajesh Kanna, G., Subhash, S. D., & Hebinson Jothi, J. (2021). Retrospective and prospective application of robots and Artificial Intelligence in global pandemic and epidemic diseases. *Vacunas*, *22*(2), 98–105. doi:10.1016/j.vacun.2020.12.004 PMID:33841058

Yuhanna, I., Alexander, A., & Kachik, A. (2020). Advantages and disadvantages of online learning. *Journal Educational Verkenning*, *1*(2), 13–19. doi:10.48173/jev.v1i2.54

Zhang, J. Z., Chang, C. W., & Neslin, S. A. (2022). How Physical Stores Enhance Customer Value: The Importance of Product Inspection Depth. *Journal of Marketing*, *86*(2), 166–185. doi:10.1177/00222429211012106

Zhao, R., Zhang, Y., Zhu, Y., Lan, R., & Hua, Z. (2022). *Metaverse: Security and Privacy Concerns*. arXiv preprint arXiv:2203.03854.

Zhao, Y., & Watterston, J. (2021). The changes we need: Education post COVID-19. *Journal of Educational Change*, *22*(1), 3–12. doi:10.100710833-021-09417-3

Zulkarnain, N., Anshari, M., Hamdan, M., & Fithriyah, M. (2021, August). Big data in business and ethical challenges. In *2021 International Conference on Information Management and Technology (ICIMTech)* (Vol. 1, pp. 298-303). IEEE. 10.1109/ICIMTech53080.2021.9534963

Related References

To continue our tradition of advancing information science and technology research, we have compiled a list of recommended IGI Global readings. These references will provide additional information and guidance to further enrich your knowledge and assist you with your own research and future publications.

Abdul Razak, R., & Mansor, N. A. (2021). Instagram Influencers in Social Media-Induced Tourism: Rethinking Tourist Trust Towards Tourism Destination. In M. Dinis, L. Bonixe, S. Lamy, & Z. Breda (Eds.), *Impact of New Media in Tourism* (pp. 135-144). IGI Global. https://doi.org/10.4018/978-1-7998-7095-1.ch009

Abir, T., & Khan, M. Y. (2022). Importance of ICT Advancement and Culture of Adaptation in the Tourism and Hospitality Industry for Developing Countries. In C. Ramos, S. Quinteiro, & A. Gonçalves (Eds.), *ICT as Innovator Between Tourism and Culture* (pp. 30–41). IGI Global. https://doi.org/10.4018/978-1-7998-8165-0.ch003

Abtahi, M. S., Behboudi, L., & Hasanabad, H. M. (2017). Factors Affecting Internet Advertising Adoption in Ad Agencies. *International Journal of Innovation in the Digital Economy*, *8*(4), 18–29. doi:10.4018/IJIDE.2017100102

Afenyo-Agbe, E., & Mensah, I. (2022). Principles, Benefits, and Barriers to Community-Based Tourism: Implications for Management. In I. Mensah & E. Afenyo-Agbe (Eds.), *Prospects and Challenges of Community-Based Tourism and Changing Demographics* (pp. 1–29). IGI Global. doi:10.4018/978-1-7998-7335-8.ch001

Agbo, V. M. (2022). Distributive Justice Issues in Community-Based Tourism. In I. Mensah & E. Afenyo-Agbe (Eds.), *Prospects and Challenges of Community-Based Tourism and Changing Demographics* (pp. 107–129). IGI Global. https://doi.org/10.4018/978-1-7998-7335-8.ch005

Agrawal, S. (2017). The Impact of Emerging Technologies and Social Media on Different Business(es): Marketing and Management. In O. Rishi & A. Sharma (Eds.), *Maximizing Business Performance and Efficiency Through Intelligent Systems* (pp. 37–49). Hershey, PA: IGI Global. doi:10.4018/978-1-5225-2234-8.ch002

Ahmad, A., & Johari, S. (2022). Georgetown as a Gastronomy Tourism Destination: Visitor Awareness Towards Revisit Intention of Nasi Kandar Restaurant. In M. Valeri (Ed.), *New Governance and Management in Touristic Destinations* (pp. 71–83). IGI Global. https://doi.org/10.4018/978-1-6684-3889-3.ch005

Alkhatib, G., & Bayouq, S. T. (2021). A TAM-Based Model of Technological Factors Affecting Use of E-Tourism. *International Journal of Tourism and Hospitality Management in the Digital Age*, *5*(2), 50–67. https://doi.org/10.4018/IJTHMDA.20210701.oa1

Altinay Ozdemir, M. (2021). Virtual Reality (VR) and Augmented Reality (AR) Technologies for Accessibility and Marketing in the Tourism Industry. In C. Eusébio, L. Teixeira, & M. Carneiro (Eds.), *ICT Tools and Applications for Accessible Tourism* (pp. 277-301). IGI Global. https://doi.org/10.4018/978-1-7998-6428-8.ch013

Anantharaman, R. N., Rajeswari, K. S., Angusamy, A., & Kuppusamy, J. (2017). Role of Self-Efficacy and Collective Efficacy as Moderators of Occupational Stress Among Software Development Professionals. *International Journal of Human Capital and Information Technology Professionals*, *8*(2), 45–58. doi:10.4018/IJHCITP.2017040103

Aninze, F., El-Gohary, H., & Hussain, J. (2018). The Role of Microfinance to Empower Women: The Case of Developing Countries. *International Journal of Customer Relationship Marketing and Management*, *9*(1), 54–78. doi:10.4018/IJCRMM.2018010104

Antosova, G., Sabogal-Salamanca, M., & Krizova, E. (2021). Human Capital in Tourism: A Practical Model of Endogenous and Exogenous Territorial Tourism Planning in Bahía Solano, Colombia. In V. Costa, A. Moura, & M. Mira (Eds.), *Handbook of Research on Human Capital and People Management in the Tourism Industry* (pp. 282–302). IGI Global. https://doi.org/10.4018/978-1-7998-4318-4.ch014

Arsenijević, O. M., Orčić, D., & Kastratović, E. (2017). Development of an Optimization Tool for Intangibles in SMEs: A Case Study from Serbia with a Pilot Research in the Prestige by Milka Company. In M. Vemić (Ed.), *Optimal Management Strategies in Small and Medium Enterprises* (pp. 320–347). Hershey, PA: IGI Global. doi:10.4018/978-1-5225-1949-2.ch015

Aryanto, V. D., Wismantoro, Y., & Widyatmoko, K. (2018). Implementing Eco-Innovation by Utilizing the Internet to Enhance Firm's Marketing Performance: Study of Green Batik Small and Medium Enterprises in Indonesia. *International Journal of E-Business Research, 14*(1), 21–36. doi:10.4018/IJEBR.2018010102

Asero, V., & Billi, S. (2022). New Perspective of Networking in the DMO Model. In M. Valeri (Ed.), *New Governance and Management in Touristic Destinations* (pp. 105–118). IGI Global. https://doi.org/10.4018/978-1-6684-3889-3.ch007

Atiku, S. O., & Fields, Z. (2017). Multicultural Orientations for 21st Century Global Leadership. In N. Baporikar (Ed.), *Management Education for Global Leadership* (pp. 28–51). Hershey, PA: IGI Global. doi:10.4018/978-1-5225-1013-0.ch002

Atiku, S. O., & Fields, Z. (2018). Organisational Learning Dimensions and Talent Retention Strategies for the Service Industries. In N. Baporikar (Ed.), *Global Practices in Knowledge Management for Societal and Organizational Development* (pp. 358–381). Hershey, PA: IGI Global. doi:10.4018/978-1-5225-3009-1.ch017

Atsa'am, D. D., & Kuset Bodur, E. (2021). Pattern Mining on How Organizational Tenure Affects the Psychological Capital of Employees Within the Hospitality and Tourism Industry: Linking Employees' Organizational Tenure With PsyCap. *International Journal of Tourism and Hospitality Management in the Digital Age, 5*(2), 17–28. https://doi.org/10.4018/IJTHMDA.2021070102

Ávila, L., & Teixeira, L. (2018). The Main Concepts Behind the Dematerialization of Business Processes. In M. Khosrow-Pour, D.B.A. (Ed.), Encyclopedia of Information Science and Technology, Fourth Edition (pp. 888-898). Hershey, PA: IGI Global. https://doi.org/ doi:10.4018/978-1-5225-2255-3.ch076

Ayorekire, J., Mugizi, F., Obua, J., & Ampaire, G. (2022). Community-Based Tourism and Local People's Perceptions Towards Conservation: The Case of Queen Elizabeth Conservation Area, Uganda. In I. Mensah & E. Afenyo-Agbe (Eds.), *Prospects and Challenges of Community-Based Tourism and Changing Demographics* (pp. 56–82). IGI Global. https://doi.org/10.4018/978-1-7998-7335-8.ch003

Baleiro, R. (2022). Tourist Literature and the Architecture of Travel in Olga Tokarczuk and Patti Smith. In R. Baleiro & R. Pereira (Eds.), *Global Perspectives on Literary Tourism and Film-Induced Tourism* (pp. 202-216). IGI Global. https://doi.org/10.4018/978-1-7998-8262-6.ch011

Barat, S. (2021). Looking at the Future of Medical Tourism in Asia. *International Journal of Tourism and Hospitality Management in the Digital Age, 5*(1), 19–33. https://doi.org/10.4018/IJTHMDA.2021010102

Barbosa, C. A., Magalhães, M., & Nunes, M. R. (2021). Travel Instagramability: A Way of Choosing a Destination? In M. Dinis, L. Bonixe, S. Lamy, & Z. Breda (Eds.), *Impact of New Media in Tourism* (pp. 173-190). IGI Global. https://doi.org/10.4018/978-1-7998-7095-1.ch011

Bari, M. W., & Khan, Q. (2021). Pakistan as a Destination of Religious Tourism. In E. Alaverdov & M. Bari (Eds.), *Global Development of Religious Tourism* (pp. 1-10). IGI Global. https://doi.org/10.4018/978-1-7998-5792-1.ch001

Bartens, Y., Chunpir, H. I., Schulte, F., & Voß, S. (2017). Business/IT Alignment in Two-Sided Markets: A COBIT 5 Analysis for Media Streaming Business Models. In S. De Haes & W. Van Grembergen (Eds.), *Strategic IT Governance and Alignment in Business Settings* (pp. 82–111). Hershey, PA: IGI Global. doi:10.4018/978-1-5225-0861-8.ch004

Bashayreh, A. M. (2018). Organizational Culture and Organizational Performance. In W. Lee & F. Sabetzadeh (Eds.), *Contemporary Knowledge and Systems Science* (pp. 50–69). Hershey, PA: IGI Global. doi:10.4018/978-1-5225-5655-8.ch003

Bechthold, L., Lude, M., & Prügl, R. (2021). Crisis Favors the Prepared Firm: How Organizational Ambidexterity Relates to Perceptions of Organizational Resilience. In A. Zehrer, G. Glowka, K. Schwaiger, & V. Ranacher-Lackner (Eds.), *Resiliency Models and Addressing Future Risks for Family Firms in the Tourism Industry* (pp. 178–205). IGI Global. https://doi.org/10.4018/978-1-7998-7352-5.ch008

Bedford, D. A. (2018). Sustainable Knowledge Management Strategies: Aligning Business Capabilities and Knowledge Management Goals. In N. Baporikar (Ed.), *Global Practices in Knowledge Management for Societal and Organizational Development* (pp. 46–73). Hershey, PA: IGI Global. doi:10.4018/978-1-5225-3009-1.ch003

Bekjanov, D., & Matyusupov, B. (2021). Influence of Innovative Processes in the Competitiveness of Tourist Destination. In J. Soares (Ed.), *Innovation and Entrepreneurial Opportunities in Community Tourism* (pp. 243–263). IGI Global. https://doi.org/10.4018/978-1-7998-4855-4.ch014

Bharwani, S., & Musunuri, D. (2018). Reflection as a Process From Theory to Practice. In M. Khosrow-Pour, D.B.A. (Ed.), Encyclopedia of Information Science and Technology, Fourth Edition (pp. 1529-1539). Hershey, PA: IGI Global. doi:10.4018/978-1-5225-2255-3.ch132

Bhatt, G. D., Wang, Z., & Rodger, J. A. (2017). Information Systems Capabilities and Their Effects on Competitive Advantages: A Study of Chinese Companies. *Information Resources Management Journal, 30*(3), 41–57. doi:10.4018/IRMJ.2017070103

Bhushan, M., & Yadav, A. (2017). Concept of Cloud Computing in ESB. In R. Bhadoria, N. Chaudhari, G. Tomar, & S. Singh (Eds.), *Exploring Enterprise Service Bus in the Service-Oriented Architecture Paradigm* (pp. 116–127). Hershey, PA: IGI Global. doi:10.4018/978-1-5225-2157-0.ch008

Bhushan, S. (2017). System Dynamics Base-Model of Humanitarian Supply Chain (HSCM) in Disaster Prone Eco-Communities of India: A Discussion on Simulation and Scenario Results. *International Journal of System Dynamics Applications*, *6*(3), 20–37. doi:10.4018/IJSDA.2017070102

Binder, D., & Miller, J. W. (2021). A Generations' Perspective on Employer Branding in Tourism. In V. Costa, A. Moura, & M. Mira (Eds.), *Handbook of Research on Human Capital and People Management in the Tourism Industry* (pp. 152–174). IGI Global. https://doi.org/10.4018/978-1-7998-4318-4.ch008

Birch Freeman, A. A., Mensah, I., & Antwi, K. B. (2022). Smiling vs. Frowning Faces: Community Participation for Sustainable Tourism in Ghanaian Communities. In I. Mensah & E. Afenyo-Agbe (Eds.), *Prospects and Challenges of Community-Based Tourism and Changing Demographics* (pp. 83–106). IGI Global. https://doi.org/10.4018/978-1-7998-7335-8.ch004

Biswas, A., & De, A. K. (2017). On Development of a Fuzzy Stochastic Programming Model with Its Application to Business Management. In S. Trivedi, S. Dey, A. Kumar, & T. Panda (Eds.), *Handbook of Research on Advanced Data Mining Techniques and Applications for Business Intelligence* (pp. 353–378). Hershey, PA: IGI Global. doi:10.4018/978-1-5225-2031-3.ch021

Boragnio, A., & Faracce Macia, C. (2021). "Taking Care of Yourself at Home": Use of E-Commerce About Food and Care During the COVID-19 Pandemic in the City of Buenos Aires. In M. Korstanje (Ed.), *Socio-Economic Effects and Recovery Efforts for the Rental Industry: Post-COVID-19 Strategies* (pp. 45–71). IGI Global. https://doi.org/10.4018/978-1-7998-7287-0.ch003

Borges, V. D. (2021). Happiness: The Basis for Public Policy in Tourism. In A. Perinotto, V. Mayer, & J. Soares (Eds.), *Rebuilding and Restructuring the Tourism Industry: Infusion of Happiness and Quality of Life* (pp. 1–25). IGI Global. https://doi.org/10.4018/978-1-7998-7239-9.ch001

Bücker, J., & Ernste, K. (2018). Use of Brand Heroes in Strategic Reputation Management: The Case of Bacardi, Adidas, and Daimler. In A. Erdemir (Ed.), *Reputation Management Techniques in Public Relations* (pp. 126–150). Hershey, PA: IGI Global. doi:10.4018/978-1-5225-3619-2.ch007

Buluk Eşitti, B. (2021). COVID-19 and Alternative Tourism: New Destinations and New Tourism Products. In M. Demir, A. Dalgıç, & F. Ergen (Eds.), *Handbook of Research on the Impacts and Implications of COVID-19 on the Tourism Industry* (pp. 786–805). IGI Global. https://doi.org/10.4018/978-1-7998-8231-2.ch038

Bureš, V. (2018). Industry 4.0 From the Systems Engineering Perspective: Alternative Holistic Framework Development. In R. Brunet-Thornton & F. Martinez (Eds.), *Analyzing the Impacts of Industry 4.0 in Modern Business Environments* (pp. 199–223). Hershey, PA: IGI Global. doi:10.4018/978-1-5225-3468-6.ch011

Buzady, Z. (2017). Resolving the Magic Cube of Effective Case Teaching: Benchmarking Case Teaching Practices in Emerging Markets – Insights from the Central European University Business School, Hungary. In D. Latusek (Ed.), *Case Studies as a Teaching Tool in Management Education* (pp. 79–103). Hershey, PA: IGI Global. doi:10.4018/978-1-5225-0770-3.ch005

Camillo, A. (2021). *Legal Matters, Risk Management, and Risk Prevention: From Forming a Business to Legal Representation.* IGI Global. doi:10.4018/978-1-7998-4342-9.ch004

Căpusneanu, S., & Topor, D. I. (2018). Business Ethics and Cost Management in SMEs: Theories of Business Ethics and Cost Management Ethos. In I. Oncioiu (Ed.), *Ethics and Decision-Making for Sustainable Business Practices* (pp. 109–127). Hershey, PA: IGI Global. doi:10.4018/978-1-5225-3773-1.ch007

Chan, R. L., Mo, P. L., & Moon, K. K. (2018). Strategic and Tactical Measures in Managing Enterprise Risks: A Study of the Textile and Apparel Industry. In K. Strang, M. Korstanje, & N. Vajjhala (Eds.), *Research, Practices, and Innovations in Global Risk and Contingency Management* (pp. 1–19). Hershey, PA: IGI Global. doi:10.4018/978-1-5225-4754-9.ch001

Charlier, S. D., Burke-Smalley, L. A., & Fisher, S. L. (2018). Undergraduate Programs in the U.S: A Contextual and Content-Based Analysis. In J. Mendy (Ed.), *Teaching Human Resources and Organizational Behavior at the College Level* (pp. 26–57). Hershey, PA: IGI Global. doi:10.4018/978-1-5225-2820-3.ch002

Chumillas, J., Güell, M., & Quer, P. (2022). The Use of ICT in Tourist and Educational Literary Routes: The Role of the Guide. In C. Ramos, S. Quinteiro, & A. Gonçalves (Eds.), *ICT as Innovator Between Tourism and Culture* (pp. 15–29). IGI Global. https://doi.org/10.4018/978-1-7998-8165-0.ch002

Dahlberg, T., Kivijärvi, H., & Saarinen, T. (2017). IT Investment Consistency and Other Factors Influencing the Success of IT Performance. In S. De Haes & W. Van Grembergen (Eds.), *Strategic IT Governance and Alignment in Business Settings* (pp. 176–208). Hershey, PA: IGI Global. doi:10.4018/978-1-5225-0861-8.ch007

Damnjanović, A. M. (2017). Knowledge Management Optimization through IT and E-Business Utilization: A Qualitative Study on Serbian SMEs. In M. Vemić (Ed.), *Optimal Management Strategies in Small and Medium Enterprises* (pp. 249–267). Hershey, PA: IGI Global. doi:10.4018/978-1-5225-1949-2.ch012

Daneshpour, H. (2017). Integrating Sustainable Development into Project Portfolio Management through Application of Open Innovation. In M. Vemić (Ed.), *Optimal Management Strategies in Small and Medium Enterprises* (pp. 370–387). Hershey, PA: IGI Global. doi:10.4018/978-1-5225-1949-2.ch017

Daniel, A. D., & Reis de Castro, V. (2018). Entrepreneurship Education: How to Measure the Impact on Nascent Entrepreneurs. In A. Carrizo Moreira, J. Guilherme Leitão Dantas, & F. Manuel Valente (Eds.), *Nascent Entrepreneurship and Successful New Venture Creation* (pp. 85–110). Hershey, PA: IGI Global. doi:10.4018/978-1-5225-2936-1.ch004

David, R., Swami, B. N., & Tangirala, S. (2018). Ethics Impact on Knowledge Management in Organizational Development: A Case Study. In N. Baporikar (Ed.), *Global Practices in Knowledge Management for Societal and Organizational Development* (pp. 19–45). Hershey, PA: IGI Global. doi:10.4018/978-1-5225-3009-1.ch002

De Uña-Álvarez, E., & Villarino-Pérez, M. (2022). Fostering Ecocultural Resources, Identity, and Tourism in Inland Territories (Galicia, NW Spain). In G. Fernandes (Ed.), *Challenges and New Opportunities for Tourism in Inland Territories: Ecocultural Resources and Sustainable Initiatives* (pp. 1-16). IGI Global. https://doi.org/10.4018/978-1-7998-7339-6.ch001

Delias, P., & Lakiotaki, K. (2018). Discovering Process Horizontal Boundaries to Facilitate Process Comprehension. *International Journal of Operations Research and Information Systems*, *9*(2), 1–31. doi:10.4018/IJORIS.2018040101

Denholm, J., & Lee-Davies, L. (2018). Success Factors for Games in Business and Project Management. In *Enhancing Education and Training Initiatives Through Serious Games* (pp. 34–68). Hershey, PA: IGI Global. doi:10.4018/978-1-5225-3689-5.ch002

Deshpande, M. (2017). Best Practices in Management Institutions for Global Leadership: Policy Aspects. In N. Baporikar (Ed.), *Management Education for Global Leadership* (pp. 1–27). Hershey, PA: IGI Global. doi:10.4018/978-1-5225-1013-0.ch001

Deshpande, M. (2018). Policy Perspectives for SMEs Knowledge Management. In N. Baporikar (Ed.), *Knowledge Integration Strategies for Entrepreneurship and Sustainability* (pp. 23–46). Hershey, PA: IGI Global. doi:10.4018/978-1-5225-5115-7.ch002

Dezdar, S. (2017). ERP Implementation Projects in Asian Countries: A Comparative Study on Iran and China. *International Journal of Information Technology Project Management, 8*(3), 52–68. doi:10.4018/IJITPM.2017070104

Domingos, D., Respício, A., & Martinho, R. (2017). Reliability of IoT-Aware BPMN Healthcare Processes. In C. Reis & M. Maximiano (Eds.), *Internet of Things and Advanced Application in Healthcare* (pp. 214–248). Hershey, PA: IGI Global. doi:10.4018/978-1-5225-1820-4.ch008

Dosumu, O., Hussain, J., & El-Gohary, H. (2017). An Exploratory Study of the Impact of Government Policies on the Development of Small and Medium Enterprises in Developing Countries: The Case of Nigeria. *International Journal of Customer Relationship Marketing and Management, 8*(4), 51–62. doi:10.4018/IJCRMM.2017100104

Durst, S., Bruns, G., & Edvardsson, I. R. (2017). Retaining Knowledge in Smaller Building and Construction Firms. *International Journal of Knowledge and Systems Science, 8*(3), 1–12. doi:10.4018/IJKSS.2017070101

Edvardsson, I. R., & Durst, S. (2017). Outsourcing, Knowledge, and Learning: A Critical Review. *International Journal of Knowledge-Based Organizations, 7*(2), 13–26. doi:10.4018/IJKBO.2017040102

Edwards, J. S. (2018). Integrating Knowledge Management and Business Processes. In M. Khosrow-Pour, D.B.A. (Ed.), Encyclopedia of Information Science and Technology, Fourth Edition (pp. 5046-5055). Hershey, PA: IGI Global. doi:10.4018/978-1-5225-2255-3.ch437

Eichelberger, S., & Peters, M. (2021). Family Firm Management in Turbulent Times: Opportunities for Responsible Tourism. In A. Zehrer, G. Glowka, K. Schwaiger, & V. Ranacher-Lackner (Eds.), *Resiliency Models and Addressing Future Risks for Family Firms in the Tourism Industry* (pp. 103–124). IGI Global. https://doi.org/10.4018/978-1-7998-7352-5.ch005

Eide, D., Hjalager, A., & Hansen, M. (2022). Innovative Certifications in Adventure Tourism: Attributes and Diffusion. In R. Augusto Costa, F. Brandão, Z. Breda, & C. Costa (Eds.), *Planning and Managing the Experience Economy in Tourism* (pp. 161-175). IGI Global. https://doi.org/10.4018/978-1-7998-8775-1.ch009

Ejiogu, A. O. (2018). Economics of Farm Management. In *Agricultural Finance and Opportunities for Investment and Expansion* (pp. 56–72). Hershey, PA: IGI Global. doi:10.4018/978-1-5225-3059-6.ch003

Ekanem, I., & Abiade, G. E. (2018). Factors Influencing the Use of E-Commerce by Small Enterprises in Nigeria. *International Journal of ICT Research in Africa and the Middle East*, *7*(1), 37–53. doi:10.4018/IJICTRAME.2018010103

Ekanem, I., & Alrossais, L. A. (2017). Succession Challenges Facing Family Businesses in Saudi Arabia. In P. Zgheib (Ed.), *Entrepreneurship and Business Innovation in the Middle East* (pp. 122–146). Hershey, PA: IGI Global. doi:10.4018/978-1-5225-2066-5.ch007

El Faquih, L., & Fredj, M. (2017). Ontology-Based Framework for Quality in Configurable Process Models. *Journal of Electronic Commerce in Organizations*, *15*(2), 48–60. doi:10.4018/JECO.2017040104

Faisal, M. N., & Talib, F. (2017). Building Ambidextrous Supply Chains in SMEs: How to Tackle the Barriers? *International Journal of Information Systems and Supply Chain Management*, *10*(4), 80–100. doi:10.4018/IJISSCM.2017100105

Fernandes, T. M., Gomes, J., & Romão, M. (2017). Investments in E-Government: A Benefit Management Case Study. *International Journal of Electronic Government Research*, *13*(3), 1–17. doi:10.4018/IJEGR.2017070101

Figueira, L. M., Honrado, G. R., & Dionísio, M. S. (2021). Human Capital Management in the Tourism Industry in Portugal. In V. Costa, A. Moura, & M. Mira (Eds.), *Handbook of Research on Human Capital and People Management in the Tourism Industry* (pp. 1–19). IGI Global. doi:10.4018/978-1-7998-4318-4.ch001

Gao, S. S., Oreal, S., & Zhang, J. (2018). Contemporary Financial Risk Management Perceptions and Practices of Small-Sized Chinese Businesses. In I. Management Association (Ed.), Global Business Expansion: Concepts, Methodologies, Tools, and Applications (pp. 917-931). Hershey, PA: IGI Global. doi:10.4018/978-1-5225-5481-3.ch041

Garg, R., & Berning, S. C. (2017). Indigenous Chinese Management Philosophies: Key Concepts and Relevance for Modern Chinese Firms. In B. Christiansen & G. Koc (Eds.), *Transcontinental Strategies for Industrial Development and Economic Growth* (pp. 43–57). Hershey, PA: IGI Global. doi:10.4018/978-1-5225-2160-0.ch003

Gencer, Y. G. (2017). Supply Chain Management in Retailing Business. In U. Akkucuk (Ed.), *Ethics and Sustainability in Global Supply Chain Management* (pp. 197–210). Hershey, PA: IGI Global. doi:10.4018/978-1-5225-2036-8.ch011

Gera, R., Arora, S., & Malik, S. (2021). Emotional Labor in the Tourism Industry: Strategies, Antecedents, and Outcomes. In V. Costa, A. Moura, & M. Mira (Eds.), *Handbook of Research on Human Capital and People Management in the Tourism Industry* (pp. 73–91). IGI Global. https://doi.org/10.4018/978-1-7998-4318-4.ch004

Giacosa, E. (2018). The Increasing of the Regional Development Thanks to the Luxury Business Innovation. In L. Carvalho (Ed.), *Handbook of Research on Entrepreneurial Ecosystems and Social Dynamics in a Globalized World* (pp. 260–273). Hershey, PA: IGI Global. doi:10.4018/978-1-5225-3525-6.ch011

Glowka, G., Tusch, M., & Zehrer, A. (2021). The Risk Perception of Family Business Owner-Manager in the Tourism Industry: A Qualitative Comparison of the Intra-Firm Senior and Junior Generation. In A. Zehrer, G. Glowka, K. Schwaiger, & V. Ranacher-Lackner (Eds.), *Resiliency Models and Addressing Future Risks for Family Firms in the Tourism Industry* (pp. 126–153). IGI Global. https://doi.org/10.4018/978-1-7998-7352-5.ch006

Glykas, M., & George, J. (2017). Quality and Process Management Systems in the UAE Maritime Industry. *International Journal of Productivity Management and Assessment Technologies*, *5*(1), 20–39. doi:10.4018/IJPMAT.2017010102

Glykas, M., Valiris, G., Kokkinaki, A., & Koutsoukou, Z. (2018). Banking Business Process Management Implementation. *International Journal of Productivity Management and Assessment Technologies*, *6*(1), 50–69. doi:10.4018/IJPMAT.2018010104

Gomes, J., & Romão, M. (2017). The Balanced Scorecard: Keeping Updated and Aligned with Today's Business Trends. *International Journal of Productivity Management and Assessment Technologies*, *5*(2), 1–15. doi:10.4018/IJPMAT.2017070101

Gomes, J., & Romão, M. (2017). Aligning Information Systems and Technology with Benefit Management and Balanced Scorecard. In S. De Haes & W. Van Grembergen (Eds.), *Strategic IT Governance and Alignment in Business Settings* (pp. 112–131). Hershey, PA: IGI Global. doi:10.4018/978-1-5225-0861-8.ch005

Goyal, A. (2021). Communicating and Building Destination Brands With New Media. In M. Dinis, L. Bonixe, S. Lamy, & Z. Breda (Eds.), *Impact of New Media in Tourism* (pp. 1-20). IGI Global. https://doi.org/10.4018/978-1-7998-7095-1.ch001

Grefen, P., & Turetken, O. (2017). Advanced Business Process Management in Networked E-Business Scenarios. *International Journal of E-Business Research, 13*(4), 70–104. doi:10.4018/IJEBR.2017100105

Guasca, M., Van Broeck, A. M., & Vanneste, D. (2021). Tourism and the Social Reintegration of Colombian Ex-Combatants. In J. da Silva, Z. Breda, & F. Carbone (Eds.), *Role and Impact of Tourism in Peacebuilding and Conflict Transformation* (pp. 66-86). IGI Global. https://doi.org/10.4018/978-1-7998-5053-3.ch005

Haider, A., & Saetang, S. (2017). Strategic IT Alignment in Service Sector. In S. Rozenes & Y. Cohen (Eds.), *Handbook of Research on Strategic Alliances and Value Co-Creation in the Service Industry* (pp. 231–258). Hershey, PA: IGI Global. doi:10.4018/978-1-5225-2084-9.ch012

Hajilari, A. B., Ghadaksaz, M., & Fasghandis, G. S. (2017). Assessing Organizational Readiness for Implementing ERP System Using Fuzzy Expert System Approach. *International Journal of Enterprise Information Systems, 13*(1), 67–85. doi:10.4018/IJEIS.2017010105

Haldorai, A., Ramu, A., & Murugan, S. (2018). Social Aware Cognitive Radio Networks: Effectiveness of Social Networks as a Strategic Tool for Organizational Business Management. In H. Bansal, G. Shrivastava, G. Nguyen, & L. Stanciu (Eds.), *Social Network Analytics for Contemporary Business Organizations* (pp. 188–202). Hershey, PA: IGI Global. doi:10.4018/978-1-5225-5097-6.ch010

Hall, O. P. Jr. (2017). Social Media Driven Management Education. *International Journal of Knowledge-Based Organizations, 7*(2), 43–59. doi:10.4018/IJKBO.2017040104

Hanifah, H., Halim, H. A., Ahmad, N. H., & Vafaei-Zadeh, A. (2017). Innovation Culture as a Mediator Between Specific Human Capital and Innovation Performance Among Bumiputera SMEs in Malaysia. In N. Ahmad, T. Ramayah, H. Halim, & S. Rahman (Eds.), *Handbook of Research on Small and Medium Enterprises in Developing Countries* (pp. 261–279). Hershey, PA: IGI Global. doi:10.4018/978-1-5225-2165-5.ch012

Hartlieb, S., & Silvius, G. (2017). Handling Uncertainty in Project Management and Business Development: Similarities and Differences. In Y. Raydugin (Ed.), *Handbook of Research on Leveraging Risk and Uncertainties for Effective Project Management* (pp. 337–362). Hershey, PA: IGI Global. doi:10.4018/978-1-5225-1790-0.ch016

Hass, K. B. (2017). Living on the Edge: Managing Project Complexity. In Y. Raydugin (Ed.), *Handbook of Research on Leveraging Risk and Uncertainties for Effective Project Management* (pp. 177–201). Hershey, PA: IGI Global. doi:10.4018/978-1-5225-1790-0.ch009

Hawking, P., & Carmine Sellitto, C. (2017). Developing an Effective Strategy for Organizational Business Intelligence. In M. Tavana (Ed.), *Enterprise Information Systems and the Digitalization of Business Functions* (pp. 222–237). Hershey, PA: IGI Global. doi:10.4018/978-1-5225-2382-6.ch010

Hawking, P., & Sellitto, C. (2017). A Fast-Moving Consumer Goods Company and Business Intelligence Strategy Development. *International Journal of Enterprise Information Systems*, *13*(2), 22–33. doi:10.4018/IJEIS.2017040102

Hawking, P., & Sellitto, C. (2017). Business Intelligence Strategy: Two Case Studies. *International Journal of Business Intelligence Research*, *8*(2), 17–30. doi:10.4018/IJBIR.2017070102

Hee, W. J., Jalleh, G., Lai, H., & Lin, C. (2017). E-Commerce and IT Projects: Evaluation and Management Issues in Australian and Taiwanese Hospitals. *International Journal of Public Health Management and Ethics*, *2*(1), 69–90. doi:10.4018/IJPHME.2017010104

Hernandez, A. A. (2018). Exploring the Factors to Green IT Adoption of SMEs in the Philippines. *Journal of Cases on Information Technology*, *20*(2), 49–66. doi:10.4018/JCIT.2018040104

Hollman, A., Bickford, S., & Hollman, T. (2017). Cyber InSecurity: A Post-Mortem Attempt to Assess Cyber Problems from IT and Business Management Perspectives. *Journal of Cases on Information Technology*, *19*(3), 42–70. doi:10.4018/JCIT.2017070104

Ibrahim, F., & Zainin, N. M. (2021). Exploring the Technological Impacts: The Case of Museums in Brunei Darussalam. *International Journal of Tourism and Hospitality Management in the Digital Age*, *5*(1), 1–18. https://doi.org/10.4018/IJTHMDA.2021010101

Igbinakhase, I. (2017). Responsible and Sustainable Management Practices in Developing and Developed Business Environments. In Z. Fields (Ed.), *Collective Creativity for Responsible and Sustainable Business Practice* (pp. 180–207). Hershey, PA: IGI Global. doi:10.4018/978-1-5225-1823-5.ch010

Iwata, J. J., & Hoskins, R. G. (2017). Managing Indigenous Knowledge in Tanzania: A Business Perspective. In P. Jain & N. Mnjama (Eds.), *Managing Knowledge Resources and Records in Modern Organizations* (pp. 198–214). Hershey, PA: IGI Global. doi:10.4018/978-1-5225-1965-2.ch012

Jain, P. (2017). Ethical and Legal Issues in Knowledge Management Life-Cycle in Business. In P. Jain & N. Mnjama (Eds.), *Managing Knowledge Resources and Records in Modern Organizations* (pp. 82–101). Hershey, PA: IGI Global. doi:10.4018/978-1-5225-1965-2.ch006

James, S., & Hauli, E. (2017). Holistic Management Education at Tanzanian Rural Development Planning Institute. In N. Baporikar (Ed.), *Management Education for Global Leadership* (pp. 112–136). Hershey, PA: IGI Global. doi:10.4018/978-1-5225-1013-0.ch006

Janošková, M., Csikósová, A., & Čulková, K. (2018). Measurement of Company Performance as Part of Its Strategic Management. In R. Leon (Ed.), *Managerial Strategies for Business Sustainability During Turbulent Times* (pp. 309–335). Hershey, PA: IGI Global. doi:10.4018/978-1-5225-2716-9.ch017

Jean-Vasile, A., & Alecu, A. (2017). Theoretical and Practical Approaches in Understanding the Influences of Cost-Productivity-Profit Trinomial in Contemporary Enterprises. In A. Jean Vasile & D. Nicolò (Eds.), *Sustainable Entrepreneurship and Investments in the Green Economy* (pp. 28–62). Hershey, PA: IGI Global. doi:10.4018/978-1-5225-2075-7.ch002

Joia, L. A., & Correia, J. C. (2018). CIO Competencies From the IT Professional Perspective: Insights From Brazil. *Journal of Global Information Management, 26*(2), 74–103. doi:10.4018/JGIM.2018040104

Juma, A., & Mzera, N. (2017). Knowledge Management and Records Management and Competitive Advantage in Business. In P. Jain & N. Mnjama (Eds.), *Managing Knowledge Resources and Records in Modern Organizations* (pp. 15–28). Hershey, PA: IGI Global. doi:10.4018/978-1-5225-1965-2.ch002

K., I., & A, V. (2018). Monitoring and Auditing in the Cloud. In K. Munir (Ed.), *Cloud Computing Technologies for Green Enterprises* (pp. 318-350). Hershey, PA: IGI Global. https://doi.org/ doi:10.4018/978-1-5225-3038-1.ch013

Kabra, G., Ghosh, V., & Ramesh, A. (2018). Enterprise Integrated Business Process Management and Business Intelligence Framework for Business Process Sustainability. In A. Paul, D. Bhattacharyya, & S. Anand (Eds.), *Green Initiatives for Business Sustainability and Value Creation* (pp. 228–238). Hershey, PA: IGI Global. doi:10.4018/978-1-5225-2662-9.ch010

Kaoud, M. (2017). Investigation of Customer Knowledge Management: A Case Study Research. *International Journal of Service Science, Management, Engineering, and Technology*, *8*(2), 12–22. doi:10.4018/IJSSMET.2017040102

Katuu, S. (2018). A Comparative Assessment of Enterprise Content Management Maturity Models. In N. Gwangwava & M. Mutingi (Eds.), *E-Manufacturing and E-Service Strategies in Contemporary Organizations* (pp. 93–118). Hershey, PA: IGI Global. doi:10.4018/978-1-5225-3628-4.ch005

Khan, M. Y., & Abir, T. (2022). The Role of Social Media Marketing in the Tourism and Hospitality Industry: A Conceptual Study on Bangladesh. In C. Ramos, S. Quinteiro, & A. Gonçalves (Eds.), *ICT as Innovator Between Tourism and Culture* (pp. 213–229). IGI Global. https://doi.org/10.4018/978-1-7998-8165-0.ch013

Kinnunen, S., Ylä-Kujala, A., Marttonen-Arola, S., Kärri, T., & Baglee, D. (2018). Internet of Things in Asset Management: Insights from Industrial Professionals and Academia. *International Journal of Service Science, Management, Engineering, and Technology*, *9*(2), 104–119. doi:10.4018/IJSSMET.2018040105

Klein, A. Z., Sabino de Freitas, A., Machado, L., Freitas, J. C. Jr, Graziola, P. G. Jr, & Schlemmer, E. (2017). Virtual Worlds Applications for Management Education. In L. Tomei (Ed.), *Exploring the New Era of Technology-Infused Education* (pp. 279–299). Hershey, PA: IGI Global. doi:10.4018/978-1-5225-1709-2.ch017

Kővári, E., Saleh, M., & Steinbachné Hajmásy, G. (2022). The Impact of Corporate Digital Responsibility (CDR) on Internal Stakeholders' Satisfaction in Hungarian Upscale Hotels. In M. Valeri (Ed.), *New Governance and Management in Touristic Destinations* (pp. 35–51). IGI Global. https://doi.org/10.4018/978-1-6684-3889-3.ch003

Kożuch, B., & Jabłoński, A. (2017). Adopting the Concept of Business Models in Public Management. In M. Lewandowski & B. Kożuch (Eds.), *Public Sector Entrepreneurship and the Integration of Innovative Business Models* (pp. 10–46). Hershey, PA: IGI Global. doi:10.4018/978-1-5225-2215-7.ch002

Kumar, J., Adhikary, A., & Jha, A. (2017). Small Active Investors' Perceptions and Preferences Towards Tax Saving Mutual Fund Schemes in Eastern India: An Empirical Note. *International Journal of Asian Business and Information Management*, *8*(2), 35–45. doi:10.4018/IJABIM.2017040103

Latusi, S., & Fissore, M. (2021). Pilgrimage Routes to Happiness: Comparing the Camino de Santiago and Via Francigena. In A. Perinotto, V. Mayer, & J. Soares (Eds.), *Rebuilding and Restructuring the Tourism Industry: Infusion of Happiness and Quality of Life* (pp. 157–182). IGI Global. https://doi.org/10.4018/978-1-7998-7239-9.ch008

Lavassani, K. M., & Movahedi, B. (2017). Applications Driven Information Systems: Beyond Networks toward Business Ecosystems. *International Journal of Innovation in the Digital Economy*, *8*(1), 61–75. doi:10.4018/IJIDE.2017010104

Lazzareschi, V. H., & Brito, M. S. (2017). Strategic Information Management: Proposal of Business Project Model. In G. Jamil, A. Soares, & C. Pessoa (Eds.), *Handbook of Research on Information Management for Effective Logistics and Supply Chains* (pp. 59–88). Hershey, PA: IGI Global. doi:10.4018/978-1-5225-0973-8.ch004

Lechuga Sancho, M. P., & Martín Navarro, A. (2022). Evolution of the Literature on Social Responsibility in the Tourism Sector: A Systematic Literature Review. In G. Fernandes (Ed.), *Challenges and New Opportunities for Tourism in Inland Territories: Ecocultural Resources and Sustainable Initiatives* (pp. 169–186). IGI Global. https://doi.org/10.4018/978-1-7998-7339-6.ch010

Lederer, M., Kurz, M., & Lazarov, P. (2017). Usage and Suitability of Methods for Strategic Business Process Initiatives: A Multi Case Study Research. *International Journal of Productivity Management and Assessment Technologies*, *5*(1), 40–51. doi:10.4018/IJPMAT.2017010103

Lee, I. (2017). A Social Enterprise Business Model and a Case Study of Pacific Community Ventures (PCV). In V. Potocan, M. Üngan, & Z. Nedelko (Eds.), *Handbook of Research on Managerial Solutions in Non-Profit Organizations* (pp. 182–204). Hershey, PA: IGI Global. doi:10.4018/978-1-5225-0731-4.ch009

Leon, L. A., Seal, K. C., Przasnyski, Z. H., & Wiedenman, I. (2017). Skills and Competencies Required for Jobs in Business Analytics: A Content Analysis of Job Advertisements Using Text Mining. *International Journal of Business Intelligence Research*, *8*(1), 1–25. doi:10.4018/IJBIR.2017010101

Levy, C. L., & Elias, N. I. (2017). SOHO Users' Perceptions of Reliability and Continuity of Cloud-Based Services. In M. Moore (Ed.), *Cybersecurity Breaches and Issues Surrounding Online Threat Protection* (pp. 248–287). Hershey, PA: IGI Global. doi:10.4018/978-1-5225-1941-6.ch011

Levy, M. (2018). Change Management Serving Knowledge Management and Organizational Development: Reflections and Review. In N. Baporikar (Ed.), *Global Practices in Knowledge Management for Societal and Organizational Development* (pp. 256–270). Hershey, PA: IGI Global. doi:10.4018/978-1-5225-3009-1.ch012

Lewandowski, M. (2017). Public Organizations and Business Model Innovation: The Role of Public Service Design. In M. Lewandowski & B. Kożuch (Eds.), *Public Sector Entrepreneurship and the Integration of Innovative Business Models* (pp. 47–72). Hershey, PA: IGI Global. doi:10.4018/978-1-5225-2215-7.ch003

Lhannaoui, H., Kabbaj, M. I., & Bakkoury, Z. (2017). A Survey of Risk-Aware Business Process Modelling. *International Journal of Risk and Contingency Management, 6*(3), 14–26. doi:10.4018/IJRCM.2017070102

Li, J., Sun, W., Jiang, W., Yang, H., & Zhang, L. (2017). How the Nature of Exogenous Shocks and Crises Impact Company Performance?: The Effects of Industry Characteristics. *International Journal of Risk and Contingency Management, 6*(4), 40–55. doi:10.4018/IJRCM.2017100103

Lopez-Fernandez, M., Perez-Perez, M., Serrano-Bedia, A., & Cobo-Gonzalez, A. (2021). Small and Medium Tourism Enterprise Survival in Times of Crisis: "El Capricho de Gaudí. In D. Toubes & N. Araújo-Vila (Eds.), *Risk, Crisis, and Disaster Management in Small and Medium-Sized Tourism Enterprises* (pp. 103–129). IGI Global. doi:10.4018/978-1-7998-6996-2.ch005

Mahajan, A., Maidullah, S., & Hossain, M. R. (2022). Experience Toward Smart Tour Guide Apps in Travelling: An Analysis of Users' Reviews on Audio Odigos and Trip My Way. In R. Augusto Costa, F. Brandão, Z. Breda, & C. Costa (Eds.), *Planning and Managing the Experience Economy in Tourism* (pp. 255-273). IGI Global. https://doi.org/10.4018/978-1-7998-8775-1.ch014

Malega, P. (2017). Small and Medium Enterprises in the Slovak Republic: Status and Competitiveness of SMEs in the Global Markets and Possibilities of Optimization. In M. Vemić (Ed.), *Optimal Management Strategies in Small and Medium Enterprises* (pp. 102–124). Hershey, PA: IGI Global. doi:10.4018/978-1-5225-1949-2.ch006

Malewska, K. M. (2017). Intuition in Decision-Making on the Example of a Non-Profit Organization. In V. Potocan, M. Ünğan, & Z. Nedelko (Eds.), *Handbook of Research on Managerial Solutions in Non-Profit Organizations* (pp. 378–399). Hershey, PA: IGI Global. doi:10.4018/978-1-5225-0731-4.ch018

Maroofi, F. (2017). Entrepreneurial Orientation and Organizational Learning Ability Analysis for Innovation and Firm Performance. In N. Baporikar (Ed.), *Innovation and Shifting Perspectives in Management Education* (pp. 144–165). Hershey, PA: IGI Global. doi:10.4018/978-1-5225-1019-2.ch007

Marques, M., Moleiro, D., Brito, T. M., & Marques, T. (2021). Customer Relationship Management as an Important Relationship Marketing Tool: The Case of the Hospitality Industry in Estoril Coast. In M. Dinis, L. Bonixe, S. Lamy, & Z. Breda (Eds.), Impact of New Media in Tourism (pp. 39-56). IGI Global. https://doi.org/doi:10.4018/978-1-7998-7095-1.ch003

Martins, P. V., & Zacarias, M. (2017). A Web-based Tool for Business Process Improvement. *International Journal of Web Portals*, *9*(2), 68–84. doi:10.4018/IJWP.2017070104

Matthies, B., & Coners, A. (2017). Exploring the Conceptual Nature of e-Business Projects. *Journal of Electronic Commerce in Organizations*, *15*(3), 33–63. doi:10.4018/JECO.2017070103

Mayer, V. F., Fraga, C. C., & Silva, L. C. (2021). Contributions of Neurosciences to Studies of Well-Being in Tourism. In A. Perinotto, V. Mayer, & J. Soares (Eds.), *Rebuilding and Restructuring the Tourism Industry: Infusion of Happiness and Quality of Life* (pp. 108–128). IGI Global. https://doi.org/10.4018/978-1-7998-7239-9.ch006

McKee, J. (2018). Architecture as a Tool to Solve Business Planning Problems. In M. Khosrow-Pour, D.B.A. (Ed.), Encyclopedia of Information Science and Technology, Fourth Edition (pp. 573-586). Hershey, PA: IGI Global. doi:10.4018/978-1-5225-2255-3.ch050

McMurray, A. J., Cross, J., & Caponecchia, C. (2018). The Risk Management Profession in Australia: Business Continuity Plan Practices. In N. Bajgoric (Ed.), *Always-On Enterprise Information Systems for Modern Organizations* (pp. 112–129). Hershey, PA: IGI Global. doi:10.4018/978-1-5225-3704-5.ch006

Meddah, I. H., & Belkadi, K. (2018). Mining Patterns Using Business Process Management. In R. Hamou (Ed.), *Handbook of Research on Biomimicry in Information Retrieval and Knowledge Management* (pp. 78–89). Hershey, PA: IGI Global. doi:10.4018/978-1-5225-3004-6.ch005

Melian, A. G., & Camprubí, R. (2021). The Accessibility of Museum Websites: The Case of Barcelona. In C. Eusébio, L. Teixeira, & M. Carneiro (Eds.), *ICT Tools and Applications for Accessible Tourism* (pp. 234–255). IGI Global. https://doi.org/10.4018/978-1-7998-6428-8.ch011

Mendes, L. (2017). TQM and Knowledge Management: An Integrated Approach Towards Tacit Knowledge Management. In D. Jaziri-Bouagina & G. Jamil (Eds.), *Handbook of Research on Tacit Knowledge Management for Organizational Success* (pp. 236–263). Hershey, PA: IGI Global. doi:10.4018/978-1-5225-2394-9.ch009

Menezes, V. D., & Cavagnaro, E. (2021). Communicating Sustainable Initiatives in the Hotel Industry: The Case of the Hotel Jakarta Amsterdam. In F. Brandão, Z. Breda, R. Costa, & C. Costa (Eds.), *Handbook of Research on the Role of Tourism in Achieving Sustainable Development Goals* (pp. 224-234). IGI Global. https://doi.org/10.4018/978-1-7998-5691-7.ch013

Mitas, O., Bastiaansen, M., & Boode, W. (2022). If You're Happy, I'm Happy: Emotion Contagion at a Tourist Information Center. In R. Augusto Costa, F. Brandão, Z. Breda, & C. Costa (Eds.), *Planning and Managing the Experience Economy in Tourism* (pp. 122-140). IGI Global. https://doi.org/10.4018/978-1-7998-8775-1.ch007

Mnjama, N. M. (2017). Preservation of Recorded Information in Public and Private Sector Organizations. In P. Jain & N. Mnjama (Eds.), *Managing Knowledge Resources and Records in Modern Organizations* (pp. 149–167). Hershey, PA: IGI Global. doi:10.4018/978-1-5225-1965-2.ch009

Mokoqama, M., & Fields, Z. (2017). Principles of Responsible Management Education (PRME): Call for Responsible Management Education. In Z. Fields (Ed.), *Collective Creativity for Responsible and Sustainable Business Practice* (pp. 229–241). Hershey, PA: IGI Global. doi:10.4018/978-1-5225-1823-5.ch012

Monteiro, A., Lopes, S., & Carbone, F. (2021). Academic Mobility: Bridging Tourism and Peace Education. In J. da Silva, Z. Breda, & F. Carbone (Eds.), *Role and Impact of Tourism in Peacebuilding and Conflict Transformation* (pp. 275-301). IGI Global. https://doi.org/10.4018/978-1-7998-5053-3.ch016

Muniapan, B. (2017). Philosophy and Management: The Relevance of Vedanta in Management. In P. Ordóñez de Pablos (Ed.), *Managerial Strategies and Solutions for Business Success in Asia* (pp. 124–139). Hershey, PA: IGI Global. doi:10.4018/978-1-5225-1886-0.ch007

Murad, S. E., & Dowaji, S. (2017). Using Value-Based Approach for Managing Cloud-Based Services. In A. Turuk, B. Sahoo, & S. Addya (Eds.), *Resource Management and Efficiency in Cloud Computing Environments* (pp. 33–60). Hershey, PA: IGI Global. doi:10.4018/978-1-5225-1721-4.ch002

Mutahar, A. M., Daud, N. M., Thurasamy, R., Isaac, O., & Abdulsalam, R. (2018). The Mediating of Perceived Usefulness and Perceived Ease of Use: The Case of Mobile Banking in Yemen. *International Journal of Technology Diffusion*, *9*(2), 21–40. doi:10.4018/IJTD.2018040102

Naidoo, V. (2017). E-Learning and Management Education at African Universities. In N. Baporikar (Ed.), *Management Education for Global Leadership* (pp. 181–201). Hershey, PA: IGI Global. doi:10.4018/978-1-5225-1013-0.ch009

Naidoo, V., & Igbinakhase, I. (2018). Opportunities and Challenges of Knowledge Retention in SMEs. In N. Baporikar (Ed.), *Knowledge Integration Strategies for Entrepreneurship and Sustainability* (pp. 70–94). Hershey, PA: IGI Global. doi:10.4018/978-1-5225-5115-7.ch004

Naumov, N., & Costandachi, G. (2021). Creativity and Entrepreneurship: Gastronomic Tourism in Mexico. In J. Soares (Ed.), *Innovation and Entrepreneurial Opportunities in Community Tourism* (pp. 90–108). IGI Global. https://doi.org/10.4018/978-1-7998-4855-4.ch006

Nayak, S., & Prabhu, N. (2017). Paradigm Shift in Management Education: Need for a Cross Functional Perspective. In N. Baporikar (Ed.), *Management Education for Global Leadership* (pp. 241–255). Hershey, PA: IGI Global. doi:10.4018/978-1-5225-1013-0.ch012

Nedelko, Z., & Potocan, V. (2017). Management Solutions in Non-Profit Organizations: Case of Slovenia. In V. Potocan, M. Üngan, & Z. Nedelko (Eds.), *Handbook of Research on Managerial Solutions in Non-Profit Organizations* (pp. 1–22). Hershey, PA: IGI Global. doi:10.4018/978-1-5225-0731-4.ch001

Nedelko, Z., & Potocan, V. (2017). Priority of Management Tools Utilization among Managers: International Comparison. In V. Wang (Ed.), *Encyclopedia of Strategic Leadership and Management* (pp. 1083–1094). Hershey, PA: IGI Global. doi:10.4018/978-1-5225-1049-9.ch075

Nedelko, Z., Raudeliūnienė, J., & Črešnar, R. (2018). Knowledge Dynamics in Supply Chain Management. In N. Baporikar (Ed.), *Knowledge Integration Strategies for Entrepreneurship and Sustainability* (pp. 150–166). Hershey, PA: IGI Global. doi:10.4018/978-1-5225-5115-7.ch008

Nguyen, H. T., & Hipsher, S. A. (2018). Innovation and Creativity Used by Private Sector Firms in a Resources-Constrained Environment. In S. Hipsher (Ed.), *Examining the Private Sector's Role in Wealth Creation and Poverty Reduction* (pp. 219–238). Hershey, PA: IGI Global. doi:10.4018/978-1-5225-3117-3.ch010

Obicci, P. A. (2017). Risk Sharing in a Partnership. In *Risk Management Strategies in Public-Private Partnerships* (pp. 115–152). Hershey, PA: IGI Global. doi:10.4018/978-1-5225-2503-5.ch004

Obidallah, W. J., & Raahemi, B. (2017). Managing Changes in Service Oriented Virtual Organizations: A Structural and Procedural Framework to Facilitate the Process of Change. *Journal of Electronic Commerce in Organizations*, *15*(1), 59–83. doi:10.4018/JECO.2017010104

Ojo, O. (2017). Impact of Innovation on the Entrepreneurial Success in Selected Business Enterprises in South-West Nigeria. *International Journal of Innovation in the Digital Economy*, *8*(2), 29–38. doi:10.4018/IJIDE.2017040103

Okdinawati, L., Simatupang, T. M., & Sunitiyoso, Y. (2017). Multi-Agent Reinforcement Learning for Value Co-Creation of Collaborative Transportation Management (CTM). *International Journal of Information Systems and Supply Chain Management*, *10*(3), 84–95. doi:10.4018/IJISSCM.2017070105

Olivera, V. A., & Carrillo, I. M. (2021). Organizational Culture: A Key Element for the Development of Mexican Micro and Small Tourist Companies. In J. Soares (Ed.), *Innovation and Entrepreneurial Opportunities in Community Tourism* (pp. 227–242). IGI Global. doi:10.4018/978-1-7998-4855-4.ch013

Ossorio, M. (2022). Corporate Museum Experiences in Enogastronomic Tourism. In R. Augusto Costa, F. Brandão, Z. Breda, & C. Costa (Eds.), Planning and Managing the Experience Economy in Tourism (pp. 107-121). IGI Global. https://doi.org/doi:10.4018/978-1-7998-8775-1.ch006

Ossorio, M. (2022). Enogastronomic Tourism in Times of Pandemic. In G. Fernandes (Ed.), *Challenges and New Opportunities for Tourism in Inland Territories: Ecocultural Resources and Sustainable Initiatives* (pp. 241–255). IGI Global. https://doi.org/10.4018/978-1-7998-7339-6.ch014

Özekici, Y. K. (2022). ICT as an Acculturative Agent and Its Role in the Tourism Context: Introduction, Acculturation Theory, Progress of the Acculturation Theory in Extant Literature. In C. Ramos, S. Quinteiro, & A. Gonçalves (Eds.), *ICT as Innovator Between Tourism and Culture* (pp. 42–66). IGI Global. https://doi.org/10.4018/978-1-7998-8165-0.ch004

Pal, K. (2018). Building High Quality Big Data-Based Applications in Supply Chains. In A. Kumar & S. Saurav (Eds.), *Supply Chain Management Strategies and Risk Assessment in Retail Environments* (pp. 1–24). Hershey, PA: IGI Global. doi:10.4018/978-1-5225-3056-5.ch001

Palos-Sanchez, P. R., & Correia, M. B. (2018). Perspectives of the Adoption of Cloud Computing in the Tourism Sector. In J. Rodrigues, C. Ramos, P. Cardoso, & C. Henriques (Eds.), *Handbook of Research on Technological Developments for Cultural Heritage and eTourism Applications* (pp. 377–400). Hershey, PA: IGI Global. doi:10.4018/978-1-5225-2927-9.ch018

Papadopoulou, G. (2021). Promoting Gender Equality and Women Empowerment in the Tourism Sector. In F. Brandão, Z. Breda, R. Costa, & C. Costa (Eds.), Handbook of Research on the Role of Tourism in Achieving Sustainable Development Goals (pp. 152-174). IGI Global. https://doi.org/ doi:10.4018/978-1-7998-5691-7.ch009

Papp-Váry, Á. F., & Tóth, T. Z. (2022). Analysis of Budapest as a Film Tourism Destination. In R. Baleiro & R. Pereira (Eds.), *Global Perspectives on Literary Tourism and Film-Induced Tourism* (pp. 257-279). IGI Global. https://doi.org/10.4018/978-1-7998-8262-6.ch014

Patiño, B. E. (2017). New Generation Management by Convergence and Individual Identity: A Systemic and Human-Oriented Approach. In N. Baporikar (Ed.), *Innovation and Shifting Perspectives in Management Education* (pp. 119–143). Hershey, PA: IGI Global. doi:10.4018/978-1-5225-1019-2.ch006

Patro, C. S. (2021). Digital Tourism: Influence of E-Marketing Technology. In M. Dinis, L. Bonixe, S. Lamy, & Z. Breda (Eds.), *Impact of New Media in Tourism* (pp. 234-254). IGI Global. https://doi.org/10.4018/978-1-7998-7095-1.ch014

Pawliczek, A., & Rössler, M. (2017). Knowledge of Management Tools and Systems in SMEs: Knowledge Transfer in Management. In A. Bencsik (Ed.), *Knowledge Management Initiatives and Strategies in Small and Medium Enterprises* (pp. 180–203). Hershey, PA: IGI Global. doi:10.4018/978-1-5225-1642-2.ch009

Pejic-Bach, M., Omazic, M. A., Aleksic, A., & Zoroja, J. (2018). Knowledge-Based Decision Making: A Multi-Case Analysis. In R. Leon (Ed.), *Managerial Strategies for Business Sustainability During Turbulent Times* (pp. 160–184). Hershey, PA: IGI Global. doi:10.4018/978-1-5225-2716-9.ch009

Perano, M., Hysa, X., & Calabrese, M. (2018). Strategic Planning, Cultural Context, and Business Continuity Management: Business Cases in the City of Shkoder. In A. Presenza & L. Sheehan (Eds.), *Geopolitics and Strategic Management in the Global Economy* (pp. 57–77). Hershey, PA: IGI Global. doi:10.4018/978-1-5225-2673-5.ch004

Pereira, R., Mira da Silva, M., & Lapão, L. V. (2017). IT Governance Maturity Patterns in Portuguese Healthcare. In S. De Haes & W. Van Grembergen (Eds.), *Strategic IT Governance and Alignment in Business Settings* (pp. 24–52). Hershey, PA: IGI Global. doi:10.4018/978-1-5225-0861-8.ch002

Pérez-Uribe, R. I., Torres, D. A., Jurado, S. P., & Prada, D. M. (2018). Cloud Tools for the Development of Project Management in SMEs. In R. Perez-Uribe, C. Salcedo-Perez, & D. Ocampo-Guzman (Eds.), *Handbook of Research on Intrapreneurship and Organizational Sustainability in SMEs* (pp. 95–120). Hershey, PA: IGI Global. doi:10.4018/978-1-5225-3543-0.ch005

Petrisor, I., & Cozmiuc, D. (2017). Global Supply Chain Management Organization at Siemens in the Advent of Industry 4.0. In L. Saglietto & C. Cezanne (Eds.), *Global Intermediation and Logistics Service Providers* (pp. 123–142). Hershey, PA: IGI Global. doi:10.4018/978-1-5225-2133-4.ch007

Pierce, J. M., Velliaris, D. M., & Edwards, J. (2017). A Living Case Study: A Journey Not a Destination. In N. Silton (Ed.), *Exploring the Benefits of Creativity in Education, Media, and the Arts* (pp. 158–178). Hershey, PA: IGI Global. doi:10.4018/978-1-5225-0504-4.ch008

Pipia, S., & Pipia, S. (2021). Challenges of Religious Tourism in the Conflict Region: An Example of Jerusalem. In E. Alaverdov & M. Bari (Eds.), *Global Development of Religious Tourism* (pp. 135-148). IGI Global. https://doi.org/10.4018/978-1-7998-5792-1.ch009

Poulaki, P., Kritikos, A., Vasilakis, N., & Valeri, M. (2022). The Contribution of Female Creativity to the Development of Gastronomic Tourism in Greece: The Case of the Island of Naxos in the South Aegean Region. In M. Valeri (Ed.), *New Governance and Management in Touristic Destinations* (pp. 246–258). IGI Global. https://doi.org/10.4018/978-1-6684-3889-3.ch015

Radosavljevic, M., & Andjelkovic, A. (2017). Multi-Criteria Decision Making Approach for Choosing Business Process for the Improvement: Upgrading of the Six Sigma Methodology. In J. Stanković, P. Delias, S. Marinković, & S. Rochhia (Eds.), *Tools and Techniques for Economic Decision Analysis* (pp. 225–247). Hershey, PA: IGI Global. doi:10.4018/978-1-5225-0959-2.ch011

Radovic, V. M. (2017). Corporate Sustainability and Responsibility and Disaster Risk Reduction: A Serbian Overview. In M. Camilleri (Ed.), *CSR 2.0 and the New Era of Corporate Citizenship* (pp. 147–164). Hershey, PA: IGI Global. doi:10.4018/978-1-5225-1842-6.ch008

Raghunath, K. M., Devi, S. L., & Patro, C. S. (2018). Impact of Risk Assessment Models on Risk Factors: A Holistic Outlook. In K. Strang, M. Korstanje, & N. Vajjhala (Eds.), *Research, Practices, and Innovations in Global Risk and Contingency Management* (pp. 134–153). Hershey, PA: IGI Global. doi:10.4018/978-1-5225-4754-9.ch008

Raman, A., & Goyal, D. P. (2017). Extending IMPLEMENT Framework for Enterprise Information Systems Implementation to Information System Innovation. In M. Tavana (Ed.), *Enterprise Information Systems and the Digitalization of Business Functions* (pp. 137–177). Hershey, PA: IGI Global. doi:10.4018/978-1-5225-2382-6.ch007

Rao, Y., & Zhang, Y. (2017). The Construction and Development of Academic Library Digital Special Subject Databases. In L. Ruan, Q. Zhu, & Y. Ye (Eds.), *Academic Library Development and Administration in China* (pp. 163–183). Hershey, PA: IGI Global. doi:10.4018/978-1-5225-0550-1.ch010

Ravasan, A. Z., Mohammadi, M. M., & Hamidi, H. (2018). An Investigation Into the Critical Success Factors of Implementing Information Technology Service Management Frameworks. In K. Jakobs (Ed.), *Corporate and Global Standardization Initiatives in Contemporary Society* (pp. 200–218). Hershey, PA: IGI Global. doi:10.4018/978-1-5225-5320-5.ch009

Rezaie, S., Mirabedini, S. J., & Abtahi, A. (2018). Designing a Model for Implementation of Business Intelligence in the Banking Industry. *International Journal of Enterprise Information Systems*, *14*(1), 77–103. doi:10.4018/IJEIS.2018010105

Richards, V., Matthews, N., Williams, O. J., & Khan, Z. (2021). The Challenges of Accessible Tourism Information Systems for Tourists With Vision Impairment: Sensory Communications Beyond the Screen. In C. Eusébio, L. Teixeira, & M. Carneiro (Eds.), *ICT Tools and Applications for Accessible Tourism* (pp. 26–54). IGI Global. https://doi.org/10.4018/978-1-7998-6428-8.ch002

Rodrigues de Souza Neto, V., & Marques, O. (2021). Rural Tourism Fostering Welfare Through Sustainable Development: A Conceptual Approach. In A. Perinotto, V. Mayer, & J. Soares (Eds.), *Rebuilding and Restructuring the Tourism Industry: Infusion of Happiness and Quality of Life* (pp. 38–57). IGI Global. https://doi.org/10.4018/978-1-7998-7239-9.ch003

Romano, L., Grimaldi, R., & Colasuonno, F. S. (2017). Demand Management as a Success Factor in Project Portfolio Management. In L. Romano (Ed.), *Project Portfolio Management Strategies for Effective Organizational Operations* (pp. 202–219). Hershey, PA: IGI Global. doi:10.4018/978-1-5225-2151-8.ch008

Rubio-Escuderos, L., & García-Andreu, H. (2021). Competitiveness Factors of Accessible Tourism E-Travel Agencies. In C. Eusébio, L. Teixeira, & M. Carneiro (Eds.), *ICT Tools and Applications for Accessible Tourism* (pp. 196–217). IGI Global. https://doi.org/10.4018/978-1-7998-6428-8.ch009

Rucci, A. C., Porto, N., Darcy, S., & Becka, L. (2021). Smart and Accessible Cities?: Not Always – The Case for Accessible Tourism Initiatives in Buenos Aries and Sydney. In C. Eusébio, L. Teixeira, & M. Carneiro (Eds.), *ICT Tools and Applications for Accessible Tourism* (pp. 115–145). IGI Global. https://doi.org/10.4018/978-1-7998-6428-8.ch006

Ruhi, U. (2018). Towards an Interdisciplinary Socio-Technical Definition of Virtual Communities. In M. Khosrow-Pour, D.B.A. (Ed.), Encyclopedia of Information Science and Technology, Fourth Edition (pp. 4278-4295). Hershey, PA: IGI Global. doi:10.4018/978-1-5225-2255-3.ch371

Ryan, L., Catena, M., Ros, P., & Stephens, S. (2021). Designing Entrepreneurial Ecosystems to Support Resource Management in the Tourism Industry. In V. Costa, A. Moura, & M. Mira (Eds.), *Handbook of Research on Human Capital and People Management in the Tourism Industry* (pp. 265–281). IGI Global. https://doi.org/10.4018/978-1-7998-4318-4.ch013

Sabuncu, I. (2021). Understanding Tourist Perceptions and Expectations During Pandemic Through Social Media Big Data. In M. Demir, A. Dalgıç, & F. Ergen (Eds.), *Handbook of Research on the Impacts and Implications of COVID-19 on the Tourism Industry* (pp. 330–350). IGI Global. https://doi.org/10.4018/978-1-7998-8231-2.ch016

Safari, M. R., & Jiang, Q. (2018). The Theory and Practice of IT Governance Maturity and Strategies Alignment: Evidence From Banking Industry. *Journal of Global Information Management*, *26*(2), 127–146. doi:10.4018/JGIM.2018040106

Sahoo, J., Pati, B., & Mohanty, B. (2017). Knowledge Management as an Academic Discipline: An Assessment. In B. Gunjal (Ed.), *Managing Knowledge and Scholarly Assets in Academic Libraries* (pp. 99–126). Hershey, PA: IGI Global. doi:10.4018/978-1-5225-1741-2.ch005

Saini, D. (2017). Relevance of Teaching Values and Ethics in Management Education. In N. Baporikar (Ed.), *Management Education for Global Leadership* (pp. 90–111). Hershey, PA: IGI Global. doi:10.4018/978-1-5225-1013-0.ch005

Sambhanthan, A. (2017). Assessing and Benchmarking Sustainability in Organisations: An Integrated Conceptual Model. *International Journal of Systems and Service-Oriented Engineering*, *7*(4), 22–43. doi:10.4018/IJSSOE.2017100102

Sambhanthan, A., & Potdar, V. (2017). A Study of the Parameters Impacting Sustainability in Information Technology Organizations. *International Journal of Knowledge-Based Organizations*, *7*(3), 27–39. doi:10.4018/IJKBO.2017070103

Sánchez-Fernández, M. D., & Manríquez, M. R. (2018). The Entrepreneurial Spirit Based on Social Values: The Digital Generation. In P. Isaias & L. Carvalho (Eds.), *User Innovation and the Entrepreneurship Phenomenon in the Digital Economy* (pp. 173–193). Hershey, PA: IGI Global. doi:10.4018/978-1-5225-2826-5.ch009

Sanchez-Ruiz, L., & Blanco, B. (2017). Process Management for SMEs: Barriers, Enablers, and Benefits. In M. Vemić (Ed.), *Optimal Management Strategies in Small and Medium Enterprises* (pp. 293–319). Hershey, PA: IGI Global. doi:10.4018/978-1-5225-1949-2.ch014

Sanz, L. F., Gómez-Pérez, J., & Castillo-Martinez, A. (2018). Analysis of the European ICT Competence Frameworks. In V. Ahuja & S. Rathore (Eds.), *Multidisciplinary Perspectives on Human Capital and Information Technology Professionals* (pp. 225–245). Hershey, PA: IGI Global. doi:10.4018/978-1-5225-5297-0.ch012

Sarvepalli, A., & Godin, J. (2017). Business Process Management in the Classroom. *Journal of Cases on Information Technology*, *19*(2), 17–28. doi:10.4018/JCIT.2017040102

Saxena, G. G., & Saxena, A. (2021). Host Community Role in Medical Tourism Development. In M. Singh & S. Kumaran (Eds.), *Growth of the Medical Tourism Industry and Its Impact on Society: Emerging Research and Opportunities* (pp. 105–127). IGI Global. https://doi.org/10.4018/978-1-7998-3427-4.ch006

Saygili, E. E., Ozturkoglu, Y., & Kocakulah, M. C. (2017). End Users' Perceptions of Critical Success Factors in ERP Applications. *International Journal of Enterprise Information Systems*, *13*(4), 58–75. doi:10.4018/IJEIS.2017100104

Saygili, E. E., & Saygili, A. T. (2017). Contemporary Issues in Enterprise Information Systems: A Critical Review of CSFs in ERP Implementations. In M. Tavana (Ed.), *Enterprise Information Systems and the Digitalization of Business Functions* (pp. 120–136). Hershey, PA: IGI Global. doi:10.4018/978-1-5225-2382-6.ch006

Schwaiger, K. M., & Zehrer, A. (2021). The COVID-19 Pandemic and Organizational Resilience in Hospitality Family Firms: A Qualitative Approach. In A. Zehrer, G. Glowka, K. Schwaiger, & V. Ranacher-Lackner (Eds.), *Resiliency Models and Addressing Future Risks for Family Firms in the Tourism Industry* (pp. 32–49). IGI Global. https://doi.org/10.4018/978-1-7998-7352-5.ch002

Scott, N., & Campos, A. C. (2022). Cognitive Science of Tourism Experiences. In R. Augusto Costa, F. Brandão, Z. Breda, & C. Costa (Eds.), Planning and Managing the Experience Economy in Tourism (pp. 1-21). IGI Global. https://doi.org/ doi:10.4018/978-1-7998-8775-1.ch001

Seidenstricker, S., & Antonino, A. (2018). Business Model Innovation-Oriented Technology Management for Emergent Technologies. In M. Khosrow-Pour, D.B.A. (Ed.), Encyclopedia of Information Science and Technology, Fourth Edition (pp. 4560-4569). Hershey, PA: IGI Global. doi:10.4018/978-1-5225-2255-3.ch396

Selvi, M. S. (2021). Changes in Tourism Sales and Marketing Post COVID-19. In M. Demir, A. Dalgıç, & F. Ergen (Eds.), *Handbook of Research on the Impacts and Implications of COVID-19 on the Tourism Industry* (pp. 437–460). IGI Global. doi:10.4018/978-1-7998-8231-2.ch021

Senaratne, S., & Gunarathne, A. D. (2017). Excellence Perspective for Management Education from a Global Accountants' Hub in Asia. In N. Baporikar (Ed.), *Management Education for Global Leadership* (pp. 158–180). Hershey, PA: IGI Global. doi:10.4018/978-1-5225-1013-0.ch008

Sensuse, D. I., & Cahyaningsih, E. (2018). Knowledge Management Models: A Summative Review. *International Journal of Information Systems in the Service Sector*, *10*(1), 71–100. doi:10.4018/IJISSS.2018010105

Seth, M., Goyal, D., & Kiran, R. (2017). Diminution of Impediments in Implementation of Supply Chain Management Information System for Enhancing its Effectiveness in Indian Automobile Industry. *Journal of Global Information Management*, *25*(3), 1–20. doi:10.4018/JGIM.2017070101

Seyal, A. H., & Rahman, M. N. (2017). Investigating Impact of Inter-Organizational Factors in Measuring ERP Systems Success: Bruneian Perspectives. In M. Tavana (Ed.), *Enterprise Information Systems and the Digitalization of Business Functions* (pp. 178–204). Hershey, PA: IGI Global. doi:10.4018/978-1-5225-2382-6.ch008

Shaqrah, A. A. (2018). Analyzing Business Intelligence Systems Based on 7s Model of McKinsey. *International Journal of Business Intelligence Research*, *9*(1), 53–63. doi:10.4018/IJBIR.2018010104

Sharma, A. J. (2017). Enhancing Sustainability through Experiential Learning in Management Education. In N. Baporikar (Ed.), *Management Education for Global Leadership* (pp. 256–274). Hershey, PA: IGI Global. doi:10.4018/978-1-5225-1013-0.ch013

Shetty, K. P. (2017). Responsible Global Leadership: Ethical Challenges in Management Education. In N. Baporikar (Ed.), *Innovation and Shifting Perspectives in Management Education* (pp. 194–223). Hershey, PA: IGI Global. doi:10.4018/978-1-5225-1019-2.ch009

Sinthupundaja, J., & Kohda, Y. (2017). Effects of Corporate Social Responsibility and Creating Shared Value on Sustainability. *International Journal of Sustainable Entrepreneurship and Corporate Social Responsibility*, *2*(1), 27–38. doi:10.4018/IJSECSR.2017010103

Škarica, I., & Hrgović, A. V. (2018). Implementation of Total Quality Management Principles in Public Health Institutes in the Republic of Croatia. *International Journal of Productivity Management and Assessment Technologies*, *6*(1), 1–16. doi:10.4018/IJPMAT.2018010101

Skokic, V. (2021). How Small Hotel Owners Practice Resilience: Longitudinal Study Among Small Family Hotels in Croatia. In A. Zehrer, G. Glowka, K. Schwaiger, & V. Ranacher-Lackner (Eds.), *Resiliency Models and Addressing Future Risks for Family Firms in the Tourism Industry* (pp. 50–73). IGI Global. doi:10.4018/978-1-7998-7352-5.ch003

Smuts, H., Kotzé, P., Van der Merwe, A., & Loock, M. (2017). Framework for Managing Shared Knowledge in an Information Systems Outsourcing Context. *International Journal of Knowledge Management*, *13*(4), 1–30. doi:10.4018/IJKM.2017100101

Sousa, M. J., Cruz, R., Dias, I., & Caracol, C. (2017). Information Management Systems in the Supply Chain. In G. Jamil, A. Soares, & C. Pessoa (Eds.), *Handbook of Research on Information Management for Effective Logistics and Supply Chains* (pp. 469–485). Hershey, PA: IGI Global. doi:10.4018/978-1-5225-0973-8.ch025

Spremic, M., Turulja, L., & Bajgoric, N. (2018). Two Approaches in Assessing Business Continuity Management Attitudes in the Organizational Context. In N. Bajgoric (Ed.), *Always-On Enterprise Information Systems for Modern Organizations* (pp. 159–183). Hershey, PA: IGI Global. doi:10.4018/978-1-5225-3704-5.ch008

Steenkamp, A. L. (2018). Some Insights in Computer Science and Information Technology. In *Examining the Changing Role of Supervision in Doctoral Research Projects: Emerging Research and Opportunities* (pp. 113–133). Hershey, PA: IGI Global. doi:10.4018/978-1-5225-2610-0.ch005

Stipanović, C., Rudan, E., & Zubović, V. (2022). Reaching the New Tourist Through Creativity: Sustainable Development Challenges in Croatian Coastal Towns. In M. Valeri (Ed.), *New Governance and Management in Touristic Destinations* (pp. 231–245). IGI Global. https://doi.org/10.4018/978-1-6684-3889-3.ch014

Tabach, A., & Croteau, A. (2017). Configurations of Information Technology Governance Practices and Business Unit Performance. *International Journal of IT/Business Alignment and Governance*, *8*(2), 1–27. doi:10.4018/IJITBAG.2017070101

Talaue, G. M., & Iqbal, T. (2017). Assessment of e-Business Mode of Selected Private Universities in the Philippines and Pakistan. *International Journal of Online Marketing*, *7*(4), 63–77. doi:10.4018/IJOM.2017100105

Tam, G. C. (2017). Project Manager Sustainability Competence. In *Managerial Strategies and Green Solutions for Project Sustainability* (pp. 178–207). Hershey, PA: IGI Global. doi:10.4018/978-1-5225-2371-0.ch008

Tambo, T. (2018). Fashion Retail Innovation: About Context, Antecedents, and Outcome in Technological Change Projects. In I. Management Association (Ed.), Fashion and Textiles: Breakthroughs in Research and Practice (pp. 233-260). Hershey, PA: IGI Global. https://doi.org/ doi:10.4018/978-1-5225-3432-7.ch010

Tantau, A. D., & Frăţilă, L. C. (2018). Information and Management System for Renewable Energy Business. In *Entrepreneurship and Business Development in the Renewable Energy Sector* (pp. 200–244). Hershey, PA: IGI Global. doi:10.4018/978-1-5225-3625-3.ch006

Teixeira, N., Pardal, P. N., & Rafael, B. G. (2018). Internationalization, Financial Performance, and Organizational Challenges: A Success Case in Portugal. In L. Carvalho (Ed.), *Handbook of Research on Entrepreneurial Ecosystems and Social Dynamics in a Globalized World* (pp. 379–423). Hershey, PA: IGI Global. doi:10.4018/978-1-5225-3525-6.ch017

Teixeira, P., Teixeira, L., Eusébio, C., Silva, S., & Teixeira, A. (2021). The Impact of ICTs on Accessible Tourism: Evidence Based on a Systematic Literature Review. In C. Eusébio, L. Teixeira, & M. Carneiro (Eds.), *ICT Tools and Applications for Accessible Tourism* (pp. 1–25). IGI Global. doi:10.4018/978-1-7998-6428-8.ch001

Trad, A., & Kalpić, D. (2018). The Business Transformation Framework, Agile Project and Change Management. In M. Khosrow-Pour, D.B.A. (Ed.), Encyclopedia of Information Science and Technology, Fourth Edition (pp. 620-635). Hershey, PA: IGI Global. https://doi.org/ doi:10.4018/978-1-5225-2255-3.ch054

Trad, A., & Kalpić, D. (2018). The Business Transformation and Enterprise Architecture Framework: The Financial Engineering E-Risk Management and E-Law Integration. In B. Sergi, F. Fidanoski, M. Ziolo, & V. Naumovski (Eds.), *Regaining Global Stability After the Financial Crisis* (pp. 46–65). Hershey, PA: IGI Global. doi:10.4018/978-1-5225-4026-7.ch003

Trengereid, V. (2022). Conditions of Network Engagement: The Quest for a Common Good. In R. Augusto Costa, F. Brandão, Z. Breda, & C. Costa (Eds.), *Planning and Managing the Experience Economy in Tourism* (pp. 69-84). IGI Global. https://doi.org/10.4018/978-1-7998-8775-1.ch004

Turulja, L., & Bajgoric, N. (2018). Business Continuity and Information Systems: A Systematic Literature Review. In N. Bajgoric (Ed.), *Always-On Enterprise Information Systems for Modern Organizations* (pp. 60–87). Hershey, PA: IGI Global. doi:10.4018/978-1-5225-3704-5.ch004

Vargas-Hernández, J. G. (2017). Professional Integrity in Business Management Education. In N. Baporikar (Ed.), *Management Education for Global Leadership* (pp. 70–89). Hershey, PA: IGI Global. doi:10.4018/978-1-5225-1013-0.ch004

Varnacı Uzun, F. (2021). The Destination Preferences of Foreign Tourists During the COVID-19 Pandemic and Attitudes Towards: Marmaris, Turkey. In M. Demir, A. Dalgıç, & F. Ergen (Eds.), *Handbook of Research on the Impacts and Implications of COVID-19 on the Tourism Industry* (pp. 285–306). IGI Global. https://doi.org/10.4018/978-1-7998-8231-2.ch014

Vasista, T. G., & AlAbdullatif, A. M. (2017). Role of Electronic Customer Relationship Management in Demand Chain Management: A Predictive Analytic Approach. *International Journal of Information Systems and Supply Chain Management, 10*(1), 53–67. doi:10.4018/IJISSCM.2017010104

Vieru, D., & Bourdeau, S. (2017). Survival in the Digital Era: A Digital Competence-Based Multi-Case Study in the Canadian SME Clothing Industry. *International Journal of Social and Organizational Dynamics in IT, 6*(1), 17–34. doi:10.4018/IJSODIT.2017010102

Vijayan, G., & Kamarulzaman, N. H. (2017). An Introduction to Sustainable Supply Chain Management and Business Implications. In M. Khan, M. Hussain, & M. Ajmal (Eds.), *Green Supply Chain Management for Sustainable Business Practice* (pp. 27–50). Hershey, PA: IGI Global. doi:10.4018/978-1-5225-0635-5.ch002

Vlachvei, A., & Notta, O. (2017). Firm Competitiveness: Theories, Evidence, and Measurement. In A. Vlachvei, O. Notta, K. Karantininis, & N. Tsounis (Eds.), *Factors Affecting Firm Competitiveness and Performance in the Modern Business World* (pp. 1–42). Hershey, PA: IGI Global. doi:10.4018/978-1-5225-0843-4.ch001

Wang, C., Schofield, M., Li, X., & Ou, X. (2017). Do Chinese Students in Public and Private Higher Education Institutes Perform at Different Level in One of the Leadership Skills: Critical Thinking?: An Exploratory Comparison. In V. Wang (Ed.), *Encyclopedia of Strategic Leadership and Management* (pp. 160–181). Hershey, PA: IGI Global. doi:10.4018/978-1-5225-1049-9.ch013

Wang, J. (2017). Multi-Agent based Production Management Decision System Modelling for the Textile Enterprise. *Journal of Global Information Management, 25*(4), 1–15. doi:10.4018/JGIM.2017100101

Wiedemann, A., & Gewald, H. (2017). Examining Cross-Domain Alignment: The Correlation of Business Strategy, IT Management, and IT Business Value. *International Journal of IT/Business Alignment and Governance, 8*(1), 17–31. doi:10.4018/IJITBAG.2017010102

Wolf, R., & Thiel, M. (2018). Advancing Global Business Ethics in China: Reducing Poverty Through Human and Social Welfare. In S. Hipsher (Ed.), *Examining the Private Sector's Role in Wealth Creation and Poverty Reduction* (pp. 67–84). Hershey, PA: IGI Global. doi:10.4018/978-1-5225-3117-3.ch004

Yablonsky, S. (2018). Innovation Platforms: Data and Analytics Platforms. In *Multi-Sided Platforms (MSPs) and Sharing Strategies in the Digital Economy: Emerging Research and Opportunities* (pp. 72–95). Hershey, PA: IGI Global. doi:10.4018/978-1-5225-5457-8.ch003

Yaşar, B. (2021). The Impact of COVID-19 on Volatility of Tourism Stocks: Evidence From BIST Tourism Index. In M. Demir, A. Dalgıç, & F. Ergen (Eds.), *Handbook of Research on the Impacts and Implications of COVID-19 on the Tourism Industry* (pp. 23–44). IGI Global. https://doi.org/10.4018/978-1-7998-8231-2.ch002

Yusoff, A., Ahmad, N. H., & Halim, H. A. (2017). Agropreneurship among Gen Y in Malaysia: The Role of Academic Institutions. In N. Ahmad, T. Ramayah, H. Halim, & S. Rahman (Eds.), *Handbook of Research on Small and Medium Enterprises in Developing Countries* (pp. 23–47). Hershey, PA: IGI Global. doi:10.4018/978-1-5225-2165-5.ch002

Zacher, D., & Pechlaner, H. (2021). Resilience as an Opportunity Approach: Challenges and Perspectives for Private Sector Participation on a Community Level. In A. Zehrer, G. Glowka, K. Schwaiger, & V. Ranacher-Lackner (Eds.), *Resiliency Models and Addressing Future Risks for Family Firms in the Tourism Industry* (pp. 75–102). IGI Global. https://doi.org/10.4018/978-1-7998-7352-5.ch004

Zanin, F., Comuzzi, E., & Costantini, A. (2018). The Effect of Business Strategy and Stock Market Listing on the Use of Risk Assessment Tools. In *Management Control Systems in Complex Settings: Emerging Research and Opportunities* (pp. 145–168). Hershey, PA: IGI Global. doi:10.4018/978-1-5225-3987-2.ch007

Zgheib, P. W. (2017). Corporate Innovation and Intrapreneurship in the Middle East. In P. Zgheib (Ed.), *Entrepreneurship and Business Innovation in the Middle East* (pp. 37–56). Hershey, PA: IGI Global. doi:10.4018/978-1-5225-2066-5.ch003

About the Contributors

Muhammad Anshari is researcher and academic staff at School of Business & Economics, Universiti Brunei Darussalam. His professional experience started when he was IT Business Analyst at Astra International. Research Fellowship from The Government Republic of China (Taiwan) at National Taiwan University (Jan-Dec, 2014). Research Fellowship from King Saud University - the Kingdom of Saudi Arabia 2009. Senior Associate Researcher of Informatics Department, Universitas Islam Negeri Yogyakarta, Indonesia.

Muhammad Syafrudin currently works with the Department of Artificial Intelligence at Sejong University, Seoul, Korea, since March 2022. Previously, he worked with Dongguk University for 3 years as assistant professor and 5 years as graduate researcher. He carries out research and development (R&D) in Industrial Artificial Intelligence (IAI), Big data, IoT, Informatics, etc. He is also an instructor with practical course on undergraduate topics in programming languages, linear algebra, big data and database systems.

Ganjar Alfian currently works as lecturer and researcher at Department of Electrical Engineering and Informatics, Vocational College, Universitas Gadjah Mada, Indonesia since 2022. Previously, he worked as Assistant Professor at Dongguk University-Seoul, Republic of Korea for five years. In July 2017, he was a short-term Visiting Researcher with the VSB-Technical University of Ostrava, Czech Republic. His research interests include Artificial Intelligence, RFID, IoT, Machine Learning, Carsharing, Simulation, etc.

* * *

Laurent Cleenewerck is an interdisciplinary researcher in global health, interfaith dialogue, international administration. Professor at EUCLID, an intergovernmental institution.

Norma Latif Fitriyani is currently with the Department of Data Science at Sejong University, Seoul, Korea. She can be reached at home.sejong.ac.kr/~norma. f563e19f-72ce-4e53-ab88-88f50ea92e77

Nur Nazihah Assyakirah Haji Isa is a research student majoring in Cybersecurity & Forensics, Universiti Brunei Darussalam.

Wardah Hakimah Haji Sumardi is an Assistant Lecturer of Marketing at UBD School of Business and Economics (UBDSBE), Brunei Darussalam. She holds a PhD in Business Management and Master in Marketing from the University of Manchester, United Kingdom. Her research and teaching focus primarily on service marketing, social marketing, transformative service, and service ecosystem.

Muhamad Danial Asyraf bin Mohamad is research student at Universiti Brunei Darussalam, majoring in Digital Science in Cybersecurity & Forensics. He was part of the students' representative council of Persatuan Mahasiswa/I Universiti Brunei Darussalam (PMUBD) as Executive of Sports & Recreations 2020/2021. He has a Higher National Diploma in Network and security from Politeknik Brunei.

Louis Rosenberg is a pioneer of virtual and augmented reality. His work began over thirty years ago in labs at Stanford and NASA. In 1992 he developed the first interactive augmented reality (mixed reality) system at Air Force Research Laboratory (AFRL). In 1993 he founded the early Virtual Reality company Immersion Corporation. In 2004 he founded the early Augmented Reality company Outland Research. He's been awarded over 300 patents for VR, AR, and AI technologies and published over 100 academic papers. He received his PhD from Stanford University and was a tenured professor at California State University (Cal Poly). He is currently CEO of Unanimous AI, the Chief Scientist of the Responsible Metaverse Alliance, the Global Technology Advisor to the XR Safety Initiative (XRSI) and a technology advisor to the Future of Marketing Institute (FMI).

Index

K

M

O

P

S

T

U

V

Recommended Reference Books

IGI Global's reference books can now be purchased from three unique pricing formats: Print Only, E-Book Only, or Print + E-Book.
Shipping fees may apply.

www.igi-global.com

ISBN: 9781799824022
EISBN: 9781799824046
© 2021; 323 pp.
List Price: US$ **195**

ISBN: 9781799867722
EISBN: 9781799867746
© 2021; 353 pp.
List Price: US$ **225**

ISBN: 9781799867548
EISBN: 9781799867562
© 2021; 420 pp.
List Price: US$ **265**

ISBN: 9781799857921
EISBN: 9781799857945
© 2021; 366 pp.
List Price: US$ **195**

ISBN: 9781799850366
EISBN: 9781799850373
© 2021; 297 pp.
List Price: US$ **215**

ISBN: 9781799849124
EISBN: 9781799849131
© 2021; 717 pp.
List Price: US$ **265**

Do you want to stay current on the latest research trends, product announcements, news, and special offers?
Join IGI Global's mailing list to receive customized recommendations, exclusive discounts, and more.
Sign up at: **www.igi-global.com/newsletters.**

Publisher of Timely, Peer-Reviewed Inclusive Research Since 1988

IGI Global
PUBLISHER of TIMELY KNOWLEDGE

www.igi-global.com Sign up at www.igi-global.com/newsletters facebook.com/igiglobal twitter.com/igiglobal

Ensure Quality Research is Introduced to the Academic Community

Become an Evaluator for IGI Global Authored Book Projects

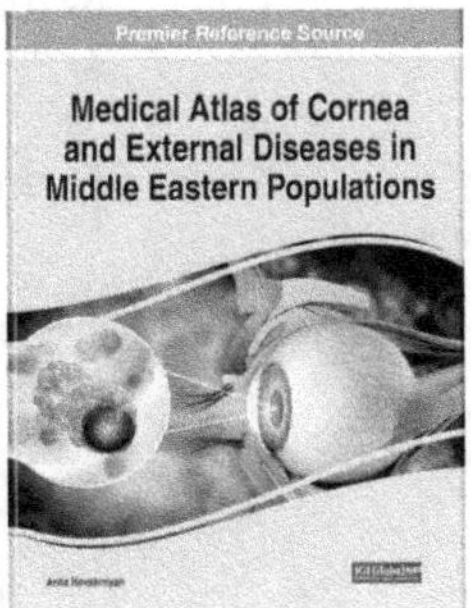

The overall success of an authored book project is dependent on quality and timely manuscript evaluations.

Applications and Inquiries may be sent to:
development@igi-global.com

Applicants must have a doctorate (or equivalent degree) as well as publishing, research, and reviewing experience. Authored Book Evaluators are appointed for one-year terms and are expected to complete at least three evaluations per term. Upon successful completion of this term, evaluators can be considered for an additional term.

If you have a colleague that may be interested in this opportunity, we encourage you to share this information with them.

Easily Identify, Acquire, and Utilize Published Peer-Reviewed Findings in Support of Your Current Research

IGI Global OnDemand

Purchase Individual IGI Global OnDemand Book Chapters and Journal Articles

For More Information:

www.igi-global.com/e-resources/ondemand/

Browse through 150,000+ Articles and Chapters!

Find specific research related to your current studies and projects that have been contributed by international researchers from prestigious institutions, including:

Massachusetts Institute of Technology

HARVARD UNIVERSITY

COLUMBIA UNIVERSITY IN THE CITY OF NEW YORK

Australian National University

- Accurate and Advanced Search
- Affordably Acquire Research
- Instantly Access Your Content
- Benefit from the InfoSci Platform Features

"It really provides an excellent entry into the research literature of the field. It presents a manageable number of highly relevant sources on topics of interest to a wide range of researchers. The sources are scholarly, but also accessible to 'practitioners'."

- Ms. Lisa Stimatz, MLS, University of North Carolina at Chapel Hill, USA

Interested in Additional Savings?

Subscribe to

IGI Global OnDemand *Plus*

Learn More

Acquire content from over 128,000+ research-focused book chapters and 33,000+ scholarly journal articles for as low as US$ 5 per article/chapter (original retail price for an article/chapter: US$ 37.50).

6,600+ E-BOOKS. ADVANCED RESEARCH. INCLUSIVE & ACCESSIBLE.

IGI Global
PUBLISHER of TIMELY KNOWLEDGE

IGI Global e-Book Collection

- **Flexible Purchasing Options** (Perpetual, Subscription, EBA, etc.)
- Multi-Year Agreements with **No Price Increases** Guaranteed
- **No Additional Charge** for Multi-User Licensing
- No Maintenance, Hosting, or Archiving Fees
- Transformative **Open Access Options** Available

Request More Information, or Recommend the IGI Global e-Book Collection to Your Institution's Librarian

Among Titles Included in the IGI Global e-Book Collection

Research Anthology on Racial Equity, Identity, and Privilege (3 Vols.)
EISBN: 9781668445082
Price: US$ 895

Handbook of Research on Remote Work and Worker Well-Being in the Post-COVID-19 Era
EISBN: 9781799867562
Price: US$ 265

Research Anthology on Big Data Analytics, Architectures, and Applications (4 Vols.)
EISBN: 9781668436639
Price: US$ 1,950

Handbook of Research on Challenging Deficit Thinking for Exceptional Education Improvement
EISBN: 9781799888628
Price: US$ 265

Acquire & Open

When your library acquires an IGI Global e-Book and/or e-Journal Collection, your faculty's published work will be considered for immediate conversion to Open Access *(CC BY License)*, at no additional cost to the library or its faculty *(cost only applies to the e-Collection content being acquired)*, through our popular **Transformative Open Access (Read & Publish) Initiative**.

For More Information or to Request a Free Trial, Contact IGI Global's e-Collections Team: eresources@igi-global.com | 1-866-342-6657 ext. 100 | 717-533-8845 ext. 100

Have Your Work Published and Freely Accessible

Open Access Publishing

With the industry shifting from the more traditional publication models to an open access (OA) publication model, publishers are finding that OA publishing has many benefits that are awarded to authors and editors of published work.

Freely Share Your Research

Higher Discoverability & Citation Impact

Rigorous & Expedited Publishing Process

Increased Advancement & Collaboration

Acquire & Open

When your library acquires an IGI Global e-Book and/or e-Journal Collection, your faculty's published work will be considered for immediate conversion to Open Access *(CC BY License)*, at no additional cost to the library or its faculty *(cost only applies to the e-Collection content being acquired)*, through our popular **Transformative Open Access (Read & Publish) Initiative**.

Provide Up To **100%** OA APC or CPC Funding

Funding to Convert or Start a Journal to **Platinum OA**

Support for Funding an **OA Reference Book**

IGI Global publications are found in a number of prestigious indices, including Web of Science™, Scopus®, Compendex, and PsycINFO®. The selection criteria is very strict and to ensure that journals and books are accepted into the major indexes, IGI Global closely monitors publications against the criteria that the indexes provide to publishers.

WEB OF SCIENCE™ Compendex Scopus® PsycINFO® IET Inspec

Learn More Here:

For Questions, Contact IGI Global's Open Access Team at openaccessadmin@igi-global.com

IGI Global PUBLISHER of TIMELY KNOWLEDGE www.igi-global.com

Are You Ready to Publish Your Research?

IGI Global
PUBLISHER of TIMELY KNOWLEDGE

IGI Global offers book authorship and editorship opportunities across 11 subject areas, including business, computer science, education, science and engineering, social sciences, and more!

Benefits of Publishing with IGI Global:

- Free one-on-one editorial and promotional support.
- Expedited publishing timelines that can take your book from start to finish in less than one (1) year.
- Choose from a variety of formats, including Edited and Authored References, Handbooks of Research, Encyclopedias, and Research Insights.
- Utilize IGI Global's eEditorial Discovery® submission system in support of conducting the submission and double-blind peer review process.
- IGI Global maintains a strict adherence to ethical practices due in part to our full membership with the Committee on Publication Ethics (COPE).
- Indexing potential in prestigious indices such as Scopus®, Web of Science™, PsycINFO®, and ERIC – Education Resources Information Center.
- Ability to connect your ORCID iD to your IGI Global publications.
- Earn honorariums and royalties on your full book publications as well as complimentary copies and exclusive discounts.

Join Your Colleagues from Prestigious Institutions, Including:

Australian National University

Massachusetts Institute of Technology

Johns Hopkins University

Harvard University

Columbia University in the City of New York

Learn More at: www.igi-global.com/publish

or by Contacting the Acquisitions Department at: acquisition@igi-global.com